W9-DGS-952

EMOTIONS

EMOTIONS

*What they are and how they affect us,
from the basic hates & fears of childhood
to more sophisticated feelings that
later govern our adult lives.*

*How we can deal with
the way we feel.*

JUNE CALLWOOD

Originally published as
Love, Hate, Fear, Anger and the Other Lively Emotions,
this edition is revised and updated.

DOUBLEDAY & COMPANY, INC.
GARDEN CITY, NEW YORK
1986

Originally published as *Love, Hate, Fear, Anger and the Other Lively Emotions*
© 1964 by June Callwood

Canadian Cataloguing in Publication Data
Callwood, June.
Emotions
Updated ed. of: Love, hate, fear, anger and other
lively emotions.
ISBN 0-385-19976-7
1. Emotions. I. Title. II.Title: Love, hate, fear,
anger and other lively emotions.
BF531.C27 1986   152.4   C86-093050-5

Library of Congress Cataloging-in-Publication Data
Callwood, June.
Emotions.
Rev. ed. of: Love, hate, fear, anger, and other
lively emotions. 1980.
Bibliography: p. 259
1. Emotions. I. Callwood, June. Love, hate, fear,
anger, and other lively emotions. II. Title.
BF531.C27   1986   152.4   85-20417
ISBN 0-385-19976-7

CONTENTS

CONTENTS

TO DREAMIE

EMOTIONS

EMOTION

HUMANS unfold into emotional maturity by a process of spontaneous branching that no one yet understands. Examination of the nature of each unique emotional tree has fascinated sages and scientists since the beginning of time. Philosophers, deists and others intrigued by inner space have sought without success to learn why one person behaves wisely and another kills.

The invention of theology is one response to the riddle; psychology is another.

In recent years investigation of emotions has become a major field of research for behavioral scientists. There are people with stopwatches in hand who hover over babies, holding up one-eyed masks to determine that babies prefer faces with two eyes; this establishes, for those who doubted, that the human species is born sociable. There are teams who have been interviewing annually for thirty years a selection of people who were chosen when they were children to represent all of North America, from which it is regularly noted that happy children become happy adults. In university laboratories undergraduates are required to express hatred before and after being verbally abused by an authority figure whose skin is black; the purpose of this is to reveal the dynamics of bigotry.

The experts speculate on the origin and composition of such emotions as love and fear but they cannot agree even on what they are. This century, empowered by the insights of Freud, his followers and his detractors, is obsessed with introspection and analysis. Because there is more understanding of the chemical components of emotion and where they arise in the brain, there is fresh excitement that neuroscientists will be able to unravel the puzzle of personality, and even rebuild a personality to order.

Most people live their lives in the middle ground between complete sanity and total insanity, veering close to one edge or the other on what seems a random and wind-driven course. They can never be certain which element in their nature will prevail in a crisis. The death-craving within everyone balances against the life-loving capacity for joy; inability to shake a grudge lives beside a capacity for lasting friendship; malice exists with a blameless sense of social responsibility. How did such a jumble happen?

Some hope, and others fear, that comprehension of human emotion will lead to chemical engineering of behavior. The insights of the importance of early environment on emotional development have been known for half a century without making much impression on society's concern for the well-being of babies, but the direction of recent research is toward manipulating adult behavior. Dangerous people might then be given chemical cocktails to make them kind. No one would have to suffer guilt or depression; male rage would vanish, rendering obsolete hostels for battered wives.

The enlightened American radicals of the eighteenth century believed that happiness was accessible to all citizens of a democracy. Accordingly, they wrote the right to pursue happiness into the Declaration of Independence. In the present Age of Anxiety, people will settle for a smaller hero: a capacity for well-being.

Everyone wants what is called happiness, yet the miracle workers who can watch a double helix drifting and parting in a cell, who with the push of a button could cause a nuclear winter that would obliterate all life, who have produced a single television show, the Oscar awards ceremony, which simultaneously bores or enthralls two billion people—these whirling brains are as baffled by human emotions as the sweaty group in bedsheets who assumed thoughtful expressions when Socrates advised them to know themselves.

Few psychologists are still attached to the early dogmas which held that personalities are inherent in the genes like the arrangement of teeth, or that babies have no participation in their fate but are empty slates available to whatever message is delivered.

Embryo humans vary in the womb in a number of ways, of which general excitability is an important ingredient. Gender has a powerful role to play in personality development despite the best efforts of egalitarian parents who give their sons dolls and encourage their daughters to play hockey. Placement in the family has a bearing: oldest children, only children and children born at the end of the litter many years after the nearest sibling all show similar traits. Long-term childhood illnesses also influence personality development, and very tall men will display some of the same assumptions that are shown by beautiful women.

Scientists currently are interested in what they have been learning about the brain's peculiar chemistry and the pathways that neuroelectricity carves in the brain's meat. Neurobiologists and neurochemists contemplate the gray three-pound pudding of the human brain and see where it can be tickled to produce a grin on the face or where it can be laced with a chemical that will cause it to explode with rage. Neurotransmitters are under investigation, no longer able to send a message that the sky is falling without alerting a scientist or a psychiatrist.

More than a hundred chemicals have been found in the brain's stew and there are an estimated 30,000 genes which occur nowhere else in the body except the cranial cavity. Much work is being done to harness this information to the treatment of such disorders as schizophrenia, Parkinson's disease, multiple sclerosis, drug addiction, Alzheimer's disease and melancholia, but for thousands of other researchers the goal of interpreting the brain better is to be able to rearrange personality.

That focus makes some people uneasy. The fear is that knowledge of how the emotions are formed will result in Orwellian control of personality according to quota—so many aggressives for commerce and war, so many submissives for tedious work, one fluke for comic relief.

Many are concerned that dissection of emotions violates a holy place. In 1641, René Descartes, the mathematician and philosopher, paid reverent respect to the brain as the seat of the rational soul. Modern neurosurgeons are no less in awe of the pulpy mass and its strange authority over health and behavior. Opponents of researchers who use chemicals and electrodes on living brains fear that when science pulls a vital thread, the inspired tapestry will be destroyed.

When it is known why a child laughs, what causes a decent person to feel guilty, how it is that anyone can put on a glove without having to think carefully where the fingers go, and why people love illogically, will the human race be better off? For some, the ignorance of science on the subject of the emotions is immensely reassuring.

Despite the qualms that are expressed, the search for control of emotion is proceeding at a rapid pace. Some psychologists are absorbed in efforts to read emotion in facial expression. Others are obtaining results from the use of mind control in fighting cancer. Another line of inquiry concerns itself with dreams, that doodling in the subconscious that teems with clues for the diagnosis of behavior.

The primary focus is the lives of newborns. Harvard's William James described a newborn's world as one of "buzzing confusion," a concept that sits well with the explanation anthropologists have for the human infant's puzzling helplessness, a vulnerability rare in the animal world which does not normally leave its young to the vagaries of the jungle, whether African or urban.

When the primates who evolved into humans first walked erect, the brain development that ensued as hunters developed an ability to make tools was felt most acutely by females, whose pelvises could not tolerate the enlarged head of their young. In order to avoid crushing the inflexible skull in the birth canal, babies would have to be born prematurely. Accordingly, the species selected itself for early delivery and what today are considered full-term newborns are in fact several months short of birth readiness.

Nevertheless, the human brain is a formidable size at birth, weighing one-seventh the baby's total weight. Soon after the child's second birthday, the brain reaches 70 percent of its adult size; it is 80 percent the size of an adult brain when the child is four. Significantly, primate babies reach that brain size before they are born.

Few scientists believe any longer that people are born with certain emotions. The prevailing theory, instead, is that humans begin with capacities, impulses and instincts, from which they build a personality according to the experiences that befall them.

A venerable study by K. M. B. Bridges in a now-vanished Montreal foundling home continues to provide a starting point. Dr. Bridges was of the opinion that the first stage of emotion is the newborn's generalized excitement, after which, at about three weeks, distress becomes distinct. The second observable emotion is delight —and following that the two parent bodies divide and subdivide as cells do, on their determined schedules.

By six months, Dr. Bridges said, disgust and anger evolve from the distress root and elation and affection from delight. When babies are a year old, their ability to observe and assimilate has enabled the development of a sense of humor, some moments of elation and a simple kind of affection. The latter is the beginning of the capacity to love, which is the brickwork of maturity.

More recent work has led to the conviction that there is an orderly progression to emotional development. It is confounding those who believe in the doctrine of original sin that it appears to be true that humans experience joy before sadness. Envy, ambition and social confidence all occur later, at a higher level of development. While there is no agreement on the precise time at which each emotion is supposed to flower, there is accord on the point of logical sequence and the problems that ensue if the baby misses a hurdle.

Doubt has been expressed about the legitimacy of a baby's emotions, on the theory that they are not innate but are reflections of the moods of the nearest adults. Walter B. Cannon, the Harvard physiologist whose prewar classic *The Wisdom of the Body* still influences scholars, declared flatly that this is impossible because the emotions of an infant as registered on the face cannot be learned: the baby is too young to have absorbed such distinctions.

Martin Hoffman at the University of Michigan has been doing some critical work on the development of a key emotional element, the ability to feel empathy. He notes that newborn babies are distressed to hear another baby cry, but he isn't certain if the babies have differentiated themselves from the sounds and objects around them to know that it is a separate person who is unhappy and not a part of themselves.

But a toddler of only thirteen months once was seen to offer an unhappy adult her cherished doll. For some, that's all that needs to be demonstrated about divinity.

The excited state of newborns has some landmasses that poke out of the cloud. For instance, a day-old baby registers disgust at an unpleasant taste. Developmental psychologists note a newborn's interest in moving lights and believe that this state of alert interest should be classified as an emotion in its own right.

Babies as young as three months feel sadness if they are abused or neglected by their parents. By ten months their range of emotions includes joy, anger, misery, surprise and fear. A biological clock seems to be governing the branching. Dr. Jerome Kagan, a Harvard psychologist, puts his theories in the context of Jean Piaget's monumental work on cognitive development and believes that emotional growth is tied to the intellect, each level of intelligence providing the setting for another group of increasingly more subtle and complex emotions.

Shadings come along as regularly as lunar eclipses. Shame develops at about eighteen months, and by the age of four children, alas, are capable of the adult experience of worry.

The ages of five and six are believed by some to be periods of major emotional development because children are gaining perspective on their physical and emotional separateness from everyone else in the world. They are ready to begin to compare themselves with others and to conform where they can and dig in where they can't. This brings forth such conflicting emotions as pride and humility, insecurity and confidence, envy and contempt.

Psychologist Justin Pikunas of the University of Detroit wrote, "The child's affections grow as he (and, presumably, she) come into contact with more people who are good to him (or, assuredly, her)."*

Infants emerge from a weightless, effortless state in a sound-muted, blood-warm uterus to the chill, glare and noise of a delivery room. The ejection is effected with more force than is required to wrench a molar from its socket and the horrified fetus is squeezed through a narrow corridor that threatens to crush it to pulp. When the birth is over, most infants understandably are shocked and dazed. But, despite the bombardment of stimuli on their newly hatched senses, they begin at once to try to figure out what has happened.

The eyes of newborns only two hours old will follow a moving light. When they are five days old, babies are so full of curiosity that they will stop feeding to look at a light jiggling on the periphery of their vision.

They crave stimulation. Harvard's Jerome Bruner worked with pediatrician Berry Brazelton in 1966 in an experiment which involved placing babies in comfortable recliners in a cream-colored space devoid of any distraction. In thirty seconds, the babies were crying with all their might. When the researchers placed objects within the area, the babies stopped complaining and examined the shapes with interest.

* Unthinking sexism is endemic in scientific reports and, indeed, in all of literature until the last decade. Whether the author was a man or a woman, the assumption was that all human beings are male. In the interests of space and to avoid repetition, the author henceforth will not amend the original text.

The same team discovered that babies turn away from pictures that are out of focus on a screen. By arranging a pacifier in such an ingenious way that sucking would bring the picture into focus, the scientists discovered that babies only six weeks old will suck hard in order to see a sharper picture, and learn to suck rapidly in order to get quicker results.

Babies are so labile, Dr. Bruner concluded, that they are easily overaroused. Unable to control their responses, they are prone to abrupt frustration, boredom or fatigue.

Even tiny babies are thinking, purposeful beings actively involved in their surroundings and able to respond to whatever they can see, smell, hear or guess. Their coordination is sufficient to permit them to follow an adult's gaze to inspect what the adult is looking at. A one-year-old, Dr. Bruner says, apparently enchanted by the discovery, can sense by the change in an adult's tone that something distracting has occurred—and the baby is avid to find out what it is.

Babies can be startled, which they demonstrate by straightening their legs, opening their arms and throwing back their heads. They can suck before they are born and immediately afterward they will turn toward a nipple. Their hands instinctively grasp whatever is placed across their palms with such tenacity and strength that newborns have been known to support their own weight while hanging from a bar.

That particular trick is a legacy from the primates who were obliged to cling for their lives to mothers who had no free hand to hold them when on the move.

No one is certain if the brain of a fetus is sufficiently developed in the final few months before delivery for the unborn person to be storing memories of the amniotic state and the trauma of birth. Many people, particularly those who undergo hypnosis, believe that they can remember details of their birth. The literature is rich in such stories as the one about a man whose left arm hurt excruciatingly when he remembered being born. On inquiry he learned for the first time that the obstetrician indeed had hauled him through the final stages of delivery by grasping his left arm. It is a compelling story— unless the man had heard that detail before and had forgotten that he knew it.

But numerous experiments have established that a fetus is listening and that the fetal brain is collecting and storing information. Anthony J. Casper of the University of North Carolina performed a charming experiment to determine if the fetus is paying attention to the muffled sounds outside the womb. Pregnant women read aloud Dr. Seuss's *The Cat in the Hat* for five hours during the final six weeks of their pregnancies, after which their newborns were given a pacifier which when sucked activated a tape recorder. Babies only hours old would suck hard to produce the sound of their mothers reading *The Cat in the Hat* but were less interested in another person reading the same book, or even in their mothers' voices reading a different book.

Some scientists believe that patterns which will control behavior for a lifetime are established before birth. They are convinced that chemical alterations in the mother, such as occur if she undergoes long periods in the grip of fear or anger, or if she sustains a high level of anxiety, will carry their toxicity across the placental barriers to flood the fetus. The suspicion is that the irritable nature of some babies, the hypertension and colic which exhaust the infants and distress their parents, are the consequences of a pregnancy marked by emotional anguish.

The emotional fragility of adopted children is often cited as evidence of this theory. Even children who were adopted at birth and were lovingly nurtured seem to be more prone to despair than children raised by natural parents. Adoption workers suspect that a woman carrying a baby she plans to place for adoption is probably in continuous emotional stress as she struggles to remain aloof from the life within her. The theory is that the fetus knows something is wrong; the message isn't the one the species intended a baby to get.

The first social relationship in human life is the one between the newborn and the food supplier. Babies are indifferent about the gender of the care-giving person or whether that person is a relative, or young or old. What matters, and matters greatly, is whether the baby's needs are met quickly and in a spirit of affection and interest, or whether care is given irregularly and with indifference or roughness.

The former creates a sense of safety in the infant, and the latter breeds anxiety.

While it is observably true that babies bloom in a steady, calm and loving environment and that erratic or insensitive care will make them slower to develop, there are variations on the themes. Even in infancy, humans are quirky and unpredictable. Some newborns are relaxed little people who can tolerate a capricious routine, while others are so edgy that even constant attendance can't reassure them.

Babies begin in an environment they can't see clearly. Their eyes focus at a point about eighteen inches from their noses, which happens to be where adults instinctively position themselves when talking to babies. Infants are sensitive to discomfort and make it abundantly clear when they are in distress. Within a few weeks they notice the fluctuations in their state and marvel that when they feel the pangs of hunger, the misery of a dirty diaper or a balloon of gas that cramps their stomachs, something always comes along to make things better. Such mysterious alterations are the basis for the delight in magic that is so acute in small children.

Gradually the infant perceives that the change from pain to pleasure comes from a certain source. With repetition, the baby can identify the care giver from all others. The person who brings warm milk and dry clothes and strokes the tired body has a distinct smell, sound and touch, to which the baby becomes habituated.

This first friend is the keystone relationship of a lifetime.

At four months, babies know how a human face is supposed to look. When they are shown a mask with the features in the wrong place, they are bored. If the mask, however grotesque, has the features properly arranged, the babies will be intrigued; most will give a gargoyle a friendly smile. But unless the mask jiggles, moving as real heads do, the baby's attention will wander.

Babies whose cries bring a quick response come to the conclusion that they are in control; by crying, they bring help. This is a gratifying discovery but not without a price: babies simultaneously become aware of the ghastly truth that their situation is precarious: they are dependent on the goodwill of the care giver. Gratitude is the baby's first experience of love and is bestowed on the care giver; also, the baby is centering hatred and anger for the first time, and these too are directed at the care giver. The intensity of this hostility is frightening to the baby, who imagines—or so psychoanalysts believe—that he or she might be able to destroy the care giver.

Alarming as this stage of development must be to a tiny person scarcely able to roll over, it is normal and desirable. The babies in peril are those whose care has been so deficient that they don't have a consistent person on whom to begin constructing an emotional life.

Among the saddest sights on earth are the babies raised in institutions, or moved many times from one care giver to another, or reared by adults who don't know how to give care, or can't. When babies are profoundly deprived of consistent nurturing, they lose hope. They are capable of suicidal depression: severely understimulated babies exhibit what is called "failure to thrive." Even when nutrition is adequate and they are kept clean, they will waste away with debilitating infections—smaller than other babies of their age and seemingly retarded.

Babies who have no experience with a dependable person who feeds and entertains them will feel little trust in what casual care comes their way. Thus they may miss the branching of emotional growth that puts forth empathy, love and stability. Unable to feel attached to others, they cannot imagine how anyone else is feeling, or that there is any compelling reason, other than self-interest or fear of discovery, to behave well instead of badly. They grow into wary adults who cannot be touched, emotional cripples who in extreme cases are given such labels as psychopath.

While such emotional coldness can be traced almost invariably to a childhood of neglect or cruelty, the reverse is not true. Not all battered children become battering adults, and it is equally true that not all children raised in what seem to be loving homes become loving people. Scientists are more interested in the former and are studying the so-called immune children who emerge from violent households with their sweetness intact.

Jerome Kagan has a sanguine view of the human potential to resist damage. Children do get off to ominous starts, he agrees, "but that doesn't mean the child can't recover. There is ample evidence that a bad beginning can be dramatically turned around."

He tells the story of a little girl whose mother locked her in a room for the first three years of her life, feeding her only once every five days. Yet when Dr. Kagan met the youngster years later, when she had grown into her teens in a middle-class caring family, he found that "she was fine. She had good grades in school, had a boy friend, and was planning to be a nurse. You would never have known from her behavior that she had such a tragic first three years."

It is accepted now, after decades of dispute among professionals, that humans are amazing and that the effects of what happened to them at any stage of life, including infancy, can be reversed. Emotional change can occur almost anywhere along the continuum between cradle and grave and appears to depend on constitutional factors and good luck. People are challenged by crisis to alter themselves; transition also occurs less convulsively, bit by bit over long periods of time.

Emotional growth is like bone growth, moving in spurts and then settling down for periods of consolidation. Unlike bones, however, emotions can regress abruptly and spill even stable adults into childhood tantrums. Much of a lifetime is spent on emotional plateaus between levels of development, the person washed forward and backward between confidence and anxiety. Since the natural tendency of the human organism is to improve and grow, the normal thrust of emotional development is always toward betterment.

Observations which established that emotions are part of orderly systems came along only recently. In the 1920s psychologists were influenced by a formidably opinionated man, John B. Watson, a phenomenon who was a professor at Johns Hopkins University at the age of thirty. Dr. Watson believed that babies are born with a fully formed portfolio of adult emotions, primarily fear, anger and love.

He experimented on living babies in tests no ethics review would tolerate today. In order to observe terror and revulsion he put three-year-olds in well-lighted rooms where he would suddenly release a small boa constrictor or in a dark room where he would start a noisy fire with newspapers. He would present children with boxes containing frogs or paper bags containing pigeons.

He also demonstrated the capacity of babies to feel fear by dropping them short distances and their ability to feel rage by trussing them like turkeys. When the babies relaxed on being stroked tenderly, Dr. Watson deduced that they were experiencing the emotion of love.

Faith in his behaviorism theories waned when psychologists who tried to duplicate his work found that they didn't know if the babies were expressing fear or anger unless they were aware of the cause of the crying. Worse, they encountered perverse babies who didn't cooperate at all, either crying when caressed or showing amusement at being dropped, or falling asleep when trussed.

Despite the potential for change as an adult life unfolds, it usually holds that emotional tone is fixed before people learn to tie their shoes. One major influence is constitutional: people are born jumpy or placid, or in between. One view is that these characteristics are inherent like red hair. It's a matter of neural gaps in the brain. Some people have short distances for messages to leap to the nerve center and others have such chasms that news travels slowly and tortuously.

One of the first to examine these neural gaps was V. H. Mottram, who described the spongeous composition of the brain and how brains differ in density. Brains are trainable, much as puppies are—some of them quick to pick up new tricks and others irresponsive to simple commands. As recent work has shown, messages which are repeated many times make pathways along the connectors so that eventually little intellectual effort is needed to reach the action center. Some messages become so familiar that behavior is automatic. The brain, like a mud road in spring, develops ruts that make for a smooth ride.

The brain operates on a simple principle but isn't simple at all. The conditioned reflex which results from practice can enable a firefighter to respond to an alarm without stopping to think of the right sequence, but the brain is nonselective and will form an equally fixed pattern for destructive behavior. The same hospitable grooves are created for emotional response. A certain kind of threat will always trigger an impulse of violence, or the reaction to a particular situation will always be avoidance.

All repetition, whether directed at learning a computer program or standing erect or acquiring social graces, eventually will wear a groove in the neural meat so that conscious thought is not required for the job to get done.

Such brain patterning is the explanation for the rituals to which humans are prone, from simple and harmless ones like the way one dresses—always the left sock before the right—to the more obvious addictions. Smokers are habituated not only to the taste of nicotine and the feel of hot smoke in their lungs but also to the movements that accompany smoking—pouring a cup of coffee, taking the cigarette from the package, tamping it once, lighting the match. Alcoholics who go on the wagon miss the smells of a bar and the look of the drink in the glass as much as they do the alcoholic blur they seek.

Similarly, a baby's emotional patterning can make such a permanent record on the brain that an adult will have difficulty changing it.

The habit of rage, for instance, seems particularly long-lasting. Angry toddlers who throw things are expressing rage in a manner normal to their age, but five-year-olds who still throw things are candidates for a life of violence. Their brains are being patterned to strike out before they think.

Therapists who work with men who batter their wives use techniques of pattern breaking and activity substitution that are not unlike those which have been successful in addiction programs such as Alcoholics Anonymous. Submissive women who persist in assertiveness training have been helped to improved self-esteem.

Neural gaps are not fixed. The average speed of the neurons is about one hundred meters a second but fatigue stretches the spaces and slows down the messengers. Stimulants do the reverse, tightening the loop. The chemicals generated by emotions reshape the network so that fear can bring either quickened response or paralysis, depending on how accustomed the person is to that situation. Depression seems to make the brain fall apart, while acute anxiety skews the whole apparatus.

On the other hand, confidence puts the brain in the pink, functioning at its best as the senses do on a spring day. Confidence is a circular process with no discernible start or finish, like chickens and eggs. When the brain has a lively battery of pathways, it can handle most input without releasing too many anxiety chemicals. Every time it demonstrates its proficiency, it gets better at being proficient.

No one is certain how much intelligence or capacity to learn tricks is inherent in the brain and how much is the result of a stimulating, encouraging and friendly environment. Children removed from homes where no one played with them will make sudden gains in IQ tests when placed in remedial nursery schools. Dr. Mottram wrote, in *The Physical Base of Personality,* that brains are individual and have widely varying ability to learn. "In some people the resistance [in the gaps] is permanently high, and in others permanently low," he said.

What brain gaps have to do with a human's appreciation of mist on a moor is too subtle to be understood. This is the territory where scientists must yield to the poets.

Back to babies. As babies grow, they learn to distinguish the care givers from others they meet. They experience jealousy for the first time when they must compete for the attention of the care givers. In order to avoid the risk of destroying the care giver with their omnipotent hate, they displace their feelings onto someone safer, such as a sibling.

In the second year, babies fluctuate between aggression, destructiveness, envy, sorrow, remorse and, more frequently than adults can imagine, contemplation. Since they are at the center of their universes, they are unable to concern themselves with the feelings of others. This is narcissism, a normal stage of development for two-year-olds but highly undesirable later on.

Somewhere between the ages of two and three, something quite wonderful occurs. Toddlers become aware of how the people who matter to them are feeling, and can begin to make associations so as to understand how those feelings were provoked. They can imagine being someone other than themselves. When asked how Goldilocks feels about the Three Bears, they tremble for her safety.

Nothing is more significant for future emotional quality than the beginning of empathy. Without sensitivity to others, people are condemned to lives of isolation and blunder.

Psychologists call the process of acquiring such skills "scaffolding." Children learn through the awareness of the care givers in their lives, who must be able to perceive what the child is able to do at a given moment, lead the child to the next stage gently without fuss, wait for that new talent to settle in and then move the child to the next goal.

Scaffolding is best observed in the way most parents almost instinctively teach their children to speak. They respond in kind when the baby babbles and seem to sense when the toddler is ready to say "da-da" and "ma-ma." A few at a time, distinctly and slowly, they teach simple words, and then short sentences. For a long while after the child has acquired a vocabulary, adults accept mispronunciations without comment, but a time comes when the child is corrected until the word is right. He or she has been scaffolded into speech.

People with talent and empathy do this naturally, without planning what they do. Their best skill may lie in the ability to judge when it is best to withdraw from teaching and allow the child to struggle alone. It is what children can do by themselves that builds confidence—and confidence in turn enables children to go on to the next level of accomplishment.

It is evident that an important aspect of what gifted parents do is to know when to stop teaching. At a point in puzzle construction or pouring juice, they stop showing the child how to do it and stand aside to let the child struggle alone until the skill is mastered. The child's triumphant "By *myself!*" is a cry of independence, a victory beyond compare for a small person.

Scaffolding is compounded of many elements, of which the essential one is empathy. If the adults have empathy in short supply, or lack it entirely, they may be unable to appreciate the child's feelings and will be unable to help the child build his or her own empathy. If the timing is missed, unhappily the opportunity to learn empathy may be permanently lost.

Skilled professionals have attempted with children as young as three and four to instill empathy skills that they failed to acquire in families where violence and neglect occurred. They find that habits of uncontrolled violence are difficult to break. They try patiently to bring the child to feel sympathy, but the child appears baffled by the concept. For a good many of them, the faculty that would have enabled them to feel sorrow for someone else's suffering and remorse for the pain they have caused seems both unformed and unformable.

Most children are not so severely devastated; they have some degree of compassion for another's woe. Three-year-olds already experience such adult miseries as inadequacy, guilt, and shame, along with the beginning of confidence and appreciation. They have a sense of their own separateness, which brings with it a glimmer of the existential aloneness which is everyone's fate. By the age of five they are able to disguise their emotions with some skill so that neither the child nor anyone else will truly know what complexities are burning within.

All lifetimes are marked by episodes of emotional storms. The period from the mid-teens to the early twenties is one. At the beginning of adulthood, teenagers are overstocked with personalities, a different set of moods and antics for almost everyone they know.

Confusing as this is for parents who are astounded to hear that the gloomy adolescent who lives at their house is elsewhere the life of the party, it is even more disturbing for the young person who inhabits all the disguises. All the masks are true, but none is wholly true. Understandably, young adults have nightmares of being fragmented or that the most awful of their selves, the one they fight to conceal, will be discovered.

Resolution must wait because the plunge into real and invented distractions begins in the early twenties. The next time when the jumbled emotions declare their presence may come in the late thirties and early forties. People either weather that crisis well, learning from it, or bury it again and move on. In the fifties, the raw keening pain of loneliness may descend again.

Some people can use periods of psychic pain to examine the nature of the anger they feel in the presence of their parents, or the drive that makes leisure time irritating. Some can't; they aren't ready to let go. They check the barricades of the familiar defenses and conclude that everything is holding well enough.

The onset of old age is a relatively calm period for most people but, as the years roll on, it becomes less possible to believe that death won't happen. The emotions flutter and whatever has been waiting all the years may escape: the resentment, the grudges, the bitterness; or, for luckier ones, more of the same friendliness.

The emotions of the elderly seem to have calcified. Habit has formed highways in the brain's transportation system that bulldozers won't alter. The tone for many is dark and grieving for lost mobility and shining face. They are possessive in the way children are, without reason. Bored, testy and rigid, they are immune to efforts aimed at diverting them from their morose self-preoccupation.

On the other hand, some old people seem purified of malice. They display benevolence, tolerance, sympathy, humor, appreciation. They give hope for the human race.

Humans begin life in a state of undifferentiated excitement. They can end with calm. Everything between is journey.

A meticulous psychologist, K. M. B. Bridges, noted more than fifty years ago that a feature of the emotions of children is that they are frequent, brief and lack shade. Adolescents gain a measure of self-control, he said, by submerging and smothering emotions so that they become opaque moods. Adults are clad in a thicket of attitudes and postures which make emotional growth difficult unless they are willing to undress.

Within these variations there are traits which persist from childhood into adult life. One of the strong ones is bossiness; others are conscientiousness, spunkiness, capacity for affection, nervousness and crabbiness. Adults will most resemble their eleven-year-old selves, eleven being a magical age when a person feels comfortable enough to be natural. As Detroit's Justin Pikunas observed, "Later

developments are to an increasing degree expanding and supplementary, rather than transforming—evolutionary rather than revolution-
ary."

Long-range behavior studies give evidence of the perseverance of
some childhood characteristics. The Fels Research Institute began a
survey of two-year-olds in the 1930s and interviewed them regularly
as they matured. Its records abound in such stories as that of the
timid and tense three-year-old girl who was a shy six-year-old and,
eventually, a meek, mild thirty-year-old still living with her parents,
afraid to leave home. Another child who was stubborn and demanding at three and competitive at five became a domineering adult.

Some linear studies of human behavior are in their fiftieth and
sixtieth years. The reports are the same. Whining children develop
into complaining adults and pugnacious little boys become belliger-
ent men.

Anxiety is the emotion which seems to have the strongest influence on emotional development. A nervous, tense person is off-balance, requiring more support and reassurance than others, seeing the
world differently, coming to conclusions on the basis of perceptions
which are warped by apprehension. Anxious people are less willing
to change, to venture into a new experience, to trust a relationship;
they have less curiosity, enthusiasm, and energy. They simply are
too exhausted by internal stress.

Anxiety differs from fear in that it is diffuse and unspecific, while
fear is vivid and has a focus. Fear disappears when the threat is over,
but anxiety is endless. One psychologist, Carroll E. Izard of Vanderbilt University, believes that anxiety isn't a single emotion but a
cluster of several, only one of which is fear. Dr. Izard sees anxiety as
a curry, a mixture which guilt may dominate in one person and
distress or shame in another.

Fearful, anxious children never seem to get enough love and attention. No matter how much comforting and praise they receive, they
are placated only briefly. Consequently they are difficult, angry, jeal-
ous little people who are hard to like. Their own conviction that no
one cares about them can become true.

Love, not hate, is anxiety's opposite. Being loved, being able to
trust that they are treasured and protected, makes children need attention less. They are free of obsession with danger and can be inter-

ested in others and outgoing. Relaxed, warm and responsive, they are full of curiosity and resilience.

They are also much more charming than anxious children are. Accordingly, they inspire admiration and affection even in people who don't normally enjoy the company of children. Teachers adore happy children; their parents beam on them; other children seek them out because they are kind and fair.

Them as has, gets.

The responsibility for the differences in the natures of children is usually placed on the backs of their parents. At a symposium on maturity held in Philadelphia a few years ago, two University of Pennsylvania psychiatrists reported, "If the personal relationships throughout childhood are good, then maturing proceeds adequately . . . If the personal relationships are poor, psychopathology of various kinds results. Psychopathology, apart from reactions to extreme current stress, is essentially the continuation of disordered patterns of human relations formed in childhood by improper treatment of the child."

They added, "Hostility, violence and cruelty of all sorts are preventable by proper child-rearing. An effective beginning would be made if we devoted to the proper raising of our children emotionally a fraction of the time, money and energy we spend on raising corn, cattle and satellites."

The Scottish psychiatrist Ian D. Suttie was equally adamant. He wrote, "Mental or nervous breakdown is merely the culmination of social strains which have existed since early childhood."

But parents aren't the only players: the child participates in whatever forces shape her or his destiny. Some babies reward their parents by smiling early and often, drawing from the adults what is best and most giving. Other babies seem to be constitutional grumps, so unresponsive that adults stop trying to please them. In a way, babies feather their own nests—or else they won't or can't.

But even if babies experience terror and pain, there is astonishing evidence that something in their natures acts as protection. Some children resist messages of unworthiness or badness. A fluke of luck, such as a sympathetic teacher or even some chance comment that provides insight, seems to reach such endangered children and keep them intact. On the other hand, others can suffer very little deprivation but are so deeply wounded by it that they are depressed for life.

Family environment, however influential on children, doesn't exist in a vacuum. People are imprinted by the expectations of the society in which they live, which turn reflects values that vary according to social class and race. Everything else being equal, children of the poor are less likely to be assured and confident than children of the well-to-do, and a black child is less likely to feel the world is safe than a white child will.

Discipline of children is less consistent in homes where the adults are under great stress, and poverty is stress without end.

Gender has a role to play, though there is no relief in the controversy over how much of male aggression is inherent in the hormones and how much is the result of the assumptions that society still makes about the nature of maleness. In settings where children play with objects which have no gender meaning for them, boys and girls are very similar in their preferences and attitudes.

Feminist researchers are reviewing the experiments that male researchers have been doing in the past century. They find the conclusions men made about female characteristics came more often from male bias than from anything that really occurred in the experiments. While they concede they may bring an equally distorting female bias to their work, they are confident that at least some of the old premises were false.

"This is not a separatist philosophy," said Carol Gilligan, a Harvard psychologist. "We're revising mainstream theory . . . the differences between the sexes are being rediscovered."

The women conclude that the ovarian imperative exists: women do have different capacities than do men for nurturing and cherishing. The sex which carries life in its body does indeed tend to value life more.

This preoccupation with the preciousness of life makes women vulnerable and more susceptible to loss, according to this theory. Motherly natures are open to masochism in the service of what is seen as a primary responsibility, which makes women punching bags and targets for economic disparities. On the other hand, those who believe in an androgynous future maintain that the so-called innate nurturing skills of women are heavily reinforced by a male-led society that needs cheap labor for raising children and providing services. If the economy was reordered, men could become nurturers.

The truth probably lies somewhere between biology and societal stereotyping. Little boys certainly are conditioned to be rough and adventurous, but also the male hormone is more fierce than its female equivalent.

Placement in the family echelon also is a factor in personality. Helen Hoch, a psychologist at the University of Chicago, tested brothers and sisters and found that firstborns were more intense, more upset by defeat, and more articulate than children born later. David F. Wrench and Chris Wrench reported almost the same finding in *Psychology: A Social Approach,* in which they noted that parents are able to give firstborns undivided attention, which accounts both for the higher intelligence of oldest children and for their obsession with perfection.

If there is a long space between the lastborn child and the nearest sibling, this child will resemble firstborns—the same drive for achievement, the same responsiveness and orientation to adults.

The Wrenches found that children other than firstborns and such singly raised lastborns will rely more on their peers than on their parents. Impulsive and athletic, they are likely to be risk takers.

The country in which people live plays a determining role in personality. The myths a nation holds about itself will shape the citizenry, as Sparta did its warrior class. Frenchmen feel reinforced in impulsive behavior by their national reputation for doing the unexpected. Americans see themselves as assertive and competitive, Canadians as conciliators.

It is curious that northerners in countries as disparate as China, Spain, Vietnam, Germany, Italy, England, Scotland and the United States generally exhibit qualities of pragmatism, grit, vigor, frugality and quickened speech, while southerners in those countries have in common languidness, ingenuousness, hospitality and slower speech.

Anthropologists note that people of basically the same stock, living in almost identical conditions on scattered Pacific islands, develop unique and different tribal personalities—generous in one village, suspicious and hostile in another. The emotional tone of the community is perpetuated, generation after generation, because child-raising techniques have been established to produce the preferred personality.

In the spring of 1984 a new organization was launched in Paris, the International Society for Research on Emotion. Its purpose is to separate the influence of culture from what is innate in its citizens. The founders, an unusual mix of philosophers and neurologists, accept that basic emotions are universal but they are eager to understand how people build ethnic variations from the same components.

Language differences complicate their efforts because some cultures do not have words for certain feelings and therefore can't describe them in a way that conforms to another culture's vocabulary. For instance, some cultures have no word for depression. When they are melancholy, they explain they have been visited by an evil spirit.

A German psychologist, Klaus Scherer, studied people in eight European cultures and reported that ethnic stereotypes don't hold up. The stolid Swiss, for example, registered on his scale as more emotional than the Spanish or Italians, while the English shattered their reputation for blandness by emerging as sensual people who find joy in food, sex and drink.

Many anthropologists believe that culture creates mind and personality as surely as the DNA creates tissue. One of them, Anthony F. C. Wallace of the University of Pennsylvania, explained that culture systems are learned by children from their parents and form "the template, as it were, for the underlying conceptions of self, society and human nature that guide all behavior in that community."

Even weather may have an effect on temperament. Researchers have observed that tempers rise in direct ratio to the fall of the barometer. On cloudy days people feel sad and cranky; Ann Landers, syndicated columnist, once observed, "When the weather is gloomy, people are apt to start fights, drink too much, break engagements and begin divorce proceedings." Sunshine is a recognized therapy for depression. On beautiful days strangers are friendly. It is notable too that people who live in very cold climates share qualities of grim tenacity; enduring the frightful winters conditions them for perseverance. Because heat is believed to relax the muscles of the body, making people lazy, slavery was long justified in southern climates, while people of northern climates, braced by the weather to be habitually energetic, saw slavery as evil.

The moon plays a strange part in human behavior. On the night when it is full, hostels for battered women overflow. Prisons and homes for the aged are swept by restlessness. People behave oddly. In shoe stores, there is a rash of requests for strange footwear. Taxi drivers relate tales of eccentrics who appear at no other time, and those who work on radio call-in shows prepare for weird telephone cranks.

Psychoanalyst Erich Fromm wrote that personality also responds to historical periods. People born in the Middle Ages tended to be cautious, circumspect, unwilling to take initiatives. During the eighteenth and nineteenth centuries, the spirit of adventure was much admired; role models emerged who were full of force and guile. Later the shopkeeper mentality appeared with its thrift and orderliness.

The present era, Dr. Fromm said, is imbued with marketing, so that personalities conform to the need to be charming, vigorous, "adjusted" and cooperative.

Of late, people are learning that the costs of maintaining the pleasant marketing personality are high. Women now are trying to express anger honestly rather than sulking for days as their mothers did, and modern men weep. It is progress.

The root of the word "emotion" is the Latin *emovere*, which connotes inner turbulence. That gets it right. Emotions have an identifiable core that can carry a label such as love or fear, but each is layered. Efforts to pin them down are as doomed as locating the edge of a fog. Besides, emotions often are masked, pretending to be what they are not. What appears to be arrogance may be insecurity, and a humble, apologetic person may be full of contempt.

Much is in the eye of the beholder. A man's friends may see him as agreeable but his sister-in-law thinks he's spineless; a woman viewed as calm and poised by one set of standards is deemed cold by another.

Psychiatrists fear for depressed people who smile a lot, since they are among the likeliest risks for suicide, and mothers who loathe their children sometimes display what seems like wholly admirable passion for their safety.

Many emotions are accompanied by distinct physical changes; entire careers have been spent studying the physiology of emotion. The species could not have survived in the wild from which it sprang without having systems that could react explosively in an emergency. Muscles tense, the mouth dries and the heart pounds as the frantic organism prepares itself either to fight or to run. The alterations are identical whatever the choice and are not useful for measuring, say, cowardice. The decision to run may reflect cool control and judgment, while the choice to make a stand might arise not from heroics but a craving for approval.

A psychoanalyst who thirty years ago addressed a famous conference on the emotions, the Mooseheart Symposium at the University of Chicago, said he had never in his career observed any emotion as a distinct entity, unshaded by any other emotions, habits, sublimations, deceptions and inhibitions. He saw in pure love some kernel of hate because loving wholeheartedly is high-risk. Fear has anger in it; outrage is often the motor that gets a petrified person moving. Grief is often full of guilt.

Before anyone appreciated the contradictions within emotions, the prevailing view was that emotions came in separate boxes, one per package, pure and undiluted. René Descartes mapped six primary emotions, which he chose to call love, hate, astonishment, desire, joy and sorrow. Immanuel Kant, the great German philosopher of the eighteenth century, described five feelings: love, hope, modesty, joy and sorrow. William James, whose brilliant *Principles of Psychology* written in 1890 is a founding document for American psychologists, said there were only four major emotions: love, fear, grief and rage.

People with time on their hands, before Dr. James and since, have listed as many as five hundred.

Surveyors now work from a different premise, that the emotional content of an individual is a range of sand dunes, so blown by the breezes that it makes no sense to give them names. What scientists prefer to calculate is the source and power of the desert's prevailing winds. Carl G. Jung made an important contribution when he established two divisions of personality, which he labeled introvert and extrovert. The latter he ascribed to those who vigorously interact with what is happening around them, realists with a practical bent, and the former term he reserved for people who lock themselves away from view and draw the blinds.

The formulation does not mean that activists never meditate upon the clouds or that unsure people never mount a podium, but that the person's dominant characteristics will be found in one of the two clusters.

A Canadian psychiatrist, John Rich, had another classification system. He used to say that there were only two kinds of people in the world: those who remembered only their successes and those who dwelt only on their failures. He preferred the company of the latter, he said.

Some years ago psychologist W. H. Sheldon divided people on the basis of body shape. Persons with broad trunks, short limbs and a tendency to middle-age fat, he said, have comfort-loving, relaxed and social natures. Those who are lean, long-limbed and narrow-faced tend to be people who are inhibited, aloof and thoughtful. Athletic types with well-proportioned bodies and good muscular development are likely to be full of vitality and push.

The flaw in Dr. Sheldon's personality-by-silhouette theory is that strong, well-coordinated youngsters are likely to excel at sports and thus will become leaders in their peer groups. Accordingly, the characteristics of authority and confidence they may develop have more to do with their home-run production than with any cosmic connection between muscles and ambition. And, similarly, chubby people may be prone to anxiety, comforting themselves with food while maintaining a sunny disposition to ward off rejection.

The fascination with the relationship of body type to well-being is not easily put off by such contradictions, however. There are many who claim that there is a link between body type and insanity. Chunky people, they say, are cyclothymic, which means they suffer from fluctuating moods; lanky people are schizothymic, which denotes a tendency to withdraw from reality; and athletes can be either.

Dr. Sheldon's grouping is a variation on what used to be called the trait theory of behavior, which has been in and out of favor ever since Hippocrates propounded *his* four temperaments—choleric, sanguine, melancholic and phlegmatic.

In 1979 two doctors at Johns Hopkins, Barbara Betz and Caroline Thomas, presented a report based on a study of 1,337 doctors who had graduated from the medical school, a piece of research that Dr. Thomas began in 1948. Her project was to study the health of the doctors, but Dr. Betz, a psychiatrist, used the data to impose a classification system which slotted the doctors as either Alpha, the slow, stolid type, or Beta, spontaneous, active and outgoing, or Gamma, the moody, irritable, demanding, often brilliant and sometimes confused ones.

The surprise in the study was that her judgment of the doctors' types proved an indicator of their health and life expectancy. The

Gammas had the most disaster in their lives—three-quarters of them had suffered such catastrophes as suicide, mental illness, heart attacks. Only one in four of the equable, cautious, well-oriented Alphas or the blithe, quick Betas experienced such disaster.

Whatever the file card reads, emotion is not socially respectable. When people say someone is emotional, they usually mean that the person is irrational, out of control. What adults strive to present is a personality devoid of anger, hate, depression, anxiety, envy or excessive hilarity. The ideal mate/friend/co-worker is an amiable person, perpetually on an even keel, who greets adversity with humor and tact. The stifling controls that must be used to maintain such a façade result in much of the dysfunction of hearts, stomachs and digestion in North America. People who remain pleasant whatever the provocation may be able to carry the performance off, but at a cost to the vital organs.

This side of the grave, there's no such state as an absence of emotion. Controlled, unflappable people in fact often have a higher degree of measurable tension than volatile types. A University of California test discovered that teenagers who were the least talkative, attention-seeking, animated and assertive, the most responsible, good-natured and cooperative—in short, the teenagers who win the approval of adults—were also the most tense. For the sake of acceptance, they were bottling up a jumble of strong emotions. The corollary is, of course, that what seem to be "weak" personalities, the people who are oversensitive, take criticism poorly, hold arrogant views and are quick to anger, were seen on measurement of their visceral changes to have a less powerful emotional content.

Epicurus, the friendly Athenian philosopher who believed that humans must locate themselves emotionally within the bounds of whatever gives them happiness, taught that pleasure is available only to those who can practice moderation. Mild emotions, he noted, give little distress while intemperate ones, even if they are such desirable emotions as joy and deliverance, are disruptive to equilibrium.

Research supports the Epicurean mean. Some of the studies are farfetched—such as the one which demonstrated that earthworms stretch themselves in apparent rapture when stroked gently but thicken convulsively when the stroking becomes firm, or that fish swim toward a weak light but avoid a glaring one, or that lab animals seem to enjoy the mild shocks which are intended to train them to fulfill some researcher's premise.

But humans behave in somewhat the same way. Mild fear isn't distressing, as witness the popularity of roller coasters and horror films, but terror is painful. A pleasant, uneventful picnic is relaxing and sweet on the senses, but exciting celebrations such as surprise parties and weddings leave the principals drained and mildly depressed. Actors would be worried about their performances if they didn't experience the anxiety of mild stage fright before their entrances and athletes depend on the edge that moderate apprehension gives their reflexes, but panic would make it impossible for either to function. Righteous indignation at an injustice feels marvelous and an angry man can be formidable in debate, but rage is terrifying to experience and temper puts one at a disadvantage.

Actors know that roles requiring strong emotion will exhaust them. The great actor Edwin Forrest could perform in *Richard III* with ease but was flattened after every performance during a run of *Othello.* "Playing with the brain is far less fatiguing than playing with the heart," the nineteenth-century actress Alma Murray said.

The Epicurean ideal is to temper emotions but that's a task requiring years of practice. Emotions can be concealed or deflected with some degree of success so they don't show, but that doesn't mean they stop tearing around in the brain, throwing the stomach into nausea. Emotions are mastered only by a simultaneous process of unlearning while bringing in the heavier guns of improved self-esteem. It's called maturity. By the time the new systems are in place, few people can describe how it works. The brain's connectors have forgotten how to take offense at a slight; the message flits along the grooves and can come up with nothing better than a shrug.

The Godot for whom people wait is perfect balance, homeostasis. Meanwhile, storms of passion rage through them, destroying more lives than war. In a sudden anger, people say the unforgivable, do the irretrievable. Emotions hold them hostage; terrorists are in command of their lives.

Physiologists have learned that emotions have a life span, and that strong emotions live for months, even years. Cats who were frightened by a barking dog were examined by X ray hours later, when they appeared restored to their former indifferent selves. It was found that they still showed the internal symptoms of fear.

The longevity of emotion is seen when people who have had a frustrating day explode over a trifle when they reach home. With repetition, such emotions as hate and fear become rooted in the brain's memory bank and will require massive determination to uproot.

Emotions have been producing startling alterations in the human body since the Sierra Nevadas heaved up from the earth's crust in the Pliocene age. From the beginning of the human species, fear, anger and hatred have caused hearts to step up their blood input by as much as two-thirds. In an emergency, livers release a flood of sugar which converts instantly to energy, the alimentary organs seize or else have an urge to empty, adrenaline sends power into the muscles and the brain circuitry approaches overload.

Such preparations for mortal combat are useful when someone faces a charging carnivore in a primeval swamp but not when the person is only responding to a phone call from a department head. The struggle to maintain a civilized exterior while one's innards are in battle is a major factor in heart disease, gastric ulcers and hypertension.

The great Canadian doctor William Osler, described as "the father of modern medicine," once remarked that "the care of tuberculosis depends more on what the patient has in his head than what he has in his chest." Since that observation a century ago, the bond between emotion and health has been acknowledged. The psychosomatic basis of ulcers and asthma were among the first to be accepted, but in recent years doctors have agreed that emotions can make one susceptible to diseases ranging from sniffles to cancer.

The study of the relationship between emotions and health has a name, psychoneuroimmunology. Specialists in this new branch of science are advising people who live under great stress to protect themselves against such collapses as lung cancer or heart disease by changing their attitude or their environment. Cancer patients are following methods designed by Fort Worth's Dr. Carl Simonton, who asks that they examine their lives to identify the emotional trauma that made them vulnerable to the disease. He believes that people can "image" their white blood cells fighting the tumor until they succeed in driving the cancer away. While the method is understandably controversial, remissions and even cures have occurred in somewhat higher ratios than might normally have been expected. Certainly it is not news that terminally ill patients who abandon hope are likely to die more quickly than those who do not.

It is possible that eventually people will be able to train their bodies to resist allergy-stimulating environments, for instance, or to block out pain naturally. As researchers see science unfolding, people will be able to give chemical instructions to their brains in order to keep their bodies healthy and their emotions pleasant.

Ortega y Gasset has written that the suppression of emotion is the greatest error of Western man since the Renaissance. Emotions, to be healthy, must be appropriate and must find expression. This discharge is pleasant when emotions are positive affirmative ones, but there are hazards in venting the darker emotions. People fear the disapproval that usually follows an outburst, however justified, so they hang on to their temper and the urge to strike. Mob violence is easily aroused in a group which has been capping frustration for a long time because it provides, at last, a socially sanctioned opportunity for the release of bottled-up fury.

There is much speculation about emotions, but no one yet knows how a human being puts together a feeling. There are scientists all over the world ransacking the brain for its secrets, for the god in the machine, as their ancestors once searched entrails for evidence of the soul.

Philosophers, psychiatrists, and psychoanalysts continue to contemplate the mind while neurobiologists and neurologists have turned to the study of living brains. About a century ago two discoveries put them on the right track, enabling them to identify the part of the brain that controlled speech. This opened the possibility that other control centers existed, but further exploration was impossible because researchers could only work with cadaver brains which yield few secrets.

A freak accident to a living brain provided the breakthrough. In 1868 Phineas P. Gage, a railway worker, suffered an accident in which a hot crowbar 43 inches long passed completely through his brain, removing and cauterizing the front lobe. To the astonishment of all, he survived, but his personality was transformed. Previously a somber repressed man, he became dissolute and promiscuous. Later a soldier involved in a motorcycle accident had a similar injury, and he too changed from being disciplined and deferential to a man who was slovenly and surly. Victims of brain-damaging sleeping sickness (encephalitis lethargica) emerge transformed from their previous cheerful and social selves to become people who are gloomy and withdrawn.

These misfortunes make it clear that the brain is not a homogeneous blob; instead it is a constellation of shops under one roof, each selling a different line of goods.

Operations on the brains of cats subsequently established that there is a lower brain, the one exposed by the crowbar accident, which is full of hatred and rage. Anthropologists call this part of the skull contents the fossil brain, believing it to be the brain with which the species began. Over the evolution of *Homo sapiens,* as food gathering and survival demanded greater skills, the brain added matter which could think and reason. These additions grew in size and sophistication until they dominated the primitive brain—but it still exists, everyone's ticking bomb.

Scientists used to believe that the brain's many compartments were so specialized that if one went out of business because of a tumor or a stroke, nothing much could be done to replace its function. Now they see the brain differently and recognize its awesome flexibility. If one control center folds, the neighbors rush to fill the breach.

Mood is a factor in the brain's performance. Jonathan Winson, an associate professor of neuroscience at Rockefeller University, explains the brain's capriciousness in computer terms. The hard wiring, he wrote in *Brain and Psyche,* "remains fixed, but the program for information processing changes with the behavioral state."

A familiar example of this is the difficulty flustered people have in remembering the name of someone they know very well. As soon as calm is restored, the memory-retrieval system in the brain works perfectly and pops in the right information.

The brain itself, three pounds of gray porridge, "a great ravelled knot," has about fifteen billion nerve cells, or neurons, together with masses of supporting cells. Each neuron has a threadlike fiber, some of them three feet long, extending from either end, which is its communicating device. The so-called seat of emotion is the optic thalamus, where the sensory impulses are generated, and below that is the hypothalamus, from which run the nerves controlling muscle response.

The neurons in these sites come in all sorts of shapes and sizes, all of them shooting messages at one another by means of enough low-watt electricity to power a twenty-watt bulb. In 1954 Dr. James Olds of McGill University in Montreal discovered where the brain's pleasure center is; since then, neuropharmacy has determined what chemicals the brain secretes for fear, rage and depression. The future is arriving apace.

Memory seems to permeate the entire brain. Dice a brain as tiny as you can and the speck that remains will remember the lyrics to "The Easter Parade," the pattern on the wall of the bedroom of childhood and the shortcut to the office. Surgeons have performed hemispherectomies, which involve removal of half the brain mass. Some patients afterwards continue to learn and remember.

Henry W. Nissen, who worked with primates thirty years ago, once mused, "What enables the musician to think of a Mozart concerto and then proceed to play it with no thought of the sequence of individual notes and chords? Or for the speaker to 'have a thought' and then express it in the proper words and correct grammar, sometimes in any one of several languages?"

He concluded regretfully, "For the present, we must detour around these questions."

"Thought," wrote philosopher Henri Bergson admiringly, "is a dance of molecules in the brain."

Neuropsychologists have found by directing mild electric charges into the brain that it likes to be tickled. Certain "pleasure centers" have been discovered in cats, dogs, monkeys, apes, the bottle-nosed dolphin and, finally, people. Hungry animals will ignore food if there is a choice between eating and the bliss of electronic pleasure.

Dr. James Olds once addressed the Nebraska Symposium on Motivation and reported enthusiastically about his experiments with brain stimulation. Abraham Maslow of Brandeis University was appalled at the implications. "If we could feel all the rewards of eating without eating, would we eat?" he asked. "So for drinking, copulation and temperature regulation? So, perhaps, for love and respect? Plugging itself into an Olds-intermittent-stimulation socket, what happens to civilization?"

Because the brain's power source is chemical, neurobiologists have been working with chemicals that fool the brain into producing whatever mood is desired. One of the first of these was developed thirty years ago for the treatment of psychotic depression. It

achieved astounding results in restoring to composure people who
had been withdrawn for years in a cocoon of madness. This breakthrough was followed by the development of tranquilizers, which
were prescribed to anxious women with such excessive zeal that
hundreds of thousands became addicted.

It became apparent that anything which gives people a buzz of
happiness will do so at the risk of addicting a substantial proportion
of those who use it. Even innocent habits which give pleasure—
long-distance running being but one example—can become psychologically addictive with characteristics similar to physically addictive
drugs as heroin. Pharmaceutical companies may be pleased that pleasure pills will be profitable, but the prospect makes many uneasy.

Pleasure is carried by the neurotransmitter dopamine, which spar-
kles through the brain's networks, blocking off receptors of dull or
worrisome news, giving the brain a good time. Appreciation of art,
the contentment of a scuba diver cruising a coral reef, the urge to
learn a craft, all derive from a network of nerve fibers in the brain
which seek to be pleased. Some seem driven to find an ever-stronger
stimulus, a drug or an activity such as gambling or satyriasis. Whatever gives the brain pleasure will be absorbed along the capering,
supple convectors, and the brain will crave more of the same.

It is difficult to escape the conclusion that people who are vulnerable to addiction are those whose brains are poorly stocked with
homemade pleasure-producing pathways. Lacking the repertoire of
people who enjoy the fall of light on a lake, or a Mozart concert, or
sitting on the front stoop, they feel estranged not only from other
people but also from the lost self within them. People whose lives
are not gratifying will be drawn to anything at hand that promises to
dissolve their terrible aloneness.

Easy delights impress the brain speedily. Craving pleasure, it is
ready to create a new pathway in its firmament for the new toy and
let weaker pleasure patterns atrophy. Thus addictions are born. Once
a surefire pleasure-route has been fixed, the brain is disinterested in
anything that can't produce the same bang, especially if it hasn't had
much experience of joy.

Despite the realization that mood chemicals inevitably will be addicting to large numbers of forlorn people, work on them goes forward briskly. The fear that society one day will order personality
components in a pharmacy is still far-fetched, however. The more

scientists learn about the brain, the less they are sure about. No chemical or electronic thrill has yet discovered the brain's center for compassion or tact or color sense. A scientist once wrote a thousand-word analysis of what is going on in the mind of a person who spends five minutes studying a painting. He wasn't sure, as it turned out. He thought it might have been directed behavior in order to impress someone else in the gallery. Or maybe the person looked at the picture in order to reduce anxiety, or to reduce drive, or to satisfy a need, or, perhaps, for simple pleasure.

England's great physiologist Sir Charles Sherrington studied brains until he was in his nineties. He declared, "I can find no explanation of the mind in terms of the brain."

When Nobel Prize-winning neurophysiologist Sir John Eccles and physiological psychologist Daniel N. Robinson spent a year together studying t'.e relationship between mind and body, the result was a book, *The Wonder of Being Human.* They wrote that they had located the exact place in the brain from which messages to the body emanate. It's at the top of the brain, straddling the two hemispheres, in what is called the supplementary motor area (SMA). When someone makes a conscious move such as opening a parcel, the SMA discharges instructions so that muscles and hand-eye coordination will function. If, however, the person is lacing up a shoe the SMA is quiet: shoelacing is in the memory bank.

The beauty of this discovery, as the two scientists see it, is that it proves people are in command of their lives. The SMA can be put to any task; behavior, even emotional patterns, *can* be changed. Ample evidence of this lies in the follow-up studies of people who had devastating childhoods which caused them to be seen as behavior problems, or even as disturbed, but whose adult lives reflect none of the early damage.

Probes of the human mind are not limited to what can be deduced by scientists working with sensors, pills, needles, knives or a phrenologist's chart. Ever since Sigmund Freud opened the dark continent of unconsciousness where people hide every event and emotion of a lifetime, there have been hopes that the answers to behavior can be found there—beyond awareness. Spelunking psychiatrists and psychoanalysts have been exploring dreams, lies, humor, fantasies and the products of unguarded free association for almost a century, but the unconscious keeps its secrets.

For a long time, the study of instinct was believed to be a promising line of inquiry, since instinct is unthought. The focus was on insects because they operate almost exclusively on instinct. Scientists, however, learned nothing useful, save an increased respect for insects.

The Russian pioneer in conditioned-reflex experiments, Ivan Petrovich Pavlov, spent twenty-five years collecting the saliva of dogs from their punctured cheeks, and an Oxford zoologist has spent his adult life transfixed by the behavior of an earnest little fish, the red-bellied stickleback, but the scientists learned little that illuminated the mystery of the human mind.

Recently, a technique for measuring emotion has been attracting attention. It is the work of two men, Paul Ekman and Wallace Friesen at the University of California Medical School at San Francisco, who have developed a way of reading people's feelings by observing movements of the eighty facial muscles. They believe that each emotion has a unique "signature" which is written on the face. These facial expressions, when examined beside such physiological changes as stepped-up heartbeat, give what they believe to be an accurate readout of emotional content.

The point of reading faces, at least at this stage, is not to facilitate communication between parents and adolescents or people whose marriage is falling apart, but to enable scientists to identify emotions better so they can understand them more. The suspicion is growing that every emotion is learned in the brain, in the sense that the neural transmitters become practiced at handling that emotion, and that a different set of nerve fibers is trained for each emotion. Accordingly, neuroscientists are now trying to locate each of the tracks that carry the freight trains of emotion.

It is believed that negative emotions activate the right frontal area of the brain's cortex and that positive emotions are on the left. Richard Davidson of the University of Wisconsin–Madison told the June 1985 meeting of the American Association for the Advancement of Science that his work, the first large-scale research on where emotion is generated in the brain, showed conclusively that happiness is the chemical stew in the left hemisphere and misery is in the right.

The decision of whether to advance or withdraw is the result of the victory of one part of the cortex over the other. With training and repetition, that side of the cortex can become more proficient and a behavior trait is established.

The model lacks the dimension of depth. The brain operates on at least three levels, possibly four. The first is normal consciousness, in which people think they know what they are feeling. Below that is the unconscious, which Freud plumbed, where powerful grievances lie suppressed. And below that is the collective unconscious, which Jung explored, where the specters of cave people sleep fitfully. Under that is something else. Physiologist V. H. Mottram asked, in *The Physical Base of Personality*, if there was also in the brain "some flickering lamp of the spirit which we may designate the real *I*, the spark of reality which the religions call the soul?"

Some experiments have been bizarre in the extreme. For instance, in a study of aversion, researchers asked women volunteers to cut off the heads of live rats. Another project in aversion consisted of putting the severed head of a chimpanzee in a cage occupied by a number of chimps.

On the other hand, some experiments are whimsical. Psychologists once disguised themselves as trippers and mingled with a group of university students vacationing on the Isle of Man, making copious notes on the young people's mating habits. Many somber reports have emerged from campuses all over North America to show conclusively that young male college students become randier when exposed to pornography. And in Florida, an enchanted scientist has succeeded in teaching dolphins to whistle; the human application of this research is not yet obvious, but nothing is lost in the universe.

Psychologists often work with algebraic formulae which they have devised for the measurement of emotion. One announced proudly that he had succeeded in transposing into a mathematical equation Hamlet's feelings as he watched his uncle praying. The language of emotion specialists has its own jargon, which is free of such subjective and sentimental concepts as "love" or "courage." They use such constructions as "need-satisfying" or "conditioned motor reflex" or "instrumental avoidance response."

Whatever the route taken, a scientist who steps back from the workbench for a moment is confronted with the realization that humans are wonders. Just as people are equipped with such safety features as an extra kidney, an extra lung, a liver ten times larger than they will need, the brain is also full of backup systems, and has infinite powers of recuperation and invention. People can endure searing grief or months of imprisonment and torture and still recover equilibrium and laughter.

"The living being is stable," wrote the French physiologist Charles Richet almost a century ago. "It must be so in order not to be destroyed, dissolved or disintegrated by colossal forces, often adverse, which surround it."

Emotions, like every other aspect of the person, mature naturally, without effort. Given a modest diet of stability and friendship, people drift from self-preoccupation and insecurity to steadiness and outward-looking. The matchless neurons bustle about, day and night, putting together cause and effect, working out rules of conduct and justice, calibrating the worth content of behavior.

The Swiss genius Jean Piaget said that learning is accretion and substitution. He referred to cognitive development but there is application as well to emotional growth. Eventually, usually in mid-life, people become adult.

The chemical lozenges and joy-popping jolts of electricity that preoccupy some researchers seem feeble when compared with the splendor of natural unfolding. A person's mind remains his or her own unique and inalienable property.

"In the latter stages of growth," remarked Abraham Maslow, the sage of Brandeis University, "the person is essentially alone and can rely only on himself."

LOVE

LOVE is the highest emotional development that humans can attain. It is an enigma: love is learned, bit by bit, from the chrysalis of an infant's gratitude for being fed, amused, made comfortable, and yet so natural and so *right* that people capable of loving are healthier than others. Their outlooks are as relaxed as their nervous system; they are at one with the universe. From the beginning of life to its end, love is the only emotion which matters.

Jesus said, "This medicine, love, which cures all sorrow."

Despite three thousand years of romantic legend about young love, it is unusual for anyone younger than thirty to develop an adult capacity for love. No love, not even a mother's love for a newborn, is instinctive or innate. Most people can love very little and only rarely; when they speak of love, they mean getting it, not giving it.

Yet there is nothing in the world that people want more for themselves, and nothing they would rather give. When a nation or community responds spontaneously and compassionately to relieve the famine in Ethiopia or help a local family whose child needs a liver transplant, the mood is pure elation.

Love is not among the tools of diplomacy but twenty years ago, at an international conference in Paris, a woman from India received a standing ovation when she called on the world to cast out fear and arm itself with love. "In the atomic age," she said, to cheers, "there is no other way whereby man can survive."

The easiest, almost surefire way to be capable of loving is to have spent the first twenty years of life in a harmonious, stable, affectionate family. The notable shortage of such environments accounts in large part for the scarcity of loving wholehearted people in society but there is abundant evidence that even when the early environment isn't stable, even when it is short on affection and harmony, people can emerge with sufficient emotional skills to home-build a loving nature.

Even childhood exposure to violence or rejection does not blight everyone. Some adults manage despite abysmal bad luck in parents, training and environment to teach themselves to trust. By refusing to accept that the harshness they experienced was deserved and fair, they steadfastly believe in themselves. They take chances: they give themselves wholly to mates, children, friends. The emotionally self-educated are among the most remarkable people on earth.

They are, alas, the exceptions. Plant a radish and you do not get a rose: wretched childhoods most frequently produce adults whose ladders are broken. Like children who missed learning to speak when their brains were ready for it, they can't double back and pick up the knack. Lacking the empathy that most people acquire around the age of three, they are stuck in a state of narcissism. Sympathy becomes a concept to be imitated but not experienced; they do not suffer to see the suffering of others.

Psychologists who work with emotionally damaged children accept considerable discouragement. Love is so vital to human development that lack of it will make a baby sick, stunted and mentally slow. Scientists classify love as a nutrient with as much influence on growth as iodine or vitamin C. Indeed, an unloved infant doesn't seem to metabolize properly; despite an adequate diet, the baby "fails to thrive." Three physicians at Johns Hopkins University School of Medicine studied children from homes torn by violence and other disruption. When the children were taken from these abnormal environments there was no significant change in diet and no administration of drugs but they immediately had growth spurts. When the children were returned home, growth rates decreased markedly.

A notable feature of children raised in old-time orphanages is that they almost all were small for the ages. A pediatrician in Halifax, John Anderson, once treated a child he thought was a dwarf. In the hospital for tests on the pituitary gland, the child suddenly grew. The problem had been a hostile mother.

Dr. Griffith Binning, medical director of schools in Saskatchewan, studied eight hundred children of school age and reported that lack of affection causes "far more damage to growth than does disease."

Internists have noted the relationship between love and good digestion. The Chicago Institute for Psychoanalysis regards gastrointestinal disease as a relative of love deficiency. Surprisingly, love is considered a factor in diabetes. A Toronto diabetic and psychiatrist, John W. Lovett Doust, once said, "We crave for love and we never will have enough love." Sandor Ferenczi believed that what heals sick people isn't medication or surgery but the "physician's love."

Something between a cult and a religion has been built around a book, *A Course in Miracles,* by the late Columbia University psychologist Helen Schuchman, whose disciples gather in living rooms to talk of replacing hate with love and testify that they are finding peace of mind.

The early absence of love is believed to be an underlying factor in delinquency, addiction and madness. It is a factor which influences the need for impersonal sex, what psychoanalyst Harry Stack Sullivan called "instrumental masturbation." It disposes its victims to make wrong choices when they mate, their craving for affection obscuring judgment. As Dr. Maslow once put it, "Non-love makes us blind."

Love certainly influences intellectual development. What the schools call motivation is in truth confidence. In the many experiments that have been done to determine the effect on learning of such methods as praise, reward, punishment, reproof and indifference, praise and reward have by far the best track records and indifference the worst. No one can force anyone else to learn. People learn for a number of compelling reasons, of which the need for approval is one. The ability to learn is a set of systems which relies to a considerable degree on whether the person believes it is possible, however faintly, that the subject *can* be mastered. The experience of being valued and admired plays a crucial role in learning skills.

Dostoevsky wrote that inability to love is the definition of hell. "Love" is a word that has been used to describe how a person feels about a new soft drink or God—or country and western music, the Toronto Blue Jays, convertibles, the entire human race, microwave ovens, a shade of blue, babies, open fireplaces, getting to work on time, birdwatching, wrestling, autumn, a clean kitchen, bicycling, libraries, working out, shopping. A clergyman found such variety within the meaning of the word that for thirty years he preached every sermon on the same text: God is love.

The word is even applied to the tools of hate. Napoleon's soldiers grew fond of the cannons they dragged over the Alps, decorated them with flowers, kissed them warmly and gave them affectionate names. The bomber that dropped the world's first atomic bomb bore the name of the pilot's mother.

However loosely or inappropriately it usually is applied, when people use the word "love" seriously they are talking about completion. Love can make existence such a personal triumph that humiliation and loss can be borne. Everyone seeks love; it inspires universal heart-hunger.

Scientists are endeavoring by pragmatic study and analysis to catch the beautiful thing so they can study its structure, know where it came from and what makes it grow, give advice on its habits and where it can be found, write a prescription. But love is the most elusive of all wild birds.

Researchers persevere, though they have noted that people most frequently look for love where it isn't. A common technique is to become gregarious because laughing crowds look so friendly and loving. Another is to have children, since it is widely believed that children invariably love their parents. Others become romantics, pinning their hopes on matching a fantasy created by narcotic books and pelvic rock stars. Some sleep a lot, or eat too much, or spend more than they can afford on clothes. Many become obsessed with power and financial success, and still others exhaust themselves with good works.

The most bitter of all commercial exploitation of love-need is a windup doll which repeats, as often as you like, "I love you . . . I love you . . . I love you."

It is not surprising that even cynical carriers of the love message are hard to refuse. A life without love is a life of destruction.

Love, the experts say, is the person's victory over the negative emotions that bloom early—self-doubt, guilt, anxiety. It begins in the pleasure a newborn experiences when fed and, when the baby is able to figure out that some large object is bringing the food, becomes pleasure-gratitude mixed with moderate fearfulness and anger if the large object is reliable but slow. If the large object is negligent or handles the infant crudely, the baby lays down a foundation of anxiety, rage and depression that can become habitual.

The baby is scarcely able to sit alone and yet must grapple with a problem that will endure for life: how to handle mixed feelings. Even the best-tended child will feel deprived several times during the day and night, and in these moments of imagined abandonment will detest intensely the care bringers. Since the baby also is acutely aware that the care bringers are essential to survival, thoughts of destroying them are horrifying.

Most of the people working in the field of human emotions have come to believe that the basic nature of newborns is friendly and cooperative; their inclinations are sociable. As proof, they cite the evidence that the cluster of emotions associated with love and contentment produce good health, while such emotions as depression and anger are harmful to organs and cognitive development.

In *Emotional Expression in Infancy*, Robert N. Emde, Theodore J. Gaensbauer and Robert J. Harman discarded the time-honored theory that when an infant smiles it is a facial tic caused by gas. Not so, the men say. Even a newborn's tiny, fleeting smile is an expression of real pleasure. In the first months of life, babies seem to have happiness attacks: their smiles come in batches and are associated with sleep and drowsiness. The scientists decided that smiles, like the frowns of infants, are organized in the brain stem. They don't know what's really going on in the baby's head, but it's clear that tickles of good feelings are moving along the neural pathways.

A famous experiment was conducted in 1941 by Wayne Dennis, who was permitted to take twin girls at birth and raise one of them with much cuddling and attention and the other coldly, without speaking to the baby or touching her more than necessary to dress and bathe her. Codes of conduct for human experimentation no longer allow such abuse, and Dr. Dennis and his wife discontinued this controlled study of the effects of parental deprivation after eight months because they could no longer bear the unhappiness of the neglected baby. However, they did satisfy their scientific curiosity about whether babies suffer dreadfully from lack of affection. The oddity was that *both* babies grew attached to their caretakers, the lonely one as well as the loved one.

Magda B. Arnold, commenting on this infamous experiment in *Emotion and Personality*, observed that while babies need love and care it is evident that they also need an opportunity to love even more.

At around two and a half months, the smiles of babies shift from the inner contemplation of private delights to rewards for attention and care. For the first time, smiles have a social meaning. Babies quickly learn that adults find their smiles enchanting. Some believe that the ability to smile is an atavistic tool designed to keep parents interested and attentive.

Babies can only judge what a human relationship is all about on the evidence of their first one, which is with the adults who give them care. Since they are helpless, their antennae are acute. If there is affection in the air, they know it and, feeling safe, can relax and enjoy themselves. If there is tension, however well the adults may conceal it, the baby will worry and be tense. A theme is established which can be either trusting and open, or wary and uncertain, or desperate.

Babies practice being sociable on the adults nearest to them. If the exchange works well, babies gain confidence and get better at being friendly. If the work is uphill, babies will clutch at whatever crumbs come their way while alarm grows in their brains. Too much neglect will crush optimism and make the baby depressed and mistrustful. Too much anxious parenting will result in babies who dread change.

The strategy a baby develops to cope with the household environment can set the tone of a lifetime. The first three years of life, and especially the span between six and eighteen months of age, are regarded as critical for emotional development. The effects of good or bad parenting at this time may be irreversible. The horticultural corollary is a young plant putting down taproots—if disturbed in that crucial period, its growth will be stunted.

The baby, however, isn't entirely a passive sponge. Newborns come equipped with their own proclivities. Some babies are readily discouraged and cannot tolerate a moment of delay, so that even parents who rush to every cry cannot provide all the reassurance the babies crave. Others are composed little people, patient about the most erratic care. Some are easily cheered or diverted; others have stubborn natures and have formidable capacities to get furious and stay that way for hours.

Balanced always between frustration and gratification, the baby looks to ways of maneuvering. The smile is not a baby's first successful social experiment. Crying is. Babies use crying as a survival device to signal need. Gradually, and in a process only partially related to the level of attentiveness they receive, they find other techniques and cease to cry except at times perceived by the child, if not by the parents, to be an emergency.

The presence of an attentive, affectionate and consistent care giver makes it possible for even easily angered and panicky infants to relax. If fear-inspiring situations and other kinds of upheaval are kept to a tolerable minimum, the baby is able to gain a sense of competence and even mastery. The flickers of hatred or rage which all babies experience don't last long enough to make an indelible pattern; the baby has no reason to fear losing control.

The baby is trying to get an answer to a basic survival question: is he or she safe, or not? The only basis on which to make that judgment is the quality of care the baby receives. If it is adequate to an average baby's needs, the baby can develop confidence that things are fine and, more importantly, come to believe that it must be a worthy person. At this early stage, nothing will make the baby feel valuable, interesting and effective except to be valued, found interesting and heeded.

Babies subjected to the vagaries of indifferent care givers become uncertain, which makes them either demanding or withdrawn. Feeling unsafe, they don't have the interest others babies do in exploring their environment. It is difficult for them to form an opinion that they matter: existence appears to be a jungle where they will have to grab what they can and be wary of changes. Unlike the babies who are treasured, their self-preoccupation and sense of outrage absorbs their energy. For them, reaching their potential either intellectually or as friendly, self-possessed personalities will be difficult.

Well-tended babies are perky, affirmative, good-humored. Innocently charmed with themselves, they are completely charming. Babies who feel vulnerable and betrayed are less giving, and accordingly are given less.

As psychologist Abraham Maslow observed, "Healthy children enjoy growing and moving forward, gaining new skills, capacities and powers. This is in flat contradiction to that version of the Freudian theory which conceives of every child as hanging on desperately to each adjustment that it achieves."

A significant branching occurs toward the end of what parents call "the terrible twos," when children occupy their entire universes and cannot imagine anything mattering except their own wishes. Like Warty Bliggens, the memorable toad invented by Don Marquis, they believe themselves to be the center of a cosmos created expressly for their comfort. Parents protest, punish, reason and beg, and finally the light dawns on the tumultuous child that throwing a toy means it may break, that kicking a sibling gives pain, that adults have feelings of sadness and disappointment just as children do.

What previously was pleasure-gratitude is changing shape. The child is distinguishing his or her small self from all others. The rest of the family is not attached to the child after all. They each are separate persons with agendas of their own, with their own sets of feelings which must be considered and respected.

This is the dawn of empathy. Without empathy, all love is dead-ended in the self.

The flowering of empathy is so poignant that parents remember the first sign of it as vividly as they can recall the first steps. For one harassed mother of twins, it was a gloomy morning when she was at the end of her rope and sat staring at the floor, close to tears. She felt a hand on her arm and looked up into the distressed face of one of her two-year-olds, who was offering her the cup of tea she had poured and forgotten.

Empathy is a skill. Toddlers have to practice to get it right. They regress and forget how to do it, most often in times of stress. If the environment continues supportive and warm, they'll eventually get very, very good at it indeed, although there is no lifetime guarantee. Even wise, compassionate adults have certain triggers that blast them backwards to become a two-year-old Warty Bliggens.

Three-year-olds move from possessive love, which saw them obsessed with security blankets of various worn and permanently soiled kinds, to loving and letting go. They can admire something without always being overpowered by the necessity to own it. They are careful with pets, respectful of property, and can enjoy the company of children or adults they have just met.

Around the age of ten, the soundly developing child is a lover. The fond adults in the child's life are at the top of the list but they are tied with buddies of the same sex and all idols. Prepuberty is a luxurious time for the growth of the ability to love. If home life is reasonably stable and friendly, the child lives in a blissfully suspended state between the frustrations of being small and the torments of being a teenager. It is a time of consolidation when the emotional patterns settle in and body size doesn't alter disconcertingly overnight.

Adolescence launches the person, ready or not, into a fire storm of physiological changes. The biological clock is programming not only for sex but also for leaving home, a process which necessarily is preceded by a deeper attachment to the about to be abandoned parents—usually unexpressed—and vast quantities of resistance and criticism, which are evinced by such classic rebellions as messiness, deviant hairstyles and noise. The period is distinguished for its conformity with peer influences, which acquire supremacy over the family's values.

Stable youngsters go through adolescence without much drama, a presage of the steadiness that will crown their lives, but for most teenagers the period is an opportunity to try on new personalities. The facility with which they can shift from sophisticate to baby alarms them almost as much as it annoys adults in their vicinity. The process is a reprise of the two-year-old's movement from self-preoccupation to consideration of others, with darting forays back and forth between the two.

Some, fixated on family, seem to change little during adolescence. Psychologists have seen in those who, emotionally speaking, never leave home a form of ancestor worship whose only difference from the same phenomenon in a primitive culture is that it is private.

Young adults are diverted from self-examination by many pressing needs—to finish their education, mate, possibly parent, get housed, find paid work, create a support network of friends. Sometime in the thirties, rarely earlier but often later, the adult has created a life that gives breathing room. There is time to reflect on the existential questions of what is it all about, and why, and *who am I?*

Their basic needs for safety, belongingness, love, respect and self-esteem have been met sufficiently well for them to move to maturity or, as Dr. Maslow used to call it, self-actualization. They have "superior perception of reality, increased acceptance of self, of others and of nature, increased spontaneity, increase in problem-centering, increased detachment and desire for privacy, increased autonomy, greater freshness of appreciation and richness of emotional reaction, higher frequency of mystical experiences, increased identification with the human species, more democratic character structure, greatly increased creativeness, improved interpersonal relations, and certain changes (improvements) in the value system."

This is the period when mature love is possible. The Quaker William Penn said that learning to love is the hardest lesson in Christendom. Being able to love, however, gives courage, compassion, strength and insight that no disaster can completely erase.

Erich Fromm, in *Man for Himself,* classified adult behavior on the basis of its approach to getting love. One he called the receptive orientation, which sees what is outside the person as the only sources of what is wanted. These are indiscriminate people who want to be loved by everybody and are highly sensitive to slights. Dependent on others, fond of food and drink, warm and helpful, they are open and appealing—but vulnerable as a sand castle.

Another orientation is the exploitive one, which also sees the outer environment as the only possible source of reward. Unlike the receivers, exploiters actively go after satisfaction. They are attracted to people from whom they can take. They don't produce their own ideas, they steal them. Full of suspicion, envy and hostility, certain that nothing will be given them voluntarily, they manipulate shamelessly to seize what they can.

The third classification is the hoarders. They don't believe, as the first two do, that there is anything in the outside world that will help them. Consequently their security lies in saving; spending alarms and angers them. Love is seen as a possession and they cling to people, rituals and memories; "the past is golden." These are the people obsessed with order and ritual. They expect the worst. Intimacy is a threat.

The marketing orientation, which Dr. Fromm saw as dominant in North America during the fifties and sixties when his books were best-sellers, is a constructed personality relying on perpetual cheerfulness. It puts on display reliability, agreeableness and ambition. People of this ilk think of themselves as commodities on a upwardly-moving conveyor belt and are devastated by anything they see as derailing. *I am as you desire me* is Dr. Fromm's withering comment on the market-minded. The individual neglects self, so that relationships can only be superficial; dignity and pride falter. There is hunger for deep relationships and much talk of knowing the self, but the person's essential hollowness precludes the development of either.

The final category is the highest level, which Dr. Fromm called the productive orientation and Sigmund Freud termed "genital character"—the achievement of someone who has passed through infantile oralism and anal compulsion. Dr. Fromm said that every human being is capable of emotional maturity, which is distinguished by the ability to do productive work, to be able to listen quietly to oneself, to accept from others, to save, to exchange, to follow authority and to lead, to be compliant and assertive.

The progression goes from I am what you desire me, to I am what I have, to—finally and triumphantly—I am me.

It is not common to make that journey. Most people suffer batterings that make them emotionally lame and oblige them to function by contortion and imitation. The earlier the injury, the more devastating the damage. Emotional tone may even be acquired in the womb. Dr. Louis Gluck, professor of pediatrics at the Yale School of Medicine, believed that the mother's state of mind during her pregnancy has a bearing on the child's emotional development.

"If she has tensions and fears during pregnancy, she will probably have a fussy child with feeding problems," he wrote.

Wars provide a laboratory in which this phenomenon can be clearly seen. Orphaned babies, cared for in wholesale lots by overworked staff, demonstrate that humans establish their foundations for loving in infancy. One of the most famous studies was the work of Dr. René Spitz, who examined 239 children institutionalized from birth in the aftermath of World War II in France. About half were with their mothers in hostels and the others were in the care of a staff so sparse that each adult was responsible for ten babies.

Despite shabby conditions in the hostels, the mothered babies had no fatalities and were progressing normally. In the other group, where nourishment was of a high quality and standards of hygiene were faultless, 37 percent of the babies died. With one or two exceptions, Dr. Spitz found that babies in the second group were "human wrecks who behaved either in the manner of agitated or apathetic idiots."

Dr. John Bowlby, a leading authority on love deprivation, once described a four-month-old baby seen after two months of hospitalization. The child was dying for no apparent reason. His weight was less than at birth and his breathing so weak that he seemed likely to give up the effort at any moment. The decision was made to send him home, since nothing further could be done to save him. When doctors saw him a day later, they were astounded to find a happy baby cooing contentedly and already showing a weight gain, though there had been no change in diet. The magical alteration was due entirely to mothering.

An interesting comment on the work of both men was made by David C. McClelland, a psychologist at Wesleyan University, who wondered if what they call "mother love" is not entertainment. He wrote that perhaps the withdrawn babies in Spitz's institution were lacking exercise and a change of scene more than cuddling. "Certainly," he added thoughtfully, "some complex questions can still be asked at the level of assumptions."

Babies deprived of warm parenting look like miniature adults with melancholia. They don't smile, they won't respond, they eat disinterestedly but don't seem to derive nourishment from their food, their sleep is broken and restless, they appear dull-minded, they are weirdly silent or else they wail and wail.

"Love hunger is a deficiency disease, exactly as is salt hunger," commented Abraham Maslow.

The consequences of raising children with insufficient affection and stimulation have been studied repeatedly. The worst cases are the psychopaths, people with skimpy emotional structure who have not developed a conscience, a sense of consequences, but gratify themselves as impulsively as babies do. Alarmingly, parents afflicted with inability to love will raise children who will duplicate their affliction: receiving no love, the infants fail to learn how as did their parents.

The behavioral sciences were satisfied for thirty years with the mathematical logic of emotion equations based on love in = love out, or rejection = rejecting, until the scientists discovered people who didn't fit. The formula looked sound enough if dangerous adults were interviewed in prisons because it almost invariably turned out that they had been violently abused as children, but it has become evident that the reverse is not true: not all abused children become dangerous adults. Even in René Spitz's heartbreaking orphanage where babies died of loneliness, there were "one or two exceptions."

A University of Chicago symposium on feelings and emotions more than thirty years ago puzzled over two sisters whose father was the town drunk and whose mother was insane. Yet the girls progressed calmly through school at the normal rate, later found excellent jobs and married sensible men. Except for rather more unaccountable aches and fevers than most people, they were thoroughly sound adults.

"How did they do it?" asked Anne Roe, a research psychologist with the U.S. Public Health Service. "I don't know. We still do not know how adjustment takes place beyond childhood levels."

The phenomenon of what some psychiatrists call "intact children" exists but usually early wounds will leave thick scars on personality. One of the most common consequences of a deprived childhood is a lifelong search for mothering. Dr. Bowlby wrote that every relationship that needy people seek is an effort to establish dependency and ask for comfort and assurance. Ian D. Suttie saw the striving as the womb-search of a person driven to create a replacement for the bliss of suspension in a warm sea. Such people covet possessions, or complete power, or uninterrupted praise; they seek the psychic stroking of endless love.

They are easily depressed and, in Dr. Bowlby's words, are "in constant danger of cracking."

A beneficial aspect of an impaired ability to love is that people who can't have a lasting relationship with a person sometimes achieve monumental love of good works. Psychiatrists call this sublimation, or guilt reduction, but the warp accounts for some magnificent contributions to society. There are philanthropists despised by their relatives for their lack of kindness but adored by their country for the hospitals, art galleries and libraries they build. Clara Barton rejected a suitor over and over because she felt incapable of love, but she organized the American Red Cross.

William James called this a kind of division of labor. When people love their family but not a "stranger," they demonstrate a limited ability to love.

Others direct the little love they can summon into activities of a less spectacular nature. A common substitute for a meager capacity to love is overwork; addiction to a briefcase is socially more acceptable than addiction to heroin but may not differ markedly in its dynamics. Many people lavish what little love they can give on cats, or the cultivation of orchids, or on comradeship with a group with which there is no commonality except enthusiasm for golf or cards.

Psychiatrist Karl Menninger warned that well-intentioned friends should not urge such people to marry, or have children, or get a divorce and find a true love. He said that a man who prefers his Airedale to a meaningful relationship with a person probably knows what he's doing.

Society tends to idealize lifelong partnerships as requiring the highest development in commitment and the ability to love. Living happily ever after, or appearing to, may be something of quite another order. People do stay together for reasons of mutual friendship, respect, satisfying sex and love, but long-term relationships can also be built on fearfulness of change or a neurotic attachment, such as between a bully and someone who is pleased to be a martyr.

People with a genuine ability to love can mate lastingly while at the same time nurturing and being nurtured by other family members and a circle of friends. Real love can't be depleted by use. The electrons in the brain are trained in the Golden Rule without hesitating over self-interest.

When asked by admirers what they can do to help him, Jacques Cousteau, explorer of the oceans, replies, "Respect life." It's a tall order for most, but people who can love do that as effortlessly as breathing.

The first step is always self-love. Unless there is self-love, existence is a poignant search for flattery. "There is nothing more conducive to giving the child the experience of what love, joy and happiness are than being loved by a mother who loves her self," Dr. Fromm said.

Self-love is not selfishness; in fact, the two are opposites. Self-love was expressed beautifully by Antoine de Saint-Exupéry as being one's own friend. It means that there has been growth beyond the level of infantile self-preoccupation. When individuals accept themselves as not being bad eggs, but rather good types—when they no longer contain so much anger that they live in fear of exploding—energy is theirs. It doesn't require conscious effort to behave in a likable manner. There is no need to be eternally vigilant in protection of one's place in the pecking order or to perceive a hint of rejection in a careless remark.

The mature, strong in a sense of their own worth, are impregnable against most adversity and resilient in a disaster.

On the other hand, a selfish person can't stop gnawing on tattered grudges. Dr. Fromm wrote, "It isn't that he loves himself too much, but too little. In fact, he hates himself." Such people must grasp and consume every crumb of comfort they can extract from what always appears to be an ungenerous world.

Unselfishness would seem to be very different from selfishness but not infrequently it too contains a strong element of self-hatred.

While it never occurs to the selfish person to give to others, the unselfish person gives relentlessly, crushing the recipient with goodness. The martyr-mother, for instance, is a figure of death. She places the burden of her sacrificial four-course meals and perfect ironing on her family in order that they will never be free of her. Her smothering servitude is, as Dr. Menninger put it, "more crippling than beatings and blows." Her poisonous love is especially destructive to sons, whose sexuality can become mired in dependence.

Promiscuity has long been recognized as indicative of an immature sex drive rather than a robust capacity to love. Don Juan figures are celebrated in fiction as great lovers but go into the annals of psychology as emotional impotent. The conquests of the singles-bar competitor are seen as impersonal acts on the order of buffalo hunting. The swashbuckling actor Errol Flynn freely admitted that he detested women, and it was no coincidence that his mother had loathed him from birth.

Rapists suffer from similar underdeveloped sex drives. Like all such brutal assaults on women, rapes are compounds of revenge against Rejecting Woman and inability to be confident of erection unless a situation of power supremacy has been clearly established. Males who had poor or malicious mothering are prone to impotency, either physical or emotional.

Romantic love dominates the sexual fantasies of women as rape does those of men. The longing for romance is the basis of a profitable Harlequin and Harlequin-clone publishing industry, and supports as well the sales of cosmetics, schmaltzy music, perfume and fluffy sweaters. Though Ortega y Gasset described falling in love as "an inferior state of mind, a form of transitory imbecility," the human mating drive is a compelling one and few escape the intensity of infatuation.

Dorothy Tennov, psychologist at the University of Bridgeport, described the features of infatuation as including preoccupation, acute longing, exaltation of the other's good qualities, seesawing buoyancy and aching in the chest. It differs from love, she wrote in *Love and Limerence*, in that it is an all-or-nothing state of mind. Using her own coinage, "limerence" for infatuation, she commented, "No one is ever just a little bit limerent, and nobody is limerent about more than one person at a time."

It is significant that people who are well mated appear to be almost immune to infatuation, while adolescents, unmated or badly mated people are susceptible to strangers across the room. The power of such attractions consumes judgment. The Moslem physician Avicenna, who lived a thousand years ago, must have had infatuation in mind when he listed love with mental diseases.

The first throes of love indeed feel like a sickness, a sweet torment that provides inspiration to poets. Psychoanalysts take a cooler approach; there is an important transaction in early loves. Dante first felt passion for Beatrice when he was only nine and she was eight, but his ardor never lost its intensity. Marriage counselors often come to believe that there were subconscious underpinnings to first choices for marriage which have more significance for happiness than the surface disarray in the relationship would suggest.

"Passion creates its ideal object before identifying it with some real being by an essentially inevitable error which is then attributed to destiny," wrote Denis de Rougemont in *The Myth of Love.* A countryman, Stendhal, agreed; he said people fall in love when their imaginations project nonexistent perfections onto another person. These individual definitions of perfection are what psychiatrists find instructive of the person's real needs. "The type of human being we prefer reveals the contours of our hearts," observed Erich Fromm.

Said Nietzsche, "One loves ultimately one's desire, not the thing desired."

Many people hope to establish whether the love they are feeling is sexual attraction or "real," by which they mean *lasting.* There is ample evidence that sex can exist in the absence of any affection or caring, but this is not usually apparent in the long afternoons when the sheets are tangled.

Psychoanalysts maintain that love and sex are entirely different systems. Theodor Reik, in *Psychology of Sex Relations,* said that sex is tied to the body and love to "the mysterious something we call soul. Sex aims at physical gratification; love, at the enrichment and enlargement of the personality." He put sex as a biological need and love as a striving on a personal level; sex as the quest for physical satisfaction and love as the pursuit of happiness; the first a call from nature, the second from culture.

The American psychiatrist, Harry Stack Sullivan, suggested that for a state of love to exist the satisfaction and security of the other person should be as significant as one's own satisfaction and security. Walter Lippmann, the political columnist and philosopher, said much the same in his distinguished book *A Preface to Morals.* "The emotion of love, despite the romantics, is not self-sustaining," he wrote. "It endures only when the lovers love many things together, and not merely each other."

This insight was grasped by the playwright R. L. Field, who examined the Cinderella legend at the point where it stops, when the prince takes Cinderella to his castle. He called it *Cinderella Married* and presented the celebrated pair as living unhappily ever after. Since they had nothing in common except their physical beauty, the handsome prince was soon involved in affairs with women of his court.

Men fall in love for different reasons than women do. As Ortega y Gasset described it, men are more likely to experience love as a violent desire to be loved, while in women the primary experience is to feel love itself, "the warm flow which radiates from her being toward her beloved." Feminists suspect that such enthronement of women is simplistic and ultimately dismissive. Women, they say, may have safety in mind when they love to a greater extent than men do, but fundamentally the need is the same: to be valued, to be important, to have attention paid—to be loved.

Sexual needs and loneliness make one vulnerable to the anguish and ecstasy of romantic love. As preparation for infatuation one need only be bored and discontented with one's mate, as Romeo was when he first saw Juliet. The goal of most people in this love-hungry age is to appear loving as well as lovable in order to attract love. Smiles play a prominent role in this performance. Agreeableness is paramount, as is expressing interest and admiration. A cocoon is spun, in which unreality can thrive undisturbed. Each presents the dearest of persons, purged of bile.

No lies are being told, at least not on the nonverbal level. As playwright Ugo Betti once wrote, inside everyone is good news. The most addicting aspect of falling in love is that it turns the person's finer self up to full power and gives it exercise. People deep into the first stage of romantic love are in love with two people, themselves and the love object.

The strategies for mating are being rewritten by the feminist movement, which rejects the role-playing rituals that have put men and women into bed since the dawn of time. The ideal now is egalitarian courtship in which two individuals sort out common objectives, ethics and attitudes toward shared parenting, house chores and careers.

That's what is happening in the script but the old dialogue is difficult to erase. Like all furred, feathered and scaly creatures, the human race has formed its bonding pairs out of one part power (male) and one part submission (female). The female of the species is coquettish and appealingly helpless; the male is controlling and strong. As surely as dawn stirs the mating instincts of pigeons, male arousal usually is piqued by a female who flutters.

Men compete for women with such buck displays as glossy cars, expensive restaurants or crime—police statistics are fattened by men showing off for women. Women compete with such representations of frailness as being thin.

In the process, people get their glasses steamed up and suffer from blurred vision. It is difficult to know, except by hindsight, whether an attraction has its basis in genuine compatibility or self-deception. Wild sexual desire can exist entirely apart from any love or knowing of the other person. Among the people most open to confusing erotic magnetism for authentic love are those who feel incomplete. They have such a piercing sense of isolation that they look for wholeness with lowered standards of common sense. As women longing for babies can wish themselves into morning sickness, the love-vulnerable imagine that this time the chosen mate is perfect, though the record of disaster is unblemished.

Psychologists believe that mate selection happens in the unconscious acting on some old childhood associations. Women who had domineering fathers they hated but were palsy with their brothers may choose a fraternal mate or else, still working on the familiarity of the paternal patterning, may select a brute like Dad. Since neither of these is wholly what she wants, she is likely to wish that her amiable husband behave more forcefully or that her wretched mate be a pal.

A man whose mother held an important job may be drawn to an efficient career woman or else may search out someone who will be more available in the nest. However accustomed he is to sharing a woman's attention with her job, though, he is bound to have moments when he feels the old maternal rejection, and however doting his other choice might be, he is likely to have days when he considers her a wimp.

Humans are too complicated to be satisfied with one dimension of what was familiar: they want a combination. As children they were ambivalent about their parents and this same inconsistency will appear when they mate.

If the marriage ends in divorce as a result of these conflicts, each partner will be at the mercy of the same old computerized predilection. Very frequently people select another manifestation of the person they have just divorced. One man, married for ten years to a flinty shrew with a loud voice, left her abruptly when he fell in love with a flinty shrew who whispered.

On the other hand, the second marriage may be a flip of the first. The daughter of a tyrant may turn in her pleasant man for a roughneck who will offend her as much as her father once did, and the son of a distracted and busy mother will turn from her replica to an easy-natured woman who will bore him.

An astute woman psychoanalyst, Joan Rivière, once mused, "How much does the need for reassurance about one's own value play a part in the decisions of men and women to marry, and how little does the feeling of love or sexual desire motivate them?"

Teenagers are not alone in their vulnerability to infatuation. Because the need to "fall in love" is a function of loneliness, middle-aged people are also susceptible. Fifty-year-olds fall in love compulsively as a way of coping with the fear of aging: it holds off the grayness. Men are attracted to younger women, as everyone knows, because they can be surer of sexual performance and it is a pleasure to be in charge; middle-aged women are drawn into affairs and marriages with young men for much the same reason: the youths look better than most older men do and there is also satisfaction in being a teacher.

La Rochefoucauld said, wickedly, "There are good marriages; there are none delicious."

The ideal of good marriages is friendliness. The notion is that success in marriage means the absence of strife and consists of one long jolly session around a campfire. This fantasy of nonending accord serves to perpetuate many bad relationships. People submerge their awareness that there is no real support in the marriage by maintaining a patter of small talk at meals, going through a stale sequence that serves for the sex act and counting the anniversaries like so many medals. Politeness is the formalization of thoughtfulness. When it exists without that content, it is the art of insult.

Such denatured marriages look fine but deplete the participants. With long practice at pretending to be hollow, a person can become truly empty.

Burying emotions to avoid a row—or self-disclosure—is a small death. Strong emotions must emerge, whether in some acceptable form such as cleaning the oven or in a high-risk outburst, or else they will turn on the organs and punish them severely. Some survive by having an enriching relationship elsewhere, such as with the children of the marriage, or in a long-lasting affair, or in a circle of friends who provide differing pieces of sustenance.

Until one or both of the marriage partners develop enough self-esteem to be honest, the relationship can lurch along indefinitely, an inspiration of perfect commitment to all.

"The variety of feelings and strivings that can be covered by the term love or that are subjectively felt as such is astonishing," said psychoanalyst Karen Horney. "For the very reason that love in our civilization is so rarely a genuine affection, maltreatment and betrayal abound."

What *is* mature love? Oswald Schwartz writes, "To be in love means to be anchored in the safest anchorage, that is in complete union with another being. It means the opening up of unlimited horizons, and the extension of our existence far beyond the boundaries of our personality; it means richness and fullness through fulfillment."

Mature love can grow, as Walter Lippmann once wrote, because its object goes beyond the mere relief of physical tension and extends to "all the objects with which the two lovers are concerned. They desire their worlds in each other, and therefore their love is as interesting as their worlds and their worlds are as interesting as their love."

Erich Fromm defined mature love as having four characteristics: responsibility, care, respect and knowledge. The core of love, he said, is that the partners undertake to preserve each other's integrity. This is an echo of the seventeenth-century Dutch philosopher Benedict Spinoza, who decided that married love should have as its source freedom of mind. The feminist position is rarely articulated so clearly.

Without the element of preservation of the other's freedom, all relationships are tyrannies.

People marry because they want transformation. Marriage is seen as acceptance into the estate of good deeds. Because it has universal approval, a reputation for blessedness which divorce records do not support, people who enter into marriage have expectations that they will be rewarded for behaving so well. The prize they want is love. They are adjusted to a child-raising, child-educating system which rewards good behavior with love. When they were young, they were loved when they remembered to brush their teeth. It doesn't seem unreasonable to expect that marriage, which society holds in much higher esteem than teeth brushing, will be given the most love of all: unwavering, unchanging, infinite love.

What people are seeking by the public act of commitment is to be reunited with their best selves. Paul Tillich explored this theme in *Love, Power and Justice,* in which he wrote that the joy experienced in finding "the loved one" is in truth self-fulfillment. "The absolutely strange cannot enter into a communion," he said. "That which is absolutely strange to me cannot add to my self-fulfillment; it can only destroy me if it touches the sphere of my being. Therefore love cannot be described as the union of the strange but as the reunion of the estranged. . . . Love manifests its greatest power where it overcomes the greatest separation. And the greatest separation is the separation of self from self."

That poignant longing to be whole, and to participate in an admired and hallowed ritual of union, makes people shiver with hope despite the knowledge that genuine success in marriage is so rare as to be almost statistically invisible. Even people who manage a loving relationship that lasts for fifty years will not have been madly in love with one another for every one of the fifty years. The explanation is simple. As Ralph Waldo Emerson once said, "Love and you shall be loved"—a stipulation that excludes most people some of the time and some people all of the time.

The dynamic of love is easier to study in its manifestation in theology than in person-to-person relationships. Freud declared that religion is a neurosis that afflicts humans who cannot tolerate being alone. Religion is also used as a device for coping with fear or death, or as reinforcement of controls to keep the inner demons from escaping.

As the human race evolves, the gods change. The Old Testament describes a wrathful, punitive God who sets hard tasks, while the God of the New Testament is sociable and compassionate. The alteration follows the pattern of human experience, which begins with the child's night terrors and the dread of punishment by powerful Others, and evolves into a sense of tribe and reduced fears.

Faith follows a growth curve which begins in a Father God, moves to a Mother God and then passes through a God Rejection phase— not unlike an adolescent's rebellion against parents—to culminate in God Within. This highest placement of God is esteemed in all religions, however outer-directed, for the spirituality that it projects. The merging of self and God in oneness is revered as a private experience by Buddhists and interpreted by Christians and Jews as holiness and social obligation.

Wholeness is the incorporation into the being of the concept that God is love. The finest wisdom of which the race is capable, it is as unusual as any other steadfast love. Friedrich Wilhelm Nietzsche, the sour nineteenth-century German philosopher, once said that the last Christian died on the cross.

However, such a sense of God is not unknown. People of any faith can develop it. Three hundred years ago, the English statesman Joseph Addison asked the distinguished physician Sir Samuel Garth what religion he was. Sir Samuel replied, "Wise men all hold the same religion." Addison inquired to know the name, and was informed, "Wise men never tell."

The power of evangelism in the past decade is in direct proportion to the rise in planet-destroying weapons and the decay of the environment. The sweet relief of finding a savior from peril and confusion compels people to suspend skepticism and throw themselves into the arms of hucksters. Dogmas of previous years have proved inadequate to the hunger for safety. Churches and temples in the middle of this century began to stress virtues of good sportsmanship, which supported Dr. Fromm's marketing mentality very well at the time but now seem naïve and inadequate to meet the threat of nuclear winter. The emphasis on the social benefits of religious observance was a desperate replacement for the collapse of faith. Religion's most spectacular and compelling promise is the denial of death. Despite a longing to believe in life-forever, many people can't manage it in their heart of hearts and they are increasingly doubtful about assurances that a God exists who watches over them. If the latter is true, God is callous in the extreme. Religious observance, where it occurs in North America, is nourished by faith beyond understanding or by the hope that faith will come.

The psychoanalyst Carl Jung wrote of the religious quest, "Theology does not help those who are looking for the key because theology demands faith and faith cannot be made: it is in the truest sense a gift of grace."

Faith is made of courage; it requires nerve to make that leap in the splendid dark. Like emotional maturity, with which it is associated, it has its own schedule and won't be hurried by evangelism. The roots of faith are established in a simple childhood transaction when parents leave their baby alone but return when needed, when they disappear from sight of a toddler for long periods but always turn up again. The child learns that it is safe to trust. What begins as information based on observation becomes the ability to believe in others and in some form of God.

Faith is society's stabilizer. Without faith in the goodwill of the community, every person would be armed. Without faith, people would not dare to love one another or have children. Those who love wholeheartedly risk disembowelment. In *The Psychology of Sex*, Oswald Schwartz said that opening up one's self is the great liberating function of love—that same exposure is also terrifying, especially to those who are unsure of their worthiness to be loved.

Hope is usually associated with love, but hope is not admired universally. Albert Camus, the great French humanist of this century, called hope a negation of life and vitality. It postpones action, he said, because it waits with cap in hand for the future. The Greeks agreed: hope was the last evil released when Pandora opened the box. Marcus Aurelius, Roman emperor and humanitarian, declared that the hope of mankind was the renunciation of hope, which would free people from their greatest enemy, disappointment.

Studies of pessimism seem to suggest that the heart of gloom is unquenchable hope. Karl Menninger said of such renowned pessimists as the despondent German philosopher Arthur Schopenhauer that their lives were spurred by hope, which filled the core of their despair.

Henri-Frédéric Amiel, the Swiss philosopher who specialized in interpreting loneliness, wrote in the nineteenth century that everything in life is based on hope. "All the activities of man presuppose a hope in him of attaining an end. Once kill this hope and his movements become senseless, spasmodic and convulsive." And Martin Luther King, Jr., said, "everything that is done in the world is done by hope."

Emily Dickinson, the poet, penned a lovely line about hope. She called it "the thing with feathers that perches in the soul."

The adult ability to be optimistic in the face of difficulties is dependent on two factors: the quality and quantity of good experiences in childhood and the duration and depth of the calamity that has befallen. Even in Nazi death camps, there were people who kept their personalities intact and did not stop believing that they would survive the ovens.

Hope is the motor in advertising. The makers of beer, toilet paper and soup promise happiness, and sales result if shoppers believe the promise that the product will make a difference in their lives. Like a child who dreams of becoming a princess, or a brain-rotted drug addict who tells counselors he plans to take computer programming, there is something poignant beyond tears in the world of dreams that advertisers present: a sun-kissed vision of capering, affectionate, carefree youth.

Love and faith are present in friendships, which Aristotle regarded as the noblest of all external aids to happiness. He had in mind quality rather than quantity. He said that a person who has many friends has no friend. Karl Menninger said much the same. There is a limit to the number of friendships that can be maintained, he wrote, because one of the two people involved in a friendship must be supportive and uncritical of the other, which puts a strain on the outgoing person.

Montreal psychiatrist Alastair MacLeod declared that variety is as important in one's friendships as in one's diet. He designed a ten-friend program, each one serving a different purpose—one of them intellectually stimulating, one relaxing and at least one a bracing annoyance who would serve to keep the personality from becoming flabby.

Aspiration to an ideal of reciprocal respect and support in relationships is relatively new in the world. In past centuries, no great emphasis was placed on mutuality. Arboreal prehumans had no concept of affection. As anthropologist Weston LaBarre explained, the male hung around the female because he had a genetically selected sexual interest in her, and her mating season was year-round because she needed to keep the male's attention while she tended her helpless young.

There is some doubt that this early woman had any emotional attachment to her babies. Some suspect one of the reasons she cared for them was in order to reduce the congestion of milk in her breasts. Modern zoos have discovered that even gorillas, a species very close to humans, are not natural parents. If they haven't seen an older animal give birth and nourish an offspring, they don't seem to know what to do with the placenta and they don't understand that their newborn is too weak to cling.

Crude as it was, the primitive version of togetherness launched the modern family, which often bears the same stamp of need, indifference and convenience. In the evolution of European family life, medieval children were considered small adults and took part in all activities that adults did, slept in the same room and dressed in clothes that were miniatures of what adults wore. With the introduction of Johann Gutenberg's wonderful printing press, aspiring merchants saw the necessity for their children to be literate, which meant separating them from adults for lessons and training. The distinction between childhood and adult life was emphasized by separate sleeping and play quarters and by identifiable clothing. Childhood has since been seen as apprenticeship.

Love was not considered a sane basis for marriage until the romantic twentieth century, when it came to be valued even by rational people as the only worthwhile, lasting reason. For most of human history husbands have regarded their wives as breeders, preferably bringing status, a dowry or a strong back for the chores. For sexual pleasure men went elsewhere than the marital bed and for intellectual stimulation there were salons and cafés.

Christianity and its concepts of selfless, responsible love were slow to be accepted because of their radical doctrine. It has required almost two centuries for notions of a compassionate and just society to take root. In the name of a Christian God who preached tolerance, Christians have butchered one another without mercy. In the Spanish revolution, a bishop blessed the guns of a firing squad; clergy are fighting in jungle wars today.

Many religions have viewed chastity as evidence of high piety but few have more sexual taboos than does Christianity, possibly because Christians believe Jesus Christ was a virgin, conceived in a virgin. The enjoyment of sex has long been considered blasphemous, an attitude which accounts to a considerable degree for the success of pornography, prostitution and topless bars. There was a period early in Christianity when unconsummated marriages were idealized for their purity and restraint. When this was seen to have a disastrous effect on the birthrate, society moved to a model only slightly less severe, in which sexual relations were condoned so long as they were joyless and had as their purpose procreation.

The oddest variant of this sexual repression is found in the period of the Crusades, when adulterous knights and ladies demonstrated their virtue by abstaining from sex. They lay naked together with a drawn sword between them to be used on the one who violated the chastity of the other. Such brinkmanship is not uncommon in the sexual tease of modern adolescents or in married couples toying with betrayal.

The evolution of romantic love went through the idealized tease of the feudal era, when operatic sorrow was thrilling and hopeless love the best kind, to the days of the troubadours whose swooning love songs stirred visions of sensuous love between perfect specimens. André Maurois, the French novelist, reflected disgustedly, "We owe to the Middle Ages the two worst inventions of humanity—romantic love and gunpowder."

The Reformation lifted the burden of guilt and sin from the marriage bed. According to Morton M. Hunt in *The Natural History of Love,* the Puritans were the first to regard marriage as a bower of tenderness and concern. The Victorians, repelled by the sordidness of the industrial age, lifted their skirts from the sewage in the gutter by sanctifying their middle-class families and corseting women. It was not until Sigmund Freud uncovered the madness of sexual repression and denial of needs that people were shaken enough to put sex back in the home. When birth-control pills were introduced some thirty years ago, sex could be enjoyed for the first time in history without fear of untimely parental responsibility.

The family of today is a curious structure which anyone can join, married or not, same sex or not, related or not. It can consist of a lesbian couple raising babies produced by artificial insemination, or a single man and his children, or a heterosexual couple with his children, her children and their children, or seven adults living in a big house and having serious meetings about relationships and the laundry, or an old woman dying in her own home, tended by the friendships of a lifetime.

This is the age of self-definition. If people believe what they have is a family, it is. A family is whatever gets one through the night.

The secret of the success of any family, however constituted, is respect, and the key to that is self-respect. When people have forgiven themselves, acknowledged themselves, come to trust that their self is not prone to do harm or think harm, they become freestanding. They are a lovely sight. Abraham Maslow noted that the emotionally healthy person, the one no longer suffering from love-deficiency disease, "does not need to give or receive love except in steady small maintenance doses, and may even do without these for periods of time."

The miracle of being human is that most people are capable of recovering from the pathology of love hunger. They attain maturity by forcing themselves to abandon a pattern of sizzling over slights. They make a conscious decision to stop nagging and to be open about what really is bothering them. They put their lives in order: more time at the top for what nourishes them, less for the demon-driven activities that lead nowhere. "Love is not a higher power which descends upon man," said Erich Fromm. "It is his own power by which he relates himself to the world and makes it truly his."

The growth of self-respect—self-love—is slow, quiet work. Happily, it becomes easier once the brain adjusts its programming to the new responses. In time, people marvel that this situation was ever tolerable or that person was admired; it all seems so, well, *childish.*

What happened? The traveler does not know. Sand has drifted over the footprints.

A research psychologist who spent twenty years studying adults in great distress and misery could find no explanation for the emotional growth of many of them. He commented, "I have come to the conclusion that maladjustment is never inevitable, and that it is not unrealistic to think that a man is capable of being responsible for himself."

The quest for love, or, rather, for the ability to love the self enough so that there is surplus love to give, has implications beyond one's own fulfillment. A loving society is a sane one. As Carl Jung wrote, "It would be very much in the interest of free society to give some thought to the question of human relationship. . . . Where love stops, power begins—and violence and terror."

HATE

HATE is the emotion which lies under all emotions, even love. In great or little amounts, people hate all their lives.

Hate sustains and inspires both the terrorist and the old woman who fiercely guards her garden against cutworms. Sigmund Freud believed that people are inherently destructive and that love is faked; he called humanity "a gang of murderers." Psychoanalysts now believe in love, but they retain the Freudian view that all people hate, even people who seem benign and forgiving. People get energy from constructive hate such as opposing a corrupt government, or they fling themselves gladly into activities which act as an outlet for hate, sports being a notable example.

Karl Menninger considered self-hatred a part of everyone's real nature. He thought of all death as suicide: "in the end," he wrote, "each man kills himself in this own selected way, fast or slow, soon or late."

These morose views have their critics. The readiness of babies to attach themselves lovingly to people, teddy bears and almost everything else they see regularly, attests to the probability that love precedes a capacity for hate. In some babies whose environment is supportive and dependable, it may be that hate doesn't develop strongly enough to influence subsequent character or behavior.

No living thing is incapable of irritability, however. Analysts of infant behavior note astutely that even babies feel intense resentment when they are thwarted. As Karl Menninger observed dryly in *Man Against Himself*, "We need no experimentation to show that this is also true of adults."

A pediatrician once observed that a person's first major decision is whether "to holler or to swaller" when the discovery is made that the two cannot be done simultaneously.

Babies have flashes of hatred that flicker in their minds when the adults who care for them are insensitive or slow to respond, but such spasms are a form of self-preservation. The babies are reacting to what seems to them abandonment, a very serious survival issue for a baby. If the periods when the baby feels hatred are rare and brief, the hate-producing structures in the brain will be weak.

The distinguished John Bowlby began studying the twining of love and hate in babies some forty years ago. He believed that if the first two years of life were constructive so that hate was much the weaker emotion, the child would be to some degree immunized against ever becoming a world-class hater. This can have significant consequences. Children who feel friendly toward adults find it easier to learn from them and accordingly will be more proficient and adaptable in school settings. Children who resent and mistrust adults will close themselves against lessons of all kinds, which adults tend to see as stubborn perversity and often seek to correct with punishment. The hard discipline, of course, reinforces the child's hatred and resistance.

Babies who come to feel that everything is against them will be mobilized to hate. If they give up belief that anything can be done about their victimization, they collapse in depression. If they can marshal sufficient confidence to fight for their rights, they can go all the way into criminality. The view that the world owes them a living is the foundation of antisocial behavior which ranges from the "spoiled child" posture of demanding treats to the berserk fanatic who throws bombs, with the grandiose and pompous in between that range.

Hate also serves a constructive role in getting the personality moving. Without hate, humans would languish in a warm stupor of passive contentment. Teenagers would never leave home. Juggling love and hate in varying combinations, people learn in early childhood to conceal the hatred they feel for parents, siblings, teachers and inconstant friends. Few adults appear to be full of hate; many believe they don't hate at all. What the human race hates most is hate.

Hatred is rarely open, except when it can find an acceptable justification. One of the most common and reasonable excuses for hating is to direct it at someone who is hating you. The process is known in psychiatry as projection. People who achieve success imagine they are hated by less successful people, and allow themselves to hate those they have bypassed. Strangeness is hated, on the presumption that whatever is foreign will be full of hatred and envy. The ease with which countries can convince their citizens that the citizens of another country hate them simplifies politics for the Pentagon and the Kremlin.

"It is possible to be fiercely partisan only against those who are wholly alien," Walter Lippmann once wrote. "When an agitator wishes to start a crusade, a religious revival, an inquisition, or some sort of jingo excitement, the further he goes from the centers of modern civilization, the more following he will attract."

Historians have long been intrigued by the number of times hysterical leaders, some of them clearly demented, have been able to sway whole populations to share their paranoia. Adolf Hitler succeeded in rousing Germans to kill millions of Jews, people who had been living peaceably in Germany for generations. Some Americans were ready to believe that ragged armies in Vietnam or Nicaragua posed a threat to the security of the residents of Des Moines; in World War II Canadians sent into prison villages some 20,000 blameless people of Japanese origin. In 1970, most Canadians cheered the War Measures Act, invoked because two men had been kidnapped and more than 500 citizens of Quebec, almost all innocent, went to jail.

Behavioral scientists are not surprised. They believe that people experience pleasure and relief when the state provides a plausible enough target for the hate citizens have bottled within. There is within everyone a maniac who sits in the fossil brain under all the coatings of civility and waits for sufficient justification and provocation to kill.

"In the end," said Karl Stern, Montreal writer and psychiatrist, "hatred becomes a strange bond of union." Fanatics are a happy band, whether striving to remove immortal literature from libraries or marching off to battle people they fancy to be evil.

It doesn't really matter what the fuss is about; the point is the joy of releasing hate. In mental hospitals all over Europe and the Americas, the inmates who rave that the forces of darkness are poised to destroy all life have identified the same interchangeable enemies: Jews, Freemasons, Communists and the Roman Catholic Church. Demagogues only marginally less insane work from the same tattered script.

When the burden of hate is enormous, only demonology will discharge it. Mild prejudice takes the form of hazy notions that certain people are inferior because they are inherently dirty or dull-witted, but the top of the line in bigotry speaks of worldwide conspiracy.

Hatred enables people to tolerate despair. Visible minorities are ready objects for animosity when unemployment figures are high. In the Depression of the 1930s, midwestern Americans hated Easterners they imagined to be prosperous and selfish. Soccer games mobilize low-income working-class people to pound out their hatred on the faces of strangers who root for the other team.

Studies of prejudice demonstrate that bigotry is a matter of convenience. A person boiling with rage must find something acceptable to hate, a minority being a safe choice, a helpless minority safer still. The attraction of hard-core pornography full of violence and humiliation is that it satisfies the need to express hatred. People unburden themselves of their hatred according to the degree of support they perceive in their community. In a society which places little value on one of its elements, whether women or Hindus, these will be selected as the targets of hatred.

Other species show the same proclivity. A male cichlid, a perchlike tropical fish, is friendly with his mate only so long as he keeps encountering another male cichlid at whom to direct his nastiness. Even a mirror in the aquarium will serve the purpose. But if other male cichlids are removed or the mirror is dirty, the cichlid promptly eats his mate. The corollary is that the families of bigots would suffer if the community did not tolerate racial or sexist hate-mouthing.

Carl Jung was convinced that people could deal with their hatred if they acknowledged it. He didn't believe it was realistic to expect that hate could be eradicated; the goal he set was to hate healthily. Erich Fromm used the term "reactive hate" to describe what Dr. Jung was getting at, which is hatred that is properly and appropriately directed. It is directed in the defense of dignity, justice and respect, a full-time occupation in any society. Without a nucleus of people whose hatred finds its outlet in attacking what is manifestly unfair, even democracies would wither.

Dr. Fromm believed that hate should be separated into two categories, one of which he labeled "reactive hate," fixed on threats to freedom, life or ideas and having as its premise respect for life. A distinguishing feature is that it disappears when the threat is removed. The other hatred is irrational "character-conditioned" hatred, which Dr. Fromm identified as "a continuous readiness to hate" which needs no stimulus from without but is enormously relieved if a suitable scapegoat presents itself.

Irrational hate, which is the opposite of Dr. Fromm's reactive hate, draws its power from a thirst for revenge that was established in the first years of life. The natural hatred babies feel for inattentive parents and for whatever diverts parental attention from them is not significant so long as the aggravation isn't beyond the baby's tolerance. If there is a high level of such destructive behavior as throwing toys, biting and pinching, the baby may be overloaded. Freudians see such violence as the toddler's substitute for acts of murder.

Avenging a perceived injustice is another factor in unconscious hatred. Children who sympathize and identify with a bullied parent store up hatred, and so do children who are held up to their disadvantage against more successful or attractive siblings. Children who feel intense hatred for a parent or sibling during the years of growing up sometimes rearrange the love-hate into a hate-love configuration. As adults they make reparation by means of costly gifts and smothering attention.

Another way of atoning for a murderous hatred in childhood is to dedicate a life to goodness. Karl Menninger wrote, "The professional work of physicians, ministers, priests, nurses, social workers and many others correspond to this formula. . . . The man who, driven by a childhood guilt over the hatred of a brother or sister, becomes a physician and ministers to thousands of other substitute sisters and brothers is not self-destructive in his solution."

Envy is a powerful element in the hatred many people bear. This form of delusional hatred holds the view that others who possess more goods or enjoy more popularity or are more talented have acquired what they hold by robbery. It is immensely comforting for people to believe, for instance, that they, instead of a brother or an acquaintance, could have been a rock star except for being crowded out of the opportunity. They can avoid putting the blame on their own shiftlessness and lack of generosity.

Psychoanalyst Joan Rivière says that the logical extension of that form of hatred is the maniacs who believe that the world is plotting to destroy them unless they act first to blow up the neighborhood.

Even young babies sense that hating is wrong: it doesn't feel good, for one thing, and it isn't safe. If the fantasy of destroying the parents could be acted upon, the baby would perish. Children seek objects they can hate wholeheartedly without the risk of becoming an orphan or of being rejected by their group. Unpopular teachers serve this useful function, as do spiders. The energy young children put into hating comes as a shock to adults, who remonstrate with them to calm down and be rational, but the device works. By dumping hatred in excessive amounts, preadolescents are free to love their idols passionately. The hazard in the bouts of *hating* math or a former playmate, however, as adults uneasily suspect, is that hatred can become a habit. The child who regularly reacts to disappointment by expressing fierce hatred is establishing brain patterning that may have ominous consequences.

The push and pull between love and hate in childhood evolves into an adult's moral code. Julian Huxley examined this in *New Bottles for New Wine.* The noted English biologist and writer believed that the guilt children experience when they feel hatred for their parents, the sense of wrongness, becomes incorporated into the personality. "When an action or impulse arouses this sense of guilt," Dr. Huxley said, "it is automatically felt as wrong."

This "proto-ethical mechanism" is the rudiment of conscience, around which people organize their sense of right and wrong. While the development of a conscience also depends on such external factors as alertness to injustice, idealism and parental models, much of what occurs when people decide how to handle ethical choices is ruled by the unconscious, where hate, guilt and love have fought it out in the caves.

Hate is never guilt-free unless it is sanctioned by society, so the developing child steers his or her course in the rough water of the family's tolerance, the community's standards and the child's own stormy needs. Where the family's rules are known and consistent factors, the task of channeling hatred is at least clearly marked. When the family's rules of conduct are shaky or contradictory, the child will turn to the community for guidance and will be vulnerable to whatever influences exist there.

Children raised by uncertain parents, or parents who handle hatred very badly themselves, have another chance if the environment is stable and constructive. Unhappily, chaotic households frequently occur among those who are very mobile. As people who operate shelters for battered women have observed, upheaval unglues children and makes them excited and mean.

Fortunately for society, most children are not raised in conditions which lack some degree of constancy. Instead they grow a conscience, so well as they are able, by avoiding acts which create guilt and self-hatred. A healthy conscience—one not loaded with illusions of sin and unworthiness, and not one infantilely weak—depends greatly on how hate is handled. If hatred turns inward to self-hate, the person is doomed to wear an inhibiting, painful hair shirt for life. "Good" children, denied all expression of normal hatred, develop heavy puritanical consciences which make the finest hating instruments in the world. No one is more viciously opposed to pleasure and sex than the person whose conscience will permit the enjoyment of neither.

Hate *must* be used up. Exercise works. People can run off hatred, become exhausted and self-satisfied in the process. Anything which uses the long muscles will suffice to relieve hatred. Team games are particularly useful because they provide the additional benefit of a sanctioned foe who can be hated cheerfully and freely. People of a sedentary bent can derive some of the same relief by watching the picturesque hatred expressed by wrestlers, or by reading books full of killer spies, while adolescents dote on computer games where electronic death prevails.

Most forms of play are hate releasers, even quiet games such as Monopoly. Bridge is particularly aggressive and Karl Menninger called poker a fighting game. According to legend, chess was invented by Buddhists as a substitute for war. Dr. Menninger said menacingly, *"People who do not play are potentially dangerous."*

Harvard's great William James advanced the theory that work is a moral equivalent for war. When people work, he said, they pit themselves against a force that they must battle daily for mastery. Whatever occupation people have, they face some form of enemy and designate in their minds a certain kind of victory. Housework is a useful subordination of hate: by scrubbing a floor mercilessly clean, something tangible—dirt—has been defeated.

People who are frantic in their neatness and punctuality, and obsessed with their status, may be carrying more hate than they can discharge comfortably.

People who cleanse themselves by means of therapeutic hate feel relaxed and friendly, as though restored to their normal good selves. Teenagers have difficulty learning the trick of it. They are still too close to their childhoods to have learned how to divert hate without being transparent. At the same time, they are striving to blend in seamlessly with their peers and must not hate unstylishly. Parents offer a handy and highly approved outlet for hatred, so teenagers talk a lot about the failings of their parents. This is cathartic for the adolescents but has never been wildly popular with parents.

Melanie Klein, who broke with Freud, once commented that adolescent rebellion against parents can't be helped. She said, "There *are* children who can keep love and admiration for their parents through this stage, but it isn't very common."

Hate creeps into personality development, like liquid into a sponge, filling up what room it can find. In some babies whose tension is high and whose lives are miserable, the brain is hospitable to the growth of hate. In others where life goes smoothly, hate is scarcely established at all.

Totally rejected babies exhibit a capacity for flaming hatred. In Detroit just after World War II, some love-starved ten-year-old boys happened into the lives of Fritz Redl and David Wineman, who supervised them for nineteen months in a group home, Pioneer House, run by the Junior League. These children, already confirmed criminals and savage street fighters, had all been abused from infancy.

"No one, not parents, brothers, neighbors, uncles, friends, cousins, took any interest in them," the two men wrote in *Children Who Hate*. "This whole vacuum in adult relationship potentialities cannot possibly be over-estimated in terms of how impoverished these children felt or how much hatred and suspicion they had toward the adult world."

Normal children who are refused something desirable, such as permission to watch television or stay up late, will experience a surge of hatred. The emotion subsides as the children turn to something else that gives comfort or promises to be fun. Moping is one of the faces that hate wears, but most children snap out of it sooner or later. On the other hand, the small boys in Detroit and other children from such barren environments can't overcome the waves of hatred that rip through them. Their threshold of frustration was so low, the psychologists reported, that they could not tolerate traffic lights being against them on the way to the zoo. They had almost no memories of good times with which to offset the frustration of the moment, and no hope that the next day would bring anything else but more pain.

In child development manuals, hate control is described as "postponing gratification." The technique consists of moving the personality along from the infantile stage where the baby demands immediate food and amusement, *this minute,* to the period around the age of three or four when children learn to wait their turn and to share. The transformation is successful in most households because adults keep their promises: when they say "In a minute," they don't mean "Never." The toddler waits a minute and the cookie appears; next time the child will be able to wait more patiently. In households where there are no attentive adults, children can't make this learning step; they clutch and snatch as best they can, boiling with hate when something is taken from them, even something they didn't really want.

The two psychologists in Detroit attempted to repair the emotional damage the boys had suffered by offering them consistent, patient affection. The boys recoiled in suspicion, confusion and alarm. What they were practiced at, and found natural and even enjoyable, was to be disliked and rejected by adults and to hate them cordially in return. Despite the best efforts of both men for more than a year and a half, the boys never really believed that the concern shown for them was sincere. They thought of the psychologists as sightseers passing through their lives, distributing trinkets from the tour bus—which, in fact, was the truth.

A controversy rages at present on the issue of the causal effect of watching violence on television or in films. Clinical studies are unconvincing because researchers find it difficult to overcome the artificiality of the situations they create. Certainly when men are encouraged to be violent, such as in wartime, they are more likely to be rapists, and it follows that in a society which admires Clint Eastwood films and depreciates women, some men will be open to the tacit message that rape is acceptable.

What muddies the waters, however, is that misogynist material is sometimes an outlet for feelings that otherwise would be expressed in action. In Denmark, there was a decrease in mild sex offenses—flashers and Peeping Toms—when pornography was legalized. For a time there were claims that rapes also decreased, but the facts don't bear this out. Similarly, sex therapists find that pornography is useful in helping people afflicted with nonintrusive deviance, but does nothing to relieve pedophilia.

The influence of such material probably varies, even within individuals. Having a satisfying life undoubtedly raises immunity to distasteful pornography and lowers interest, but a humiliating failure or rejection could bring about a change. The best customers for hardcore violent pornography and for violence on video are the people, most of them men, who resemble the group of boys the psychologists tried to help in Detroit: they are the haters in society.

One theory about hate, the Freudian one, maintains that people behave well *because* they hate. Good deeds are seen as the effort people make to conceal how much they detest others. Noting that firstborn children often select occupations in the caring professions of medicine and education, the Freudians claim that oldest children come to loathe the siblings who usurp their place at the center of the family's attention. The responsibility and concern they show for their younger brothers and sisters derives from their anxiety to hide their true sentiments.

Dr. Freud wrote, "It is interesting to learn that the existence of strong 'bad' impulses in infancy is often the actual condition for an unmistakable inclination toward 'good' in the adult person. Those who have as children been the most pronounced egoists may well become the most helpful and self-sacrificing members of the community; most of our sentimentalists, friends of humanity, champions of animals, have been evolved from little sadists and animal-tormentors."

Psychiatrists no longer accept that Freud was infallible on the subject of hate or anything else. His Scottish critic, Ian D. Suttie, complained in *The Origins of Love and Hate*, "Freudian theory is based on hate. Freud's own childish rage and despair find expression in antifeminism, the subjection of love to sex, the acclamation of hate and aggression as universal—a complete social pessimism."

Most feel that Freud was dead wrong in his conviction that infants are basically hostile and adult sweetness is always simulated, but that there is merit in his analysis of goodness as having a hidden agenda of offsetting guilt, fear and even hatred. However, there is also ample evidence that people perform acts of great kindness and generosity purely because it is a pleasure to do so, and that the content of what seems like simple goodness is indeed simply goodness.

Goodness isn't plentiful; most people have a lot of hatred to disperse. Some make a show of supporting charities or giving fond attention to individuals. The complexity of their attachments is demonstrated by the rage they display over ingratitude or lack of sufficient appreciation. When love is a mask for hate, as in the "inquisitional love" of a Torquemada, it is an expression of self-righteousness—as Joshua Loth Liebman wrote in *Peace of Mind*, "human aggression and frustration wearing the mantle of love." Rabbi Liebman saw this kind of non-love in parents who dominate their children into submissiveness, "because it is for your own good," rather than allowing them discussion and independent thought.

Oscar Wilde wrote that each man kills the thing he loves, but a truer reading of the line would recognize that insufficient love is marbled with hate. Elizabeth I beheaded her lover, the Earl of Essex, and Henry II had his beloved friend Thomas à Becket slain, both of them to suffer prostrations of grief because killing what they could not abide also destroyed what they adored. The Nazi Adolf Eichmann, who presided over death camps, displayed extraordinary ambivalence toward Jews: in his youth he was strongly drawn to Judaism, learned Yiddish, relished Jewish cooking and socialized in the Jewish community.

Much of the punishment administered by judges, prison wardens, clergy, teachers and parents is vengeance and hatred, sanctimoniously disguised as justice and rule enforcement. What is presented as character building and constructive discipline is in reality thinly concealed hate. People martyr themselves to causes, taking themselves to the brink of collapse in their dedication to a political campaign or a poor people's organization, while displacing the hatred in their natures onto their families or the staff.

A conspicuous example of the latter is John Brown, the abolitionist who fought tirelessly against slavery for twenty years, while his wife and children suffered from starvation and madness. When his sons were grown, he sent them into battle, where they were killed. The tendency for people to be cruelest to those they love is a familiar one. Psychoanalysts are endlessly intrigued by the duality of love and hate, and how suddenly they can flip.

High principles can be a disguise for hatred. Zealots who labor in

laboratories, social agencies, surgeries and the halls of academe neglect their families and friends in the service of what the community
is obliged to regard as a noble calling. Psychologists see in such dedication a poor ability to love and a fine talent for hating. "The pretense of honesty and fairness," wrote psychoanalyst Karen Horney,
"is most frequently found in the aggressive type, especially when he
has marked sadistic tendencies."

Some kinds of humor, particularly racist jokes and the character
assassination known as ribbing, contain a great deal of hate. Comedians are among the grouchiest of all entertainers, and wits are notoriously depressed and mean-minded. Dean Swift, whose classic *Gul-
liver's Travels* is still the most savage satire in the language, said he
laughed only twice in his life. He was a great hater, with a special
place in his catalogue of the despised for England: he advised the
Irish to burn everything that came from England except the coal.

Hate is an element in all religions. Many establish a special deity
for the convenience of haters, so that the god who is worshipped can
be accorded generous, unmixed love; in Christianity, the devil performs this useful function. Religions which don't accommodate the
vagaries of human nature substitute a fallible god for one wholly
good, so that adherents can place their hatred on the god's faults.
Almost every religion features some form of sublimated killing in its
ceremonies. Christians have refined the pagan sacrificial altar to the
rite of communion, when they eat symbolic flesh and drink symbolic
blood.

Flattery oozes hatred. When fans slavishly imitate an idol's dress,
there is mockery and dislike biding its time, waiting for the fall. This
hidden agenda in public adulation accounts for the overnight rever-
sals when heroes show a clay foot. If the hero dies, as Elvis Presley
did, as John Kennedy did, as Martin Luther King, Jr., did, the dislike
and envy are purged. The public is left with pure love—and loss.

"A fallen leader," Freud said, "is often deified by the mob that
killed him."

Hate must eventually make a move. In many people, most, it goes
inward. Apologetic people are full of it. Hatred of a superior adversary turns into servility, which marks the attitude of many women
toward men, while hatred of an inferior adversary converts to anger
and impatience, the attitude of many men toward women. Charles

Darwin was one of the first to comment on this; though he was studying animal behavior, the application to humans is inescapable.

Hatred, however it is displayed or dissembled, is always the overflow of self-hatred. Self-esteem takes up room in brain patterning and depletes the circuitry that makes hate possible. The oldest part of the brain, the primeval core, can have little impact on behavior or emotional color if the civilized brain is full of connections worn smooth by positive feelings. Hating oneself is so painful that people cannot bear it. They must move it out and place the source of the hatred somewhere else, imagining themselves to be the object of someone else's dislike, or the target of the bigotry of some other race or religion. As Melanie Klein noted in *Love, Guilt and Reparation,* the practice of establishing imaginary malevolent figures becomes a self-fulfilling prophecy. As one's behavior toward these projections grows unpleasant, the selected targets react with matching dislike.

Self-hatred also compels people to overload their schedules. Martyrs to the work ethic put themselves in a no-lose position: either the strain will kill them, which is fine with them, or else they might make such a success of their careers that their self-hatred will ease. They exhaust themselves in a quest for praise or oblivion, whichever comes first.

Suicides among high-achievers have been explained as a sudden failure of this balancing act. Deprived for some reason of hope that they eventually will like themselves, they are left with only the wish to be dead. Whatever contrivance the person has invented, social zeal or perpetual motion in the workplace, they are vulnerable to sudden deflation. The self-loathing that floods into the vacuum then is beyond tolerance.

Self-hatred stalks everyone, watching for weakness in order to go for the jugular. Some people avoid struggling with their dislike of themselves by sinking into alcoholism, illness, chain smoking, drugs, inordinate sleep or television-viewing, or whatever opiate presents itself. Like peevish sensitivity, the hemophilia of emotional distress, all are forms of self-mutilation.

The statistics on suicides in America do not begin to reflect the true numbers. No one can estimate how many who die of curable cancer have willed themselves dead, or how many drivers whose cars crash in accidents have planned it that way.

According to Erich Fromm, hate and self-destructiveness are forms of an unlived life. Hate imitates death in its physical manifestations; it strangles. Joan Rivière observed that babies in the throes of a hate attack scream with such intensity that they can't draw a breath and their stools are full of digestive acids that scald their bottoms. Adults endure similar pain when hate is dominant. Their silent screams are stifling, so they breathe erratically, and their bowels roil.

Hating people have the senstion of struggling against a clamp. The vise that grips them is their rigid inability to unbend and love. Though they may go through the motions of relationships and commitments, their essential hatred cannot be contained and will break through in acts of thoughtlessness. Mild and controlled though they may seem, the chaos within is taking a frightful toll on blood pressure and digestion, which by some medical diagnoses are evidence of self-contempt rather than organ failure. The precepts of the Christian Science faith, which believes that love heals, are based on the insight that hate causes disease.

A document from a Paris physician of the nineteenth century notes the postures and habits that people full of hate demonstrate, among which were listed nail-biting, a withdrawn, backward-leaning stance, pinched nostrils and narrowed eyes. The behaviorist John B. Watson elaborated on this and added a clenched jaw, much display of teeth, sardonic laughter, redness of face, jerky movements of the body.

Carl Jung once noted sadly, "Since it is universally believed that man is merely what his consciousness knows of itself, he regards himself as harmless and so adds stupidity to the iniquity . . . The evil that comes to light in man and that undoubtedly dwells within him is of gigantic proportions."

The evil not only destroys the possibility for individual happiness but also contributes to hostility internationally. Jingoistic nationalism and fanatical patriotism are the tools of personalities that cannot love without displacing the enormous hatreds of their natures somewhere. In order to love, they must invent enemies.

When it is out for blood, hate takes care to carry a flag. Those who butcher other human beings do so in the name of a beloved country, a superior political faith or a religion. Voltaire wrote bitterly, "It is forbidden to kill; therefore all murderers are punished unless they kill in large numbers and to the sound of trumpets."

A saintly American Trappist monk, Thomas Merton, spent much

of his life attempting by intellectual argument to refute the emotional proposition of the radical right that a war which kills a multitude of Communists will advance Christianity.

With humanity so far short of dissolving its high levels of hatred, it may be true that the world keeps what equilibrium it has by abiding by psychologically sound principles of finding target countries, races and religions to hate.

This warped adjustment can be seen in microcosm within families. The strategy is known to family counselors as scapegoating. One family member is designated as the evil one, the troublemaker whose wicked nature is the sole cause of the group's unhappiness. The family's venom is then drawn off, leaving all but the scapegoat rather pleased with themselves.

If the designated villain "reforms" or the group is compelled by a therapist to share blame, the unit may fall apart. Harmony will be restored only if there is real change and growth in the individuals or if, as more commonly occurs, a new scapegoat can be constructed; the therapist is the handiest subject, for a start. Nations perform the same ritualistic dance if they happen to sign peace treaties. The nationals on each side will very quickly perceive new and terrible enemies.

In the Austro-Hungarian empire, as historian J. H. Denison pointed out, Czechs distrusted Germans, Germans feared Hungarians, Hungarians despised Serbs, Serbs hated Rumanians, and the Rumanians detested Hungarians and Germans. The empire split into fragments, most of which have been attached by the Soviets, so that all the former constituents of the Austro-Hungarian empire can continue to dislike one another almost as much as they do the Russians. "The history of the world is essentially a series of race-murders," said Sigmund Freud.

As Erich Fromm said in *Man for Himself,* "We do not find great destructiveness against others in people who have little hostility against themselves."

Nevertheless, human nature shows improvement over the long history of the race. Humane postures are demanded of leaders and societies wish to be seen as compassionate. Philosophers and neuroscientists say this process of discouraging hostility can be accelerated by reinforcing what people and nations do out of kind hearts. As love becomes stronger, hate can only diminish. Buddha said that "hatred does not cease by hatred, but only by love; this is the eternal truth."

Benedict Spinoza agreed. He noted that when hatred encounters hatred, both hatreds are enlarged, but when hatred is met with affection it is puzzled and confounded. The power of passive resistance lies in the energy it saps from opponents. The bloodshed in Belfast and Beirut is evidence of force begetting force, accelerating into mutual slaughter.

Booker T. Washington, the black educator at the turn of the century who fought for economic equality for his race, was speaking of an effective strategy for a revolution when he said, "I shall never permit myself to stoop so low as to hate any man."

The end of hating begins with acknowledging that it exists under its many disguises. Carl Jung said that "only a fool can permanently neglect the conditions of his own nature. In fact, this negligence is the best means of making him an instrument of evil."

What preserves hate best is pretense that it is love. Hatred can never be entirely dissipated, but it can find worthy targets. When people can forgive themselves and accept what can't be changed, they can move their hatred from themselves to such targets as hypocrisy, apathy, despotism. Mohandas Gandhi said in the 1920s, when his crusade for the freedom of his country was just beginning, "I am anti-untruth, anti-humbug and anti-injustice."

Another way to come to terms with hatred is to take stock of "love" relationships that are fraught with dissension. The quotient of hate in them must be high: one or the other must go, the relationship or the unexpressed hate.

The purge of hate leaves peace. People who murder in a fit of hate are among the safest of all discharged criminals. As Montreal criminologist Bruno Cormier discovered when he investigated wife killers in Quebec prisons, the shock of what hatred had done was so great that the men were drained and, Dr. Cormier said, "greatly changed for the better."

Carl Jung agreed that people who deal with their hatred will have a different perspective on the world. Having less hate to give, they find otherness less hateful; racial tolerance grows by this process. "As man is," William Blake wrote, "so he sees."

All attempts to confront one's own hatred are acts of virtue and courage. John Dewey, the great American philosopher and educator, defined the good person as "the man who, no matter how morally unworthy he has been, is moving to become better."

He added thoughtfully, "Such a conception makes one severe in judging himself and humane in judging others."

FEAR

FEAR is the paralyzing emotion. In 1943 during the bombing of London, two hundred people died of fear in a shelter when a bomb exploded nearby and put out the lights. As nearly as doctors could determine, they all stopped breathing. Fear is the cause of voodoo deaths and contributes to the fatalities from cancer and heart disease. Fear also causes people to die less spectacularly, by inches.

Normal fear is that which preserves life in a threatening situation; abnormal fear imagines the danger to be greater than it really is. Such a fear makes a nation act docile toward a small cruel army; it is not rational—it causes effective people to feel impotent. It is evil, in the sense that Hannah Arendt used the word to describe the apathy of Germans as trains hauled Jews and others to the slaughter in concentration camps. On a smaller scale, fear contributes to the spectator mentality which causes people to ignore a scream for help or to tolerate a racist joke.

Most adult fears are so easy to analyze that they are something of a parlor game for psychologists. Fear of aging is common to everyone but people obsessed by thinning hair or wrinkled cheeks are simply directing their real fears of impotence and death at a natural alteration in appearance. Those who fear death most tend to be people who also fear every aspect of living.

Fear of the dark is related to fear of isolation and dates back to the child's experience of nightlong separation from the comfort of parents. Disproportionate fear of intruders is associated with people who feel deprived and have nothing to spare. They are the ones with the most locks on their doors, on their lives; they are likely to suffer chronic constipation.

The root of many fears is the fear of being discovered, of having one's true nature found out. A zeal for pacifism may be spurred by fear of one's own inner violence. Extreme fear of guns, expressed by soldiers who commit suicide rather than handle live ammunition, may be the fear of giving in to impulses to murder. A large-scale study in 1955 of a black community in the rural South found a population almost immobilized by the fear that its anger would get out of control.

Fear is one of the fundamental human emotions, recognized for so long that it is recorded in ancient Egyptian hieroglyphics. Fear is primal and unlearned; it is fear's objects that are individually perceived or invented. Benedict Spinoza declared in the seventeenth century that fear was "a weakness of mind and therefore does not appertain to the use of reason."

Fear, however, is a fence behind which people feel safer. In *Landscapes of Fear,* Yi-Fu Tuan, a geographer at the University of Minnesota, wrote that fears exist to contain chaos, that they are shelters built by the mind "in which human beings can rest, at least temporarily, from the siege of inchoate experience and doubt." However longingly people idealize what seems to be a pastoral past in which life was simple and free of danger, Professor Tuan says that humanity has always lived in a state of overwhelming fear, and always will.

In the 1920s, John B. Watson, the behavioral psychologist whose work made a strong impression in his day, perpetrated a horrid experiment on a nine-month-old baby named Albert. Albert was shown a variety of creatures, including a white rabbit, a cat, a pigeon, a dog, a goldfish, a green frog and a young boa constrictor. He was afraid of none of them. Then he was shown the fluffy white rabbit again, and when he reached to touch it, Dr. Watson struck a metal bar with a hammer right behind Albert's head. The baby screamed, was soothed, and again reached for the bunny, at which Dr. Watson repeated the frightful noise. Rapidly Albert learned to be terrified of the sight of the bunny and would howl. Eventually he was afraid of everything fluffy, including a ball of wool, a hat with feathers, cotton batting and a fur rug. Dr. Watson concluded, "Fear of all other objects is home-made."

Happily, Albert was deconditioned by the same Dr. Watson. A white bunny in a cage was introduced into a room where Albert was playing happily with three other children. When the child could tolerate that, the caged rabbit was put into a room where he was alone. After some time, Albert could accept the rabbit without concern, at which point the rabbit was allowed out of the cage. In less than two years, Albert could tolerate having a white rabbit nibble his fingers. How he felt about other fuzzy objects was not part of Dr. Watson's report.

Many authorities believe that all human fears are conditioned as Albert's was. In the main, people fear what their parents fear, though they may direct the fear differently. A mother, so frightened of thunderstorms that she would take her son into a closet to wait them out, raised a fearful man who refused to fly. Studies have shown a correlation between the number of fears held by a mother and the number her children will exhibit.

In *Children's Fears*, a monograph written at Columbia University, A. T. Jersild stated that efforts to rid a fearful child of a certain fear, of dogs, say, or the wind, will only result in the child's moving the fears elsewhere. "As long as there are underlying difficulties that press upon the child from many sides," Dr. Jersild wrote, "the elimination of one particular expression of fear may shortly be followed by other fears of a slightly different cast."

In *Fear and Courage*, S. Rachman wrote of desensitizing adults of their fear of spiders in only five sessions. He had subjects imagine a spider, then relax; look at pictures of spiders briefly while thinking tranquil thoughts, and then relax, and so on.

On the other hand, certain fears begin with the growth of imagination. An infant who is ten weeks old doesn't mind being put in a box; in fact, it feels cozy. At twenty weeks the same infant is definitely uneasy and at thirty weeks will protest heatedly. The capacity to imagine a dire consequence and feel fear is firmly in place by eight months of age.

Fear of separation, the basic fear which diffuses itself into anxiety over the absence of safety, spikes all other fears. Most babies show an early fear of falling and of sudden noises. Throughout their lives, people are unpleasantly startled by abruptness but the operative aspect of the reaction is that it was unexpected and the degree of the reaction depends on underlying fearfulness.

A loud noise that begins softly and builds will not disturb a baby, but the same child will scream in terror if a newspaper unexpectedly crackles nearby. Similarly, adults retreat from a friendship offered too quickly and are frozen momentarily in dismay at even minor mishaps they didn't foresee.

In the first two years of life, toddlers develop other fears, such as of objects associated with sudden loud noises and all forms of strangeness. They are not afraid, however, of darkness, slimy or furry animals or horror masks except when there is an unhappy association.

Researchers asked fifty-one children and ninety adults to handle a selection of snakes. Of all the age groups, only the two-year-olds were relaxed and curious. The three-year-olds showed a degree of caution, while the four-year-olds were definitely apprehensive. Those most upset by the experiment were the ninety adults.

Concrete fears, such as a fear of horses or swimming, begin to disappear as the child grows. If they remain into adolescence, chances are the person will have to deal with them into adult life.

It is fortunate for the human race that babies can feel fear, for there are real dangers they must learn. Babies reach for a burning match, for instance, and must be taught fear of fire. They are casual about stairways and, later, indifferent to traffic. For the sake of survival, it is necessary to learn respectful fear of stormy water, precipices, and dark laneways in neighborhoods where teenagers are poor and frustrated.

Children soak up dozens of useless and damaging fears, however, mainly from their parents. If the adults are nervous about entertaining, the children will read it as fear of outsiders. If the adults are unduly upset when the child is injured or ill, the child's imagination opens up the possibility that the bleeding will never stop or that the illness is fatal.

The renowned psychoanalyst Ernest Jones once treated a man almost incapacitated by his fear of heights. He discovered that when the patient was three his crying annoyed a boarder, who held him by his heels over a barrel of water and threatened to drop him if he wasn't quiet.

Fear differs markedly from anxiety in that it knows what it is about, whereas anxiety is diffused and objectless. Fear, in fact, relieves anxiety. Civilian populations in cities wracked by violence are less neurotic than those who live in peaceable kingdoms where free-floating anxieties have no focus. Some anxious people are drawn to a dangerous situation because it provides something real to fear.

The differences in the levels of fear found in individuals are the result of the interaction between each one's basic nature, which can range from tense and alarmable to placid, and the emotional tone and behavior of the adults who cared for the person as a baby. A nervous baby makes parents apprehensive, so it is only the calmest or most experienced parents who will be able to reassure the child. A jumpy baby in a household of edgy people is likely to be patterned to be afraid twenty times a day, and even an easygoing baby will be infected with the general unrest.

One certain way to raise a child who will be consumed by fear is to inflict pain. Parents who punish their children severely, descending upon them in sudden, inexplicable wrath, will instill habits of fearfulness. Babies who are beaten or fed and changed in a hostile manner will conclude, quite realistically from their point of view, that they may be killed. Intervention by child-protection workers sometimes succeeds in reversing a high level of fear but such deconditioning takes many years of patient, relaxed and affectionate treatment and a child who is amenable.

Left to the devices of fate, fearful children often protect themselves by becoming dangerous. Some of the most violent people in society justify what they do to helpless victims as being no worse than what happened to them as children. The rationale is that they must attack in order to avoid being attacked. The look of savagery so prevalent in dress fads among the young owes something to this reasoning. One young man who had been beaten in twelve of the sixteen foster homes where he was placed by a child-care agency had himself heavily tattooed when he started living on the streets and dressed himself in a biker's black leather and chains, though his nature was amazingly gentle. He felt safer by looking brutish.

The superpatriots who can't get enough of the flag often have the same motivation. Overly fearful of being harmed, they want their country to be able to wipe out the planet five thousand times over.

Studies of people who torture others reveal that they are not inordinately cruel outside the cells where they do their bloody business. They are ordinary men, as the world understands ordinariness, who have been persuaded to believe that they are saving their country by mutilating dangerous men, women and even children.

Child-raising techniques based on coddling and overprotection will make children excessively fearful. When children are cautioned, pampered and contained to an abnormal degree, they conclude shrewdly that the world is an exceedingly dangerous place in which they are ill equipped to survive on their own. Such children become clingers. They do not dare to assert their individuality but are drawn into a dependent relationship out of a need for protection. As adults they are distressed by change and hostile to reform.

Children who have the lowest levels of fear tend to be those raised in a warm and friendly environment where discipline is fair and can be anticipated. No child can be protected against all disaster, but a strong sense of safety will give children resistance against lasting emotional consequences. One young woman crippled in a near-fatal car accident later commented to sympathizers, "Look, *all* that was hurt was my body."

No one can be immunized against all fear this side of a coma but children raised in sound households are less likely in later life to be destabilized by bad experiences. Experts who work with sexually abused children observe that some seem to tolerate even a terrorizing incident while others crumble over something comparatively mild. They feel the difference lies in part with the child's own emotional resources, which are too often underestimated, and in the parents' attitude immediately following the molestation. If the child already is fearful and off-balance, and if the parents blame or disbelieve the child, the outcome of the sexual abuse may be lifelong impairment of normal sexual functioning.

Major fears of young children concern imaginary dangers such as storms, the supernatural, death and nuclear war. Psychologists cannot begin to imagine what is going on in the emotional lives of an entire generation of North American children who tell pollsters that they do not believe they will live to be adults.

The fear of inadequacy, which no one ever overcomes entirely, begins at the age of nine and is most acute in teenagers. The great fear of adolescents is that they will be criticized, mocked and rejected by their peers. The passion with which teenagers dress alike, use the same language and worship the same rock idols testifies to their dread of being outsiders.

Adults' fears often center on sex—on whether they are sexually attractive and whether they can perform acceptably or at all. Some adults have exaggerated fears of authority. People who grouse continuously about the boss are usually at heart fearful people who dread the uses of power for reasons buried deep in their childhoods.

Fearful people are contagious. In a crowd undecided what to do in an emergency, one fearful person can create a stampede. Armies try to keep them out of battle areas, for obvious reasons, and all police training stresses the importance of remaining calm in a crisis.

Bigotry is the hallmark of fear. Prejudice is an extreme form of fear of strangers. Building on centuries of fear-fed stereotyping, bigots create a demonology to justify what they say about and do to people of other religions and races. They reveal themselves by what they fear in others: a male lack of sexual confidence becomes hatred of women or prejudice against a race believed to be sexually better endowed; inadequacy in business rises up as hatred of successful shopkeepers. People want to destroy what they fear, *need* to destroy it, and therefore feel betrayed by those who talk of tolerance and democratic ideals.

Fearful people want containment. They cannot bear freedom.

Selma G. Hirsh wrote a five-volume study of prejudice in which she noted that bigots rarely had childhoods that were loving and affectionate. Instead they lived in fear of harsh and arbitrary punishment. Those childhood fears congeal into hatred, she wrote. Bigots are bursting with anxieties they can't identify, frightened of their weakness, which they disclaim, and haunted by loneliness, but fear rules them. "Without the outlet of prejudices," she said, "they might become insane as a result of the pressures on them."

Fear rises when there is premonition of pain. The fear of a baby is for the pain of being abandoned. The fear of a teenager is the pain of unpopularity. The fear of an adult is the pain of being diminished.

Extreme fear takes the person to the edge of death. It is a protective device used by several species, including those living fossils, the opossums, who seem almost to be in a state of rigor mortis when they are frightened. The silence of terrified humans is eerie. A doctor who arrived on the scene of a train wreck only a few minutes after the derailment heard nothing but the sounds of pastoral animals and the wind in the fields, though a hundred injured and dying people were strewn about. Screaming is a common reaction, especially in women, to sudden fear, but in situations of utter terror, most people are mute.

Doctors are uncertain how fear alone can kill a healthy person, but they acknowledge that it happens. Some believe that the victim dies of a disastrous drop in blood pressure and others that the chest muscles become so rigid that the person can't breathe. The surviving member of the original Siamese twins died of fright in 1874, a few hours after the brother who was attached to his body died peacefully in his sleep of a stroke. Postmortem examination found that the one who panicked had "an extended bladder which seemed to point to a severe disturbance of the emotional system."

Surgeons dread even simple operations on patients who are full of agitated fear that they will die on the table. In such cases, Charles Mayo, son of one of the founders of the famed Mayo Clinic, would refuse to perform the operation, no matter how simple the procedure. He said, "The damn thing about it is that when they say they are going to die, they often will—and nothing we can do will stop them."

In a state of cataleptic fear, the heart scarcely beats. Breathing is light and shallow, and there is no hunger. Thirst, however, is acute. A man who was taken hostage and believed that he was about to be shot said after his rescue, "My tongue began to swell and my mouth to get dry. This rapidly became worse until my tongue clove to the roof of my mouth and I could scarcely get my breath."

Clown makeup is a parody of the face of fear with its raised eyebrows, sagging lines and widened eyes. Charles Darwin believed that the wide-eyed look of fear was a legacy from our primitive ancestors, who stretched their faces in order to see predators better. When people are frightened, their bodies prepare to fight or flee with an impressive marshaling of resources. J. Gray, in *The Psychology of Fear and Stress,* made note of some of the changes. The sphincter loosens and there is an urge to empty bowel and bladder, for lightness. Appetite ceases. Blood pressure rises because the peripheral blood vessels have contracted to minimize bleeding from wounds and because the arteries are demanding a richer supply for the long muscles; this causes the skin to become ashen and cold, hence "blanching with fear."

Vascular constriction causes shivering, gooseflesh and the sensation of hair standing on end. A Sutherland Highlander sergeant in the relief of Lucknow discovered by the light of a flaming torch that he was standing ankle-deep in loose gunpowder and later reported that his hair so stiffened that it raised the bonnet from his head.

A cold sweat appears before the warm sweat of activity, so that the body shivers, its technique for keeping warm. Yawning becomes irresistible. Breathing almost ceases. A substance is released to promote blood clotting and the liver puts out extra sugar for energy.

Digestive activity is suspended and sometimes the stomach empties itself by vomiting. Because gastric juices have stopped flowing, there is no saliva in the mouth.

All this involuntary activity is directed by the thalamus and diencephalon of the lower and middle brain, which is the primitive part of the brain normally dominated by the thinking part, the cerebral cortex. Dr. Gray commented that the next step depends on what the cerebral cortex makes of the situation. In most cases it will try to tone down the reaction.

It is significant, he noted, that because infants have developed very little reasoning power, they cannot deal with the flood of their automatic responses to fear, which is why they are difficult to console after a fright. Mature adults, however, can succeed rapidly in getting control by "cortical differentiation." Confident people have the best sympathetic system for overruling their parasympathetic reactions.

After a near traffic accident or the sudden fright caused by a bat skimming silently overhead, there is often a sweeping sensation of weakness as the system makes a turn and points itself back toward normalcy.

Stark fear can cause fainting, paralysis, seizures, mental disturbances and premature aging, renowned in fiction as hair turning white overnight. In real life, change is not so swift, but people do age in obvious ways after a catastrophe. A young man with no history of early graying in his family became almost white-haired after a few months of nonstop financial crisis.

Arthur Epstein of Tulane University studied epileptics and came to believe that fear breaks down brain tissue. Among his examples was a thirteen-year-old girl who was chased by a bulldog and subsequently had recurring nightmares of being attacked by mad dogs. Ten months after the original fright, nighttime grand mal seizures began.

The most destructive fears are those which permit no remedial action. Women overpowered and raped have difficulty recovering emotionally because feeling trapped is an unbearable fear. The shelling of trenches during World War I broke the sanity and health of men on both sides of the lines. This is the fear that translates into "combat fatigue," when the system rebels against the punishment fear inflicts on the body.

Wherever choices exist, fear galvanizes itself into explosive activity which is almost pleasurable. The extra adrenaline and sugar in the system power fight or flight. Overfed muscles don't feel fatigue and can deliver spectacular bursts of speed or strength. Blood shifts away from stomach and intestines to enrich brain and limbs. Breathing becomes rapid and deep to get more exhilarating oxygen into the system. Because the brain is so enlivened, frightening experiences are unforgettable.

An athlete recounts how, as an eleven-year-old boy being pursued by a bull, he cleared a fence and ditch that he wasn't able to jump again until he was a man. The brain and reflexes are so accelerated, indeed, that everything else may seem to be in slow motion. A man whose car went out of control on the edge of a cliff related later that time seemed to stop while he unhurriedly took the precautions that saved his life—straightening the wheels so the car wouldn't roll, switching off the ignition to prevent a fire and flinging himself to the floor. An RAF combat pilot in the Battle of Britain tangled with a German fighter and watched machine-gun bullets stitching along his wing so lazily that he was able to pull his body out of the way.

That's rational fear, but some people are afraid much of the time. Their physical symptoms include diarrhea, incontinence, poor digestion, heart disease, sleeplessness and aching muscles. Karl Menninger once observed, "The same doctor who would immediately understand how a man could have an involuntary bowel movement in a moment of great fear is utterly amazed and incredulous at the proposal that chronic diarrhea may express chronic and continuous fear."

Eventually, with such abuse, the weakest organ in the chain will wear out. A. M. Meerloo, a Dutch psychiatrist, wrote in *Patterns of Panic*, "In periods of latent panic, people go more frequently to the cardiologist than to the psychologist."

Fear is very close to anger. Physiologically they cause much the same bodily changes, and therefore anger, when it takes action, relieves fear. Children who live in battle-torn cities such as Belfast and Beirut seldom show fear of gunfire but are easily irritated by trivialities. Psychiatrists in these tormented cities note widespread depression and drug dependency.

A cornered animal or person finds fear so distressing that nothing but a furious attack will relieve it. In tense negotiations, skilled participants take care to leave the enemy some room.

One of the curious side effects of fear is that it increases sexual desire. Psychiatrists believe that danger impels men and women into intense longing for physical union both because it holds a measure of creature comfort and release from tension and because sex is a confirmation of power, a victory over helplessness. Panic results in impotence, but milder fears are erotic. Much lovemaking occurs during storms and electrical blackouts.

There is a delayed reaction in some fearful situations. While there is work to be done after a flood or hurricane, people labor with every appearance of normalcy, but when there are no diverting tasks, they may collapse under the full force of fear. Following such disasters as Boston's Cocoanut Grove dance hall fire forty years ago or the collapse of a mine shaft in Springhill, Nova Scotia, psychologists who treated victims observed that some of the strongest among the survivors and their families—the people who behaved best in the crisis— were later ill and hysterical.

When the psychologist Allan Fromme was in a plane crash, he behaved calmly for hours afterwards but that night, lying in bed, he broke into a cold sweat.

Following a period of intense panic, people have felt so shattered that they cannot believe they'll ever be whole again. Behavior is eccentric for a long while. Adults become testy and restless. They prattle, crave sweets and sleep curled in the fetal position. Children regress to thumb-sucking and bed-wetting. A few are broken: suicide, divorce, mental illness and physical breakdown are not uncommon among survivors of such castastrophes as hostage-taking. After a saturation bombing of Cologne, Germany, in 1942, some of those who crawled unharmed out of the ruins threw themselves into the river.

People behave oddly when they are afraid. Some withdraw from reality, a tactic which performs the same merciful service as fainting. Told the house was on fire, a man opened his closet and began to consider what to wear. Jewish women being collected for trips to the concentration camp would protest that they had to clean the kitchen first. In a state of alarm, people straighten the contents of their handbags or wallets, make irrelevant lists, attack their cuticles.

Biologists call this "displacement activity." It can be observed in some species of birds who, when threatened, start busily to build nests.

Another technique to avoid the full impact of fear is simply to sleep. Just before a stressful event such as a television appearance or a wedding, people long to nap. In a prolonged crisis sleep becomes a compulsion.

Apathy is another way to reduce consciousness. The dull look on the face of prisoners of war is not entirely induced by fatigue. They have deadened their imaginations in order to avoid going out of control. "Withdrawal from reality," T. R. Dellen, a syndicated columnist, once wrote, "is a sign of complete surrender." Underground workers in World War II, warned that they are about to be discovered, were so demoralized by fear that they couldn't plan an escape but waited in a daze to be arrested.

People can become adjusted to fear, even life-threatening fear, and will be shocked and dismayed when the cause of the fear is removed. Citizens of Dover, shelled intermittently by German guns across the English Channel for years, showed no sign of distress until the bombardments ceased. Then they exhibited "nerve flop" and rushed to their doctors with complaints of exhaustion, insomnia and a sense of impending doom.

Fear is even enjoyable in mild forms, as witness the popularity of motorcycles and suspense films, mild shock treatments that tone up the metabolism. Fear sports such as downhill skiing and hang gliding offer the same kick in the brain, as do such fear activities as gambling and cheating on one's mate. Children are titillated by such brief-lasting, conquerable fears as those provided by a jack-in-the-box toy or a game of hide-and-go-seek at dusk. Many performers and after-dinner speakers are stimulated by their preparatory fears.

Fear is seductive, as people who have stood mesmerized by the glossy green brink of Niagara Falls can testify.

Social fears are like an adolescent's panic over being unacceptable. Psychoanalyst Karen Horney wrote that social fears are caused by a misplaced center of gravity which is found in people who have so little self-esteem that they base their sense of worth on the opinion of others. People who count heavily on goodwill to keep them from collapse live in almost perpetual fear that they will make a misstep and lose all.

Men suppress their fears more than women do, which places a greater burden on their blood pressure and digestive systems. There is no shame involved for a sensible woman to refuse to ride in a

shaky funicular up the side of a mountain but most men would feel
they must do it, however pointless the bravado. Women can scream
at the slightest noise in the house but men are obliged to turn on the
lights and calmly confront whatever caused it. When a child is lost, a
mother can go to pieces while the father talks in a matter-of-fact
tone with the police. In a crisis, even couples who have managed the
miracle of an egalitarian relationship may regress into sexual stereotypes, he being manly and controlled while she has society's permission to wail.

Psychoanalyst Otto Rank divided fear into two groups: the death
fear and the life fear. The life fear, he said, was the more destructive
one since it stems from the infantile fear of separation, the loss of
protection which begins when an infant is torn from the womb. As
he saw it, people ruled by life fear are in retreat; they cling to helplessness, resist their own individuality and attach themselves longingly to strength, however destructive. The death fear, on the other
hand, stimulates people to live more acutely. They feel compelled to
leave some sign that they existed. Their vitality is defiance of stagnation and death.

Dr. Rank believed everyone is ruled by one or the other fear. The
tone of all lifestyles is either a retreat from the commitment of living
or a confrontation with the inertia of decay.

Most people select a safe, conventional fear rather than tolerate
the greater pain of existential fear. They seize on newspapers for
something acceptable to be afraid of, cancer being a heavy favorite.
Street violence is another acceptable fear, and so are fears of polluted
water and killer bees. Maurice Duhamel, author of *We Are Not Afraid,*
compiled a list of everyday things some people fear, which included
machinery, cows, ice, blood, dust, thunder, the color black, women,
men, airplanes, ladders, horses, mice, feathers, strangers, nudity, ridicule, dreams, poverty and failure.

In a simpler age, people directed their fears at heavenly portents or
the elements. People today are careful to avoid being afraid of something wholly absurd because they don't wish to appear ridiculous
but, happily for them, the twentieth century abounds in respectable
reasons to be terrified.

People prefer to be afraid to being anxious, so they look for a hook
on which to hang their fears. A man riddled with anxiety noted that
he felt worse just before making important business trips by plane.

He concluded that he was afraid of flying and almost overnight could not board a plane unless semi-unconscious from pills and alcohol. A nervous woman who dreaded the pressure of her job selling perfume converted the unbearable apprehension into a fear of falling, which was suggested to her distressed brain by an escalator well behind her counter.

It's fool's work to use logic to rid someone of a pet fear, which is not a fear at all but only the symptom of fearfulness. One young man who traveled to remote areas fastened on a conviction that he would have an attack of appendicitis far from a doctor and would die. All abdominal pain terrified him and he was almost unable to travel beyond the range of hospitals. He pleaded with a surgeon to remove his healthy appendix but the doctor refused.

"If I take out your appendix," he explained, "you'll only switch to being afraid of something else, like a heart attack. A ruptured appendix fear is much easier to deal with, believe me." The young man picked up the suggestion. He now lives in dread of a heart attack and has switched jobs to stay in the city.

Shyness is a form of fear. Blushing is the system's way of hiding the face—not a very good one, but the brain thinks it is. Charles Darwin's epic *The Expression of the Emotions in Man and Animals* contains the information that even apes blush. Women blush more than men do and young people more than the old, except for babies—who don't blush at all.

Shyness is sensitivity to the opinion of others and is therefore endemic among adolescents of every age. A feeling of weakness always accompanies shyness, which results in uncoordinated movements that make accepting a fragile teacup a potential disaster. The mind seems blank, so that names of dear ones can't be recalled to make introductions and sentences are begun so thoughtlessly that they require crazy inventions to save them from disaster. There is interference with speech, so that the shy person may stammer and stutter.

The shy person seeks to become smaller to the point of invisibility, and will shrink in size by a series of head-lowering, loose-kneed, bent-back adjustments, meanwhile turning sideways. The dog who cringes low, with tail between legs, is attempting the same disappearance trick.

Studies of poise suggest that such social equilibrium comes when people believe they can manage the situation, and is absent when the ego feels unprepared and at a disadvantage. With repetition, social ordeals become more bearable and eventually what emerges is called poise.

No one, even the most composed, is immune to panic. When there has been no preparation and no warning, fear simply overloads the system and the frantic body craves escape. Before the thinking brain can take over, a lunatic is at the controls. Women have trampled their own children and men have throttled friends who tried to restrain them. A drowning person is so wild with fear that lifeguards do not dare approach within clutching distance but instead are trained to extend a long pole to the thrashing swimmer.

"Panic is a contagious flight reflex," Dr. Meerloo wrote. "A panicky person causes more fear than the danger itself." In the instant when a crowd of people perceive danger, there is a moment of shock and hesitancy when a stampede hangs in the balance. The freeze most often is broken when someone starts to run, but sometimes the cool head that comes of training for disaster will assert itself. A psychologist was aboard a plane that crashed at a New York airport during a blizzard in 1960. Much of his career had been devoted to studying how people behave in a crisis but in his panic he could not register what was happening, except for the crew member who opened the escape door and called out calmly, "This way, please."

Later the psychologist analyzed why the passengers behaved so well: it was the opened door. He observed, "In most cases of crowd panic in a confined area, fear of not being able to escape is the cause of virtually all terror."

A good deal of fear is simply that: not knowing what to do. Within the areas of their expertise and experience, people have little fear. Psychologists at Yale University conducted two interesting studies to illustrate the importance of preparation in preventing fear. The first took place soon after World War II, when there were rumors that the U.S.S.R. had learned the technology of atomic bombs. A group of high school students was given sophisticated information on the Soviets' progress. Three months later, President Harry Truman announced that the Soviet Union had succeeded in testing its own atomic bomb. The students who had been alerted to the possibility were noticeably less alarmed than those who had not.

The other study involved men who underwent major surgery.

Some of them were highly agitated and made their distress plain; others seemed equally upset but behaved with arrogance. Neither of these two groups wanted any medical information about their condition or prognosis, and both were difficult, angry patients after the operations. A third group behaved differently. These men asked for complete details of what they could expect in the way of pain and recovery, and this group was markedly composed and unruffled after the surgery.

A three-year-old boy of audacious temperament was warned not to play near a steep railway embankment because if he fell he would be difficult to find. One morning he disappeared and his mother eventually found him halfway down the embankment, clinging to a bush but quite tranquil about his situation. He had expected a long wait and prepared himself accordingly.

An experienced driver is cool when a car goes into a skid; a novice forgets all instructions about what to do. A sense of accomplishment is the world's best antidote to fear. For that reason, fear stimulates people beneficially to learn skills that will protect them in a crisis. Philosophers from Statius to Santayana have said that fear has a praiseworthy side because it causes humans to invent gods. John Milton said that hope would not exist without the presence of fear. Psychologist Frederick H. Lund wrote, "We could not be stirred by the possibility of success if there was no possibility of defeat."

Anticipatory fear helps people develop emotional stamina. They rehearse what the risk involves and worry it down to a manageable size. Constructive worry can lead to solutions, alternatives and useful adaptations. Like the work of grief, worrying can convert a paralyzing state into a genuine gain. The fearfulness of children is connected to their lack of skills and becomes a motivating force for learning.

Psychologists who studied young delinquents in a halfway house in Detroit noted that the boys were determined to learn defense skills. Having been severely abused when they were small, they were tireless in pursuit of such knowledge as how to box.

"The three big musts of panic prevention," wrote Columbia University's Joost Meerloo, are "preparation, information and action. When people are well prepared, fear loses its mystic penetration; when people are well informed there is no magic unknown; when people have to work and act there is no time for boosting up a fearful fantasy."

Fear sometimes brings people together. Antoine de Saint-Exupéry said people travel side by side for years, "exchanging those words which carry no freight," until danger comes and with it "they discover that they belong to the same family."

Fear has other important uses. Human achievement, the sages say, owes much to the fear of being insignificant.

Those who carry too many fears can deal with them only by going forward, wading through them with teeth clenched. The fruits of victory are more than the reduced stress on the system; learning to be unafraid is empowering. In *We Are Not Afraid*, Maurice Duhamel wrote, "A man is stronger morally, and physically too very often, for he has been able to find strength he did not know he possessed . . . his fibre has been toughened, his soul firmed, his muscles flexed, his mind sharpened."

Unvanquished fear is destructive of decency and compassion; it makes communities unsafe. When fear is in the air, few people are wise and kind. As Seneca observed two thousand years ago, "Nothing is terrible in things, except fear itself."

ANGER

ANGER, a primitive emotion, is one of the easiest to recognize. While the more disabling emotions of hate, fear and depression can be masked to appear their very opposites, few people can hide anger successfully. It's noisy, for one thing, and destructive. Anger is also ubiquitous: even the gods thunder in wrath. Some anthropologists maintain that the present species of humanoids, which are the most quarrelsome of all the apes, are in fact the missing link between anthropoids and humans.

When people speak of getting control of their emotions, what they have in mind is getting a grip on their tempers. Men and women have more regrets over a loss of temper than about any other aspect of their personalities. Psychiatrists may assure them that it is healthy to release anger appropriately, but practical experience has amply demonstrated that discharges of anger lead to broken marriages, lost jobs, arrests and evictions.

One of the most appalling discoveries people make about themselves comes when they are in a situation which causes them to unleash all the rage at their disposal, which turns out to be enough to kill. A glimpse of this inner savage leaves people shaken and depressed; it will be a long time before they can persuade their egos that they are really civilized, decent and harmless people.

Luckily, the civilized part of the human brain usually is in charge of behavior. Only occasionally does anyone have evidence that lodged in the oldest and deepest part of the brain are primitive systems which can produce a homicidal chain reaction. Many millennia ago, the human race began to grow the enormous brain mass called the cerebrum in which reason flourishes. This was an addition to the tiny primitive maniac brain, not a replacement. When surgery or a severe injury to self-esteem removes the controls, the person in the cave comes out with a club.

The phenomenon, unhappily common to all human existence, has been demonstrated repeatedly in laboratories. Electrodes placed against the hypothalamus of cats can induce instant rage at the flick of a switch. Harvard's great physiologist Walter B. Cannon was one of the first to discover that "rapid removal of the cerebral hemispheres was followed by an extraordinary exhibition of rage." Later work confirmed his hunch that the site for fear and anger was located in a living fossil within the brain. Albert Fax, at the University of Washington School of Medicine, observed that anger showed more strongly on testing equipment than did its physiological look-alike, fear, "indicating a greater organizing or integrating during anger than during fear." He concluded that anger is preparation for aggression, which needs more resources than fear, the body's trigger for either anger or flight.

When people have been deeply afraid, their subsequent anger is truly awesome.

The latest work on anger centers in the hot new field of neurochemistry. The brain apparently releases a chemical, seratonin, when it is trying to get rage under control. Yale's Michael Sheard is one of many trying to find a drug that will reinforce this natural substance to help people with a low threshold for anger.

Brain damage, such as occurs in a stroke, can result in normally mild, pleasant people becoming grouchy and intractable. In some cases of brain injury, the person becomes a psychopath capable of killing and must be restrained with drugs. The last emotion left in a paralyzed or diseased brain is wild, strong anger.

As everyone knows, the thoughtful and kind part of the human brain seems to wilt away when anger takes over. Outlandish courses of action suggest themselves and seem entirely reasonable and justified. The imagination boils with schemes of revenge, complete with dialogue, from which the rational person would cringe.

Alcohol is almost as effective as surgery in removing common sense. By dulling the effectiveness of the cerebral person, it opens the gate for the lunatic.

Annoyance and irritation, the mildest forms of anger, are much more common than full-blown rage. According to a monograph by Hulsey Cason in the *Journal of Experimental Psychology,* more than half of what annoys adults is the behavior of other adults. Only 16 percent of the 2,581 hard-core annoyances Dr. Cason listed were the result of nonhuman things and activities. Topping the list: people who loiter after saying goodbye, excessive politeness, other people losing their temper, argumentative people, being told how to drive by a passenger in the car, affected manners, gushing, loud laughing, gum chewing, children who don't obey, borrowers, unsought advice, funerals, being laughed at, "I told you so," cleaning ears in public, cheaters, high-pressure salespeople, crowding in ahead of people in line, petty liars and a mosquito in the bedroom.

When irritations accumulate, people can explode in anger over a misplaced glove.

One theory holds that the first emotion a baby experiences is anger. The first cry of newborns, as some behavioral scientists hear it, is an expression of wrath at the mauling they have endured in the birth canal. Karl Menninger was a firm supporter of this view. He wrote, "The human child begins his life in anger."

More recently, the experts disagree. The most prevalent view of emotional development is that infants have undifferentiated feelings which don't sort themselves out into the family of emotions until months after birth. Anger is the sharp branch of distress, the specialists say, but even this theory accepts that anger is one of the most distinct and earliest of all human emotions. Carroll E. Izard, in *Patterns of Emotions,* listed anger as one of the fundamental ones, along with interest, joy, surprise, distress, contempt, shame and fear.

Studies of anger in adults illustrate that grown men and women lose their tempers for the same basic reasons that babies do. The dynamic is a loss of invincibility. In babies, anger is provoked by domination and interference, a situation described as the babies "not getting their own way." In adults, anger rises fastest in reaction to a blow to self-esteem, in which case "not getting their own way" refers to approval, support and affection.

The observable truth is that people wax angriest at those they love. This is due, at least in part, to the fact that people depend most on their nearest and dearest for self-definition. Anger follows any blow that damages a precarious person's self-esteem; human nature can more easily forgive a casual acquaintance being disloyal than a gesture by a loved one that seems less than adoring. It follows that people who have adequate resources of confidence and self-approval are more impervious to an attack of anger.

Jean-Paul Sartre, the French existentialist philosopher, believed that anger is an expression of the person's temporary defeat. He noted that when people fail to solve some problem, they fall back on the primitive neural circuitry of anger, as when a person trying in vain to fix a lawn mower eventually may kick it over, or throw the wrench, or turn the air blue. Sartre observed that when friends are trading good-natured insults, both remain cheerful only so long as the exchange is even. If one continues to be inventive while the other has run out of material, however, an element of nastiness will ensue.

Temper is a universal technique for dealing with loss.

Two-year-olds are among the angriest people in the world. They've become aware that they're small and helpless at a time when their skills are only beginning to develop. Everything they attempt, they do poorly—and they know it. Their frustration makes them difficult, causing the adults around them to be exasperated, and this further increases the two-year-old's sense of hopeless failure. One researcher, only half trying, compiled a list of over a hundred sure ways to make a two-year-old furious; estimates of the true number run into the thousands. Even one-year-olds are pretty ferocious.

"Children between the ages of one and two, when put together in a playpen, will bite each other, pull each other's hair and steal each other's toys," noted Anna Freud, who observed toddlers in nurseries in wartime London. "The more their independence and strength are growing, the more they will have to be watched."

Florence L. Goodenough, professor at the esteemed University of Minnesota's Institute of Child Study, wrote in *Anger in Young Children* that there seem to be three kinds of childhood anger. In a situation, say, where a pull toy is stuck behind a chair, some toddlers will display what Dr. Goodenough called undirected anger: they simply stand and scream. Other children demonstrate resistance by pulling frantically to free the toy. The third variety is retaliation, where the child kicks the chair or tries to break the toy.

As children grow, retaliation becomes the preferred method of dealing with anger. This is the point where societal conditioning becomes evident. Most parents are shocked when a little girl does something destructive in a fit of anger. She is likely to be lectured severely or punished, on the grounds that she's behaving in a totally unacceptable way. The infrastructure in this drama is that traditional women survived in male-led families and a male-led world by developing skills of negotiation and compromise, in which arsenal confrontation is an aberration. A historical imperative is at work. For the sake of the child's future happiness and well-being, her hostility must be subdued. What she learns to do, in fact, is to hide it.

Male superiority, on the other hand, is acquired by aggression. Even enlightened, feminist-minded parents are imbued with this stereotype of male-female roles. On the subconscious level, they are less disturbed by a son who throws his toys than by a daughter who does so. He will be rebuked, but there isn't the same urgency and alarm in the parent's voice and the punishment will not be significant. He is getting permission to expose his temper; she is not.

Retaliation is not always overt, even in the unsophisticated repertoire of two-year-olds. One of the reasons for prolonged thumbsucking is how satisfyingly upset parents become, and the child who musses a fresh change of clothes may be getting revenge on a fastidious mother. Three-year-olds are starting to differentiate themselves from others in their family and begin to demonstrate charming social skills. This identification of self, however, has consequences for behavior with other children: competition begins and children can become exceedingly angry at a playmate or sibling who is more adept, or adept in different ways. The most common manifestation is a fight over toys, which is really a primitive battle for territory and prominence. Little girls stamp their feet when angry; little boys are more violent and their anger lasts longer. Around the age of seven, children exhibiting retaliatory anger against their parents will sigh, "Rebecca's mother is *so* pretty."

All preschool children are touchiest when hungry or sleepy, and when there are visitors in the home (particularly if the visitors include other children) and when they are ill. They see routine as an invasion of their independence. Unless the parents give adequate warning, they will seethe at the imposition of bedtime, putting toys away, coming in to eat, washing. Almost half the anger of three-year-olds arises from disputes with playmates or siblings; by the age of four, they become more agreeable, so that only a quarter of their anger occurs in social situations.

At this point, parental handling of the child's anger may have lasting consequences. Studies show that children who suffered from too much frustration do not learn to endure it better, as parents might hope, but become adults who cannot bear frustration at all. Karl Menninger noted that children who are frustrated too much, too rapidly or too inconsistently will permanently feel that they have been robbed or cheated.

In coping with anger in children, bribery, spanking, threatening and isolation are the usual methods employed by parents, who are dismayed to discover that coaxing, reasoning and soothing aren't very effective. Psychologists recommend instead removing the source of the trouble and making the consequences logical and consistent. "Large-minded tolerance, mixed with humor, a reasonable perspective of small misdeeds, no nagging afterwards—all result in children who are less frequently angry," advised Florence Goodenough in her important work *Anger in Young Children.*

Anna Freud observed, "If education is handled intelligently, the main part of these aggressive impulses will be directed away from their primitive aim of doing harm to somebody or something and will be used to fight difficulties of the outer world."

Unfortunately, male children raised by angry parents are very likely to be angry and aggressive themselves. Daughters raised in tumultuous, violent homes are apt to be depressed and submissive. Curiously, when the level of violence is truly terrifying, the boys may emerge as crumbled human beings and the girls impulsively cruel.

Angry children generally become angry adults. A study published in 1984 by two University of Illinois researchers, L. Rowell Huesmann and Leonard D. Eron, described some 800 youngsters followed from childhood into their twenties and thirties. Severely punished, angry children became angry adults who punished their own children severely. The Chicago team concluded sadly that aggression and anger are communicable traits.

The founder of the Institute of Child Study at the University of Toronto, psychologist William E. Blatz, also studied anger in children. He concluded that retaliatory fighting reaches its peak during the first year of formal education, at about age six, and thereafter diminishes until it has almost disappeared by the early teens. Adolescents demonstrate anger most frequently by sulking (women) and resistance (men). Their anger is aroused when they believe siblings or others have imposed on them, when they feel confined (an anger related to one of the first sources of anger after birth, namely the binding of a newborn's arms), when they think they have been lied to or treated unfairly, when they are the object of sarcasm and when they have a general sense that things aren't working out.

Parents deal with the anger of children, in the main, by driving it underground rather than looking at causes and prevention. No one expects that anger can be eliminated, but society is nervous about anger and prefers that it not be shown or, if dissembling is impossible, that anger be a brief burst of steam, evaporating immediately into sunniness. Little children, apes and the insane display this kind of anger: an explosion lasting five minutes, followed with bewildering rapidity by a return to normalcy. Most adult anger, however, has a different characteristic. The person is convulsed with it for perhaps twenty minutes, sometimes much longer, after which it does not evaporate. There are hours or even days of withdrawal, irritation, sullenness, brooding and guilt.

Like children, adults are more likely to be irritable when they are hungry, tired or ill. Holidays and weekends may also be periods of increased testiness in those who need schedules and rituals to give them stability.

People shape their lives and their personalities around their anger content. As Daniel R. Miller and Guy E. Swanson pointed out in *The Study of Conflict,* "The literature is filled with cases which illustrate the relationship to conflict and to defense of such varied forms of expression as the jokes a person appreciates, the content of his dreams and fantasies, the structures of his doodles, his vocational interests, his styles of physical expression, his reactions to threat of failure."

Anger levels vary strikingly in individual lifetimes. Some people who were crabby children become easygoing adults; others grow more cranky as they age. The curiosity for researchers is the variance between individuals, even among individuals raised together in the same family and born of the same pool of genes. To understand the latter, they look at the phenomenon of "dethronement," the birth of a sibling before the toddler has finished with symbiotic attachment to the parents. Where the ideal spacing between children once was thought to be two or three years, scientists now recommend either one year, at which time the older child is not yet sufficiently aware of self to pay much attention to a new arrival, or four years, when it can be expected that the child is steadied by a measure of independence.

Reporting on widespread research in this area in the New York *Times* of May 28, 1985, Daniel Goleman wrote that a two- or three-year-old suffers a blow to self-esteem when another child is born. Jeannie Kidwell, a psychologist at the University of Tennessee, surveyed more than 1,700 teenaged boys, for instance, and found that those who had the most negative view of themselves generally had a sibling about two years younger. If the sibling was one year or four years younger, the negativity was absent. Dr. Kidwell reported that children born about two years apart are "likely to have the most intense competition for parental attention throughout their lives."

Middle children appear to be particularly stressed, having neither the prestige of being the firstborn nor the protections of the youngest. The highest anger levels are found in these children who have no special place in the family hierarchy. If they are boys, they are likely to fight for attention, becoming scrappy and accident-prone. If they are girls, they may be very difficult to please and capable of week-long sulks.

One theory suggests that the attitude of the mother while she is carrying her baby will have a bearing on the anger level of the child. If the mother is taut and upset during her pregnancy, the fetus may be bombarded with furious messages that cause its own evolving neural circuitry to produce tension. Even six-pound newborns, displayed in swaddled rows in hospital nurseries, will exhibit emotional differences ranging from those who are serene and peaceable to the ones who scowl even when asleep.

The influence of heredity on anger level cannot be ignored. Investigators have found that automatic responses differ greatly, even within families. Identical twins will measure the same in tests of skin resistance, salivation, pulse and respiration, while other siblings will show wide variances. These divergencies have a bearing on the child's tolerance of stress, however sweetly the parents behave.

Infants who begin life in a foul mood will be reinforced in their pessimism if they happen to have parents who are unsure or combative. Even a pleasant little person can be roiled into habitual temper tantrums if the care is erratic and lacks consideration. Because bad-tempered children meet universal rejection, the misfortune of their personality development is unlikely to be relieved until they are old enough to assess their situation and lucky or strong enough to be able to correct it.

Some studies have found that anger levels are lower in breast-fed babies than in bottle-fed babies. The idea that babies fed by bottle feel mistreated seems somewhat farfetched, but what might be behind the simplistic assumption is that mothers who breast-feed babies offer a tactile and symbiotic experience. Parents who bottle-feed their babies tenderly, holding them close, assuredly give the child the same sense of safety.

Early illness seems to be a factor in the development of anger levels. One study found that adults who had sickly childhoods before the age of six were significantly more easily affronted and more wrathful than adults whose childhoods were sturdier. Illness not only is isolating for a young child but can be highly alarming, and conditions which make children fearful are likely to make them angry and resentful as well. Again, the anger of little girls appears most often to turn inward and may manifest itself as depression, while the anger of little boys emerges as crankiness and periods of destructiveness.

One of the most important determining factors in the anger of adults is the personality of the care giver who was the primary person in their babyhood. The anger of infants is always directed against the woman-made environment of the nursery. If the woman —or, more rarely, the man—who has responsibility for the baby is punitive, unresponsive or indifferent, the baby will be in a state of perpetual fright and indignation. The constitution of some babies is such that they can tolerate a great deal of rough treatment with equanimity, but most infants are highly sensitive to rejection. The weakest of these collapse in despair, but the feistier ones will be furious.

If the parent is overly solicitous, hovering over the child every waking moment, fearful to let the baby try to crawl or walk, all the growth instincts in the baby will fill with rage. Constant restrictions against movement and exploration are difficult for even a phlegmatic baby and placid toddler to tolerate, since they are so contrary to the child's interest in mastering the environment. With repetition, a pattern is laid down and anger becomes a ready response to even minor irritations.

In *The Fears Men Live By,* an epic work on prejudice, Selma G. Hirsh explored the link between habitual anger in childhood and adult bigotry. "It was startling to see how often the anger expressed by the prejudiced adult turned out to be nearly as old as he was himself," she wrote.

The engine that drives racial intolerance is self-dissatisfaction and anger. Hatred of strangers, as demonstrated in xenophobic wars and racism directed at those with visible differences such as color, is harbored by people who are permanently angry because they feel deprived. Even a temporary state of anger will cause reasonable, tolerant people to turn on a weaker group. Yale University conducted an interesting experiment with some undergraduates who were anticipating an exciting evening's entertainment. One half of the volunteers were asked to express their views about Japanese and the other half about Mexicans. Both demonstrated liberal, nonracist attitudes. Then they were informed that the entertainment had been canceled because it was necessary to complete some dreary task. The questionnaires were then switched. The first group were asked their views about Mexicans and the other group their views about Japanese. This time both responded with sharp animosity.

Angry people are profoundly negative. The views they express are full of hopelessness, skepticism and disapproval. When they talk about their friends, they list the faults; when they speak of themselves, they describe disappointments and injustices. Psychoanalyst Karen Horney observed of angry people that they "demand power and prestige and personal infallibility as a major mode of coping with a hostile world."

The habitually angry, she wrote, will show exaggerated independence along with a tendency to distrust and exploit others. Rapists and men drawn to violent pornography are exceedingly angry people, working out on women their rage at their own sexual insecurity and failed dreams. Angry women may also use sex as a weapon by withholding it or having punitive affairs.

Entire cultures can be suffused with anger if their child-raising techniques are harsh. The controversial reports of anthropologist Margaret Mead described the Iatmul, a tribe of headhunters, who placed their babies on a high shelf and left them untended for hours, screaming with hunger, to toughen them for a rigorous life. The Iatmul, Dr. Mead wrote, possess excruciatingly bad tempers.

A high level of anger has been observed in militant people, such as Prussians, whose child-raising techniques featured severe discipline. Since a child raised sternly is likely to be a stiff, unyielding parent, the trait persists through generations. As psychologist William Mc-Dougall pointed out, even the character of German religious thinkers is a reflection of the national mood: Martin Luther was a wrathful and bellicose man.

Alex Shand, a psychologist, listed the qualities of a child raiser which are most likely to produce angry children. At the head of the list were cold, demanding parents, followed as a category by syrupy, smothering ones and, next, those who are self-righteous and martyred. One couple who kept a ledger of how much their daughter cost them from the moment of her birth produced a child who ran away from home in her teens and became the sex toy of a gang of bikers.

When anger first began to attract the attention of psychologists at the turn of the century, it was assumed that all anger came from a well of discontent, self-dislike and irritation, and that no one would become angry if this basic character disorder wasn't present. Simple observation destroyed this theory in short order. *Everyone,* even a saint, can fly into a rage. The only difference is that saintly people are less prone to anger.

Sudden rage has some intriguing peculiarities. When normally controlled people reflect on their periods of temper, they are likely to find a common thread that is closely tied to a childhood rejection. Certain situations produce a conditioned reflex: the person will always be angry when specific factors come together. For a man with an undiagnosed learning disability, temper control is almost impossible when he feels intellectually patronized. A woman whose family were social outcasts in a prim, judgmental community cannot bear the suggestion of a snub. A man dominated by an authoritative mother and bossy sisters grows hot at criticism by women.

A common outlet for male anger is pugnacity. The Roman philosopher Seneca composed the earliest-known analysis of anger, in which he described its "glaring eye, wrinkled brow, violent motion, the hands restless and perpetually in action, wringing and menacing, the speech false and broken . . ."

Henry Siddons, one of a family of great British actors, in 1807 advised other thespians to portray anger with "an inflamed and rolling eye, a heavy and impetuous step, increased speed of all body movements." Small children bite when they are angry. Charles Darwin said that children are like "young crocodiles who snap their little jaws as soon as they emerge from the egg." The baring of teeth in anger was believed by Darwin to be a leftover primitive instinct to spread terror in the enemy by showing sharp teeth ready to devour the foe. The scowl which also accompanies anger in modern people was attributed by Darwin to early humans who assumed that expression to protect their eyes as they prepared to do battle. And the loud voice of anger is a throwback to ancestors who wanted to appear larger and more powerful to enemies.

According to a University of Maine professor, Roy F. Richardson, in *Psychology and Pedagogy of Anger,* the second most frequently exhibited show of anger is contrariness. Angry people cannot be persuaded to go along with the crowd even when they want to. They punish their family or friends or associates by being difficult to please and by objecting to every proposal not originated by themselves.

A less obvious form of the same perversity underlies some shows of pleasantness. Dr. Richardson estimated that one in five angry people will elect to appear polite, even obsequiously so, toward those who annoy them most. Overweight people, using food as solace, often contain considerable amounts of anger but are obliged to compensate for their unattractive bulk by assuming the face of a jolly friend. Their idle chatter gives them away: it flicks like a cat-o'-nine-tails, drawing blood. The adage "killing with kindness" didn't come out of thin air.

The least used expression of anger is to appear devoid of it. People who shrug off a wounding insult may feel that they haven't the emotional resources to take on a fight, or they may fear that once their control starts to slip they'll be lost, or they may be at such a social or economic disadvantage that they have no choice but to appear indifferent to the abuse. This pretense of no anger is seen most often in women, or in men with inferior looks or income. The consequence, of course, is that they brood a lot.

When angry people scheme, some of their plots are laced with cruelty. They imagine how they will inflict pain, either by means of an instrument or poison or by causing humiliation or loss. The work of anger keeps adrenaline running, so that people can't sleep for the excitement of planning revenge. The task consumes them even as they go about mundane chores, travel to work, stand in a shower, stare at a street scene without seeing it. Angry people become scriptwriters. They picture themselves doing this or that, saying this or that, getting satisfaction from the consternation and misery they cause. They write letters, rejecting draft after draft as not being hurtful enough. They explore ways of exposing the object of their anger as a fool or thief; they will *reveal all.* Until the anger is used up, they can't concentrate and they appear distracted. It was Seneca who said, "The greatest remedy for anger is delay."

The period when anger is simmering is a treacherous one for the unwary who come within range. The jokes of angry people are mean-minded, the friendly clap on the back will bruise and their generalizations "inadvertently" flay someone's race, or gender, or hometown. A man who lived in sixteen foster homes in Canada after his widowed mother decided to return to England with a younger brother finally traced her and sent the money for her to cross the Atlantic to meet him. He met her at the plane with a delighted smile on his face, put his arms around her and broke four of her ribs.

The blood pressure of angry people takes a fearful beating that can damage hearts or lead to strokes. Because anger increases the rate of respiration, breathing becomes irregular and people may stammer. Suppressed anger does great damage to health. A report in the *Archives of General Psychiatry* noted that people who express their anger openly get off lightly, but those who sizzle inwardly have hypertension and elevated rates of heartbeat. Some skin disorders are the body's signal that the systems are in trouble because of sustained anger. Other common symptoms are headaches, ulcers, restlessness, chronic fatigue and poor coordination resulting in physical clumsiness.

Many see a link between suppressed anger and such grave diseases as cancer. The typical cancer patient, research shows, is a self-disciplined person who is easy to get along with. Reports to cancer societies repeatedly describe cancer victims as controlled and well adjusted, rarely showing anger or upset. Even if there has been a disaster in their lives, they insist they feel no stress. As compared with heart attack patients, however, they typically describe their childhoods as "bleak and dissatisfying," as psychologist Claus Bahnson once told the American Cancer Society. If they don't get cancer, reported George F. Solomon, of Stanford's Medical School in Palo Alto, they might develop an autoimmune disease such as rheumatoid arthritis, which is also the result of something the body makes itself.

Bottled anger is a sour concoction that afflicts every organ in the body. Frustrated anger against the self is particularly wounding. This occurs in such situations as when someone important in the person's life, say a small child's mother or an infatuated person's beloved, punishes an error by appearing excessively pained, though forgiving. Miscreants shudder with merciless guilt and anger, which they direct at themselves. If this pattern continues overly long in the life of a vulnerable person, a habit of self-blame may be established. The excessively apologetic chew up their insides; anger can shorten their lives.

Many share Karl Menninger's conviction that a good deal of depression, particularly in women and vulnerable men, is mixed liberally with anger that they can't direct outside of themselves. An experiment at New York's Bellevue Hospital with patients who were recovering from suicide attempts seemed to bear this out. The staff tried handling them with open hostility, so unfair that the feeblest of the patients could not avoid being incensed. As the ward rocked with indignation, the gratified staff noted that apathy and withdrawal had vanished and recovery was speeded.

A psychiatric facility for disturbed children tried the same method to treat the unreachable. The staff looked for "anchor points," something impersonal such as untied shoes about which to berate the youngsters so severely that they would lose their tempers. After the tirade, with the child weak and relieved, the staff would hold and rock them.

Anger shouldn't be contained inappropriately but for the bad-tempered the trick of living is to find something constructive to do with it. Sigmund Freud was a cold, bitter and quarrelsome man who used his anger against colleagues who disagreed with him by pushing knowledge beyond their expertise. John Calvin, his body ravaged by the effects of his terrible wrath, founded a religion to serve the angriest God in Christendom. Abraham Lincoln, who converted his anger into morose depression, showed his genius in his capacity to be kind.

"There is actually no productive activity in which some aggression does not enter in one way or another," commented the eminent psychoanalyst Melanie Klein. Work is a healthy outlet for anger: men chop wood, women clean the oven. All activities using the long muscles, such as jogging, bicycling, swimming, will ease anger. Something allowing for short, sharp blows also works; an outraged child will find comfort in kicking a pillow around the room.

Some people get out of hearing distance and then swear fulsomely. Others yell. One woman screams when alone in her car traveling at top speed on a highway with the windows up. She says she arrives at her destination refreshed. A few hum or sing tense little tunes. Others slam doors, bite their nails, deliberately break something and claim it was an accident. Parents spank their children and children kick the family pet. Angry children also cry, a technique which also works for women.

"Some persons have greater mental versatility than others in finding successful expressions of anger," wrote Maine's Dr. Richardson. "Consequently they have a greater proportion of pleasantness."

Even the best of controls will slip, despite admirable efforts at suppression and deflection. When people are actively trying to improve a crabby disposition, it is a disheartening blow to confidence that something trivial can loom out of a blue sky and arouse in them the foot-stamping wrath of a child. Self-respect is deeply wounded when people who felt themselves beginning to improve catch fire from a spark and burn down a relationship. Most frightening of all, the rage may be so disproportionate that there is a brief urge to kill. After such an episode, people grow dizzy with fear that they could become insane.

The only solution for unbridled anger, the psychologists say, is to lessen vulnerability. The more solidly rooted people are in self-esteem and a network of family and friends they trust, the less likely they are to be angry. Negligence or tactlessness do not wound unduly a person who has a busy, productive, satisfying life. Mature people take a realistic view of their own shortcomings; failure hurts, but they don't kick themselves around the block.

Maturing takes half a lifetime and is beset with regression. In the interim, there are strategies for handling anger. One way is a stern review of the entire circumstance that provoked the most recent bout of anger. What needs to be understood is not the details of the event but the element that hit a nerve. For one man, it was simply shoddiness: his early humiliations centered on having cheap clothes and bottom-of-the-line toys that broke. When he noticed that most of his rages were directed against low-quality goods and deceitful people, his temper lost its mystery and became more manageable.

People who figure out what makes them angry have taken a giant step. Another handle on anger is to analyze the incident that incurred the wrath from a different perspective. By rolling the entire exchange through the mind from the other person's point of view, the cause of the uproar may not seem the same. New information also helps: the facts were misunderstood, the remark was taken out of context, there were extenuating circumstances.

It's a fine idea, usually, to explain to people involved what caused the anger. In the wake of a tirade, in the friendly glow that accompanies remorse and guilt, people are sometimes able to be clear about the real causes: the persistent habit of correcting minor errors, for instance, or the failure to be sensitive to fatigue.

One aunt received into her home a five-year-old whose parents were getting a divorce. The child was in a foul mood. "Do you want to go on a picnic?" the aunt asked. "No, I hate picnics," the child replied. After a few days of this, the aunt sat down with the child and said, "You shouldn't be mean to people who love you, because they are the people who will help you, and if you go on being mean to them, they won't want to help you. Also, you should tell people who love you why you are so angry. You can talk to any one of us here because we all love you. Now stop being a little bitch."

For a day or two, the child eyed her aunt warily. The aunt behaved sweetly. One morning the child woke up, sunny and cooperative, and remained her happy self for the rest of the visit.

People recover from anger when they succeed in rearranging their self-regard to a semblance of what it was before the event. A common shortcut to this desirable end is to denigrate the opposition. Those who punch their critics are using a direct approach to assert superiority but subtler methods of demolishing opponents are in the same category. For instance, some regain their sense of superiority by doing their enemies a conspicuous favor; others spread malicious stories to reduce the status of those who have angered them; some deal in hints of knowledge of dark misdeeds; some employ the sly meanness of being ostentatiously silent when everyone else is speaking praise; still others apply the wrong end of the telescope to those who have hurt their egos, diminishing them with "He means well, but he isn't very bright," or "It's a pity she's so fat, she's really very pretty." Putting the blame elsewhere is an emotional dead end.

Angry people are also well advised to consider what they hope to accomplish and whether anger will help them do it. In *Anger: The Misunderstood Emotion,* Carol Tavris dryly observes that the goal, which may be to change the attitude and behavior of the person who caused the anger, is not likely to be compatible with an inclination to shout insults. Take time out, the author suggests; don't ventilate on the spot. "I think it's an important point that what people do when they're angry is a learned habit. It can be unlearned, relearned. People can learn to control, not necessarily the feeling of their anger, but they can learn what to do next."

Specialists who delve into the layers of illusion in which people swaddle their worst fears about themselves have a theory that adults who have been unable to acknowledge how angry they are at parents who disappointed them will instead spend their lives being angry at the rest of the world, nursing what Selma Hirsh called "a permanent grievance against most of the people in it."

One aim of anger therapy is to take out the worry. "It is a normal emotional manifestation," Florence Goodenough said. "It need cause anxiety only when it becomes excessive either in frequency or intensity, or when the attitudes aroused during anger show an undue tendency to persist in the form of grudges and feelings of persecution."

Anger can even be a positive pleasure. Anger defends territory, beginning with one's own integrity and extending to personal space and beyond. Every species fights when its ground is invaded—songbirds, goats, elephants, moose, stickleback fish, wolves, rats and humans.

A man inflamed over an invasion of his home or a social injustice is delighted with himself. Nothing is more beneficial to self-approval than a good hearty indignation over something which is unfair, which William McDougall called "the anger of society." In nurseries, schools and the adult world, righteous anger always will have "a great and proper part to play in the training of the individual for his life in society," he wrote. This constructive anger turns into codes of ethics and humane law. All over the world, anger defends the weak.

"A large part of education is to teach men to be angry aright," said a pioneer American psychologist, G. Stanley Hall. "Man has powers of resentment which should be hitched onto and allowed to do good and profitable work."

Two hundred years ago Immanuel Kant mused that the race would stagnate without its capacity for anger, and thanked the fates for the cantankerous human nature. "Man wishes concord, but nature knows better what is good for the species."

COURAGE

COURAGE is the quality humanity most admires, though few people recognize it in themselves. Mostly, it is considered a male attribute and derives some of its urgency from the disquieting placement of men's vulnerable genitalia on the outside of their bodies. Manhood is measured in most species by display intended to distract attention from the conspicuous and frail male organ to something less susceptible to damage, such as plumage or a roar. From the onset of puberty until they mature, human males are inspired by the presence of women to perform. Whether it is a boy doing a wheelie in a schoolyard or a matador facing a bull, the showy courage of men is not unrelated to fear of impotence.

The courage of women is associated with nesting. Women are often valiant in defense of their children or their hearth, but their bravery in those situations is seen as acts of self-defense and therefore is considered less remarkable than the wild strange courage of men who climb Everest.

Heroism is suspect. When people are filled with hate and rage, the necessity to discharge the violence of their emotions can propel them into battle against overwhelming odds. Guilt can cleave a person to a sick parent and appear to the world like high-minded dedication. Envy powers the leap beyond the muscle-mind limitations of highboard divers and shyness of salespeople. Loneliness pushes people into the limelight. Fear of humiliation, of self-dislike, of reprisal is often a driving force in fearlessness.

The French essayist and wit Montaigne wrote in the sixteenth century, "That man whom you saw so adventurous yesterday, do you not think it strange to find him such a coward the day after? Either anger or necessity, or company or wine, or the sound of a trumpet had put his heart in his belly. This was not a courage shaped by reason."

Erich Fromm agreed. "Courageous behavior may be motivated by ambition so that a person will risk his life in certain situations in order to satisfy his craving to be admired," Dr. Fromm said. "It may be motivated by suicidal impulses which drive a person to seek danger because, consciously or unconsciously, he does not value his life and wants to destroy himself. It may be motivated by sheer lack of imagination so that a person acts courageously because he is not aware of the danger awaiting him. Finally, it may be determined by genuine devotion to the idea or aim for which a person acts, a motivation which is conventionally assumed to be the basis for courage."

Selfless courage, the last of Dr. Fromm's catalogue, is often quiet. The steadfastness of people in monotonous jobs which support their families is one example. Another is the thousands of parents who raise handicapped children and provide, through imagination, love and sacrifice, what comes very close to normality. People who lose their homes, lose their health, lose someone they adored and then carry on without bitterness have courage.

The highest form of courage is moral courage; people who have it are often overwhelmed but are never destroyed.

Much of what appears to spectators as courage is actually the result of preparation. The men of Canada's Olympic ski team, whose frightening velocity earned them the title of "the Crazy Canucks," had been on the slopes from childhood. Astronauts are so drilled in emergency procedures that their pulses may flutter in a crisis but their voices sound bored. When brains are rehearsed, peril causes the neural pathways to click out efficient messages; inexperienced people freeze in a crisis because they have nothing ready in the memory banks.

A woman who had a collection of venomous snakes was bitten in the arm by a king cobra. She called for an ambulance herself and then calmly directed first-aid treatment. People marveled at her courage but it was a danger she had anticipated and accepted for years.

The courage of soldiers is a complex of emotions but repetitious training is a large factor in getting them to their feet when the order comes to move out. The British light brigade rode into the "valley of death" because the cavalrymen had followed the command to advance a thousand times and, in the emergency, could think of no other response.

What seems heroic to bystanders is rarely so for the hero. Practice makes even skydiving or high-wire walking almost routine and people in dangerous trades always know someone who has taken more chances, demonstrated more skill, pulled off a more impossible stunt.

After the Korean War, a wounded Canadian soldier became a legend in a veterans' hospital because of the pain he was enduring. A sniper's bullet had shattered his hip, sending a shower of bone splinters through the soft organs of his abdomen. When dressings were changed on the huge open wound, the agony was so great that he bent the steel pole he gripped. He was embarrassed when interviewed by a reporter who wanted to write of his ordeal. He was better off, he insisted, than the amputees: *they* were the brave ones. The amputees, however, considered themselves luckier than those who had been blinded, and the blind were grateful they were not paraplegics. The paraplegics didn't regard their disaster as the worst —the really brave man in the hospital was the one who was cheerful despite a terminal cancer. But that man was convinced he would recover.

Group courage, on the other hand, is acknowledged by participants without modesty. When a community behaves well in a flood, spirits rise higher than the waters. Six Nations Indians walk the steel beams of rising skyscrapers deeply pleased with themselves, recognized by white construction workers as a race apart, nerveless and unknowable as their ancestors were. The comradeship of men in battle is fixed in history, as is the gallantry of citizens under siege.

People like themselves when they are able to be brave collectively. Affection and consideration abound. Overflowing with self-esteem, they have no need to maintain the fretwork of defensive moats, walls, barbed wire, lances and masks which normally gets them through the day.

Some leaders, generally men whom psychologists would characterize as father figures, have the ability to inspire others into ecstasies of courage. Julius Caesar was such a one. Plutarch described how fanatical Caesar's soldiers were in battle. One had his right arm severed by a sword but fought on, weapon in his left hand, and captured a ship. Another had an eye put out by an arrow, a shoulder and thigh pierced by javelins and one hundred and thirty darts in his shield, but he continued to engage the enemy.

In 1917 a Dutch general confronted his cowering troops, gave them a fatherly scolding, stuck a cigar in his mouth, raised his wrong-war saber and led them against the foe. During battle near Königshof in 1865, when an army refused to cross a bridge for fear of shelling, the commanding officer called for an armchair and placed it on the bridge, where he lolled in comfort as if admiring the view. His sheepish soldiers filed across.

Heroism comes easily to people with a particular kind of mental imbalance. Many of the world's most fearless people were raving megalomaniacs. Among those believed to be certifiably insane are Alexander the Great, Joan of Arc and Napoleon. Their visions of greatness inspired armies but their bravery was mostly egocentricity.

Self-image motivates much of what is seen as courage. People who view themselves as humanitarians develop a mental attitude which causes them to spring forward helpfully in an emergency. The choice for them is performing nobly in the crisis or giving up the picture they have of being worthwhile people. Those who prize their qualities of loyalty and tenacity will remain at their posts unto death. For them, it would take more courage to jump into a lifeboat and risk loss of self-esteem than to stay with the ship.

Such heroism is an enigma. It was demonstrated most conspicuously in January 1982, when an Air Florida plane struck the bridge over the Potomac soon after takeoff from Washington National Airport and spilled its passengers into the icy river. An unidentified man—"balding, probably in his 50's, an extravagant moustache"— found himself in the water along with five other gasping survivors clinging to the floating tail section. A helicopter lowered a rope-and-ring rescue device and the man helped one of the people into it. The helicopter returned four times more and the man continued to give the ring to someone else. When the rescuers returned for him, he was gone.

"At some moment in the water he must have realized that he would not live if he continued to hand over the rope and ring to others," wrote Roger Rosenblatt in *Time*. "He *had* to know it, no matter how gradual the effect of the cold . . . The man in the water pitted himself against an implacable, impersonal enemy; he fought it with charity; and he held it to a standoff. He was the best we can do."

One of the rescue team later commented to a reporter that there is someone like the man in the water in every group—only no one can ever guess which person it will be.

The presence of spectators can result in a stupid form of courage. Teenagers on motorcycles are tempted to squeal around corners at an alarming tilt if there are people to impress. The impulse to be a hero in front of a crowd has resulted in such embarrassments as the man who jumped off a bridge to save a drowning person, forgetting that he himself could not swim. The stalwart cry of "Women and children only in the lifeboats" was perfectly in accord with the male code of chivalry but made little sense if the women and children could not navigate. Clerks who bravely defend the petty cash against frantic, drugged robbers have had their heads blown off.

Some courage is laden with a death wish. Harry Houdini, the escape artist, thrilled millions with his daring but, as Louis J. Bragman noted in the *Psychoanalytic Review,* "almost every stunt staged by Houdini represented a form of pseudo-suicide." It was Nietzsche who wrote that Christianity permits only two forms of suicide—the slow death of an ascetic and the bloody demise of a martyr. Erich Fromm observed that socially useful sacrifices, such as those of scientists who expose themselves in lethal experiments and patriots who lay down their lives for freedom, are seen to be victories of the constructive side of human nature rather than evidence of private despair.

People starved for admiration seek danger and may respond valiantly in a crisis. A burst of spunk in a mild woman or self-effacing man owes much to this hope; everyone believes that a drab life can be redeemed by one act of supreme heroism. The reward of a brave deed is a flash of self-liking that Antoine de Saint-Exupéry called the birth of the sleeping prince within every man.

In a moment of abrupt danger, when people are frozen, the first person to react can determine what the crowd will do. When a fire broke out in a wooden theater in what was then called Petrograd, a police officer leaped to a chair and shouted, "In the name of the Tsar, everybody remain in his place." Though the ceiling was aflame, people filed out in orderly rows.

In *Social Psychology,* Stanford University's Richard T. LaPiere and Paul R. Farnsworth, observed, "It occasionally happens that a leader will arise—sometimes an inconspicuous member of the crew or an otherwise undomineering passenger—who will organize the people around him in a most efficient manner. With such leadership under crisis conditions, people are capable of Herculean efforts."

Dr. Fromm doesn't think much of rash bravery, which he describes as "the courage of nihilism, a willingness to throw life away because one is incapable of loving it." D. H. Munro, a New Zealand philosopher, took an even colder view. He saw a mean streak of bigotry in "strenuous heroism," a contempt for others demonstrated by imperious, condescending rescue.

Men committed to a lifestyle built on exhibitions of courage suffer acutely in middle age when their bodies will no longer cooperate. As they mourn the death of strength and timing, their envy of youth makes them exceedingly critical as fathers or employers. They find it too painful to give up the habits of bravery, whatever prudence may dictate. Winston Churchill, for instance, exulted in his participation as a young soldier in Egypt in one of the world's last cavalry charges and as wartime leader of Britain continued to take reckless chances with his life.

Another example is Lieutenant General Sir Adrian Carton de Wiart, who was wounded eleven times in various British Empire wars. His left hand was shot off at Ypres in 1915 but he continued to lead an attack, pulling pins out of grenades with his teeth. "I was thankful my teeth were my own," he commented cheerily. When he lost an eye in Somaliland, he was delighted. "Thank God," he chortled. "This will take me out of this tin-pot show to the real battle in France." In peacetime he had to content himself with pigsticking and fighting cobras.

Ernest Hemingway, who coined the surpassingly fine definition of courage as "grace under pressure," celebrated manly bravery all his life. When he wasn't putting himself to brinkmanship tests, he watched others risking their lives—bullfighters, big-game hunters, soldiers. He destroyed himself with a gun, driven mad by his sexual impotence. As with the English poet Rudyard Kipling, his admiration of bullies was rooted in his own nihilism.

Jean Anouilh made an observation about such courage in his play *Becket*. During a wild-boar hunt, the King asks Thomas à Becket why he seems to crave danger. Becket replies gaily, "One has to gamble with one's life to feel alive."

Anxious people sometimes seek danger as a catharsis. The floating, crawling, objectless fears of anxious people vanish when there is something real and terrible to be faced. Jeopardy addiction is prevalent in North America—witness the prosperity of gambling casinos, racetracks, bookies, contact sports, car racing and collection agencies.

"People often prefer fearful reality to fearful fantasy," the Dutch psychiatrist A. M. Meerloo wrote. "The audacious deeds of the Partisans were not always courage, but the dangerous wish to end insecure tension."

Some of what passes for courage is dull-wittedness. Peasant armies that trampled stolidly through thousands of years of carnage, blinking in the sun at Antioch, Hastings and Waterloo, were composed mainly of unimaginative men. "Yokel soldiers, with the courage of a vacant mind," wrote Lord Moran, British physician, in *The Anatomy of Courage*. Lord Moran spent three years in the trenches in World War I and tended Royal Air Force fighter pilots in World War II. He reached the conclusion that true courage is demonstrated only by cultivated people, because they can image their own death. The uneducated he dismissed as one would vegetables.

"They drew no pictures of danger for their own undoing," he declared of armies in every century except his own. "Phlegm, that was the yokel's virtue as a soldier; it was the distinctive quality of his race." He added, "Men suffered more in the last war [1914–18], as it seems to me, not because it was more terrible but because they were more sensitive."

Today's sensitive people, however, can be reduced to a state of dazed childhood when their brains refuse to tolerate any more noise, terror and pain. After a tornado, survivors wander about aimlessly, staring without comprehension at the wreckage. A Spitfire pilot in the Battle of Britain recalled the action for which he received the Distinguished Flying Cross. He had been in a prolonged dogfight over London and had run out of ammunition when a German bomber crossed his sights. In his exhausted state, he decided to ram it. "It was either very childish of me, or insane," he said later. "It was not brave, not in the least. It just never occurred to me that my aircraft would even be damaged in the collision."

Dr. Meerloo related how a Dutch soldier became a hero. Planes and ground forces had been attacking his part of the line fiercely for hours and, finally, a retreat was ordered. The man was too frightened to move. He remained at his position, firing hysterically. The enemy panicked at this unexpected defense and retreated. The soldier became a national hero.

A Canadian, Brigadier Dollard Menard, who charged a pillbox single-handedly on the bloody beaches of Dieppe even though wounded four times, later dissected his feelings during his crazy attack. There were four elements, he decided, and none was courage. The first was egoism, optimism or thoughtlessness; the next, discipline; the third anger because a good friend had just been shot in the stomach; and, finally, he didn't give a damn.

The commander of a Royal Air Force Spitfire squadron was asked to account for the bravery of his pilots during the Battle of Britain. He replied that it was leadership and good equipment.

Discipline and instinct are factors in many deeds of courage. People normally have a tendency to protect someone vulnerable for whom they feel responsible. The golfer Ben Hogan, for example, had no time to form a conscious thought when a bus skidded in front of his car in 1949, but he instantly flung his body in front of his wife seated in the passsenger seat. She escaped with scratches but he had bones broken from his collarbone to his ankle.

A young grandmother picnicking with her two-year-old granddaughter near Toronto one summer afternoon snatched the child out of the path of horses bolting toward them with a heavy wagon. The child was saved but the iron wheels of the wagon passed over the woman's body and left her crippled.

In wartime, when green soldiers inadvertently pull the pin on a grenade, officers and noncommissioned officers will run toward it out of reflex. Some succeed in picking it up and throwing it away to explode harmlessly, but countless others have been killed, or blinded, or have had their hands blown off.

When a training balloon burst over England in 1962, the instructor realized that one student in the gondola was too terrified to use his parachute. He stayed with him and, as they neared the ground, shouted in a parade-ground voice, "Brace yourself and lift your feet!" They walked away with minor injuries.

Andrew Carnegie, the American robber baron who became a philanthropist, took note of this kind of courage and excluded it from eligibility for his Carnegie awards for bravery. He felt a distinction should be made between courage that was the consequence of a sense of duty and that which was a free gift. Among those who are not considered for the award are police, firefighters, soldiers and those who save someone who is a relative or for whom they have responsibility.

The fund was established in 1904 with an endowment of five million dollars in U.S. Steel bonds. The annual list of citations is a moving testimonial to the greatness of which so-called ordinary people are capable. It catalogues the deeds of men, women and children who dive in front of falling objects, or descend into pits filled with lethal gas, or rush into burning buildings full of flame, or dive into roaring water—all to rescue someone they have never met.

A Silver Medal and a thousand dollars, for instance, went to a New York waiter who climbed four floors in a tenement building that was collapsing around him and carried to safety an eighty-three-year-old woman. A young woman swam to the aid of a man being devoured by a shark and towed him to shore while the shark continued to attack; she also received a Silver Medal.

The judges make fine distinctions. A man who lost his left arm as he chose to crash his disabled gravel truck into a tree rather than chance hitting a school bus was given a Bronze Medal. Gold Medals are exceedingly rare. In 1924 one was awarded the widow of a man who walked into a small house that literally was full of fire and succeeded in saving one of the two small children inside at the cost of his own life. Gold Medals mounted on bronze tablets have twice been presented to groups: one was given in memory of the passengers and crew of the *Titanic*, which sank in 1912, and another to the survivors of the Springhill mine disaster in Nova Scotia in 1958.

The history of the human race is radiant with examples of individuals who somehow find the inner resource to perform a filthy, dangerous, horrifying act that they could have avoided without blame. Fate puts them in a position to do something difficult, and they accept that they can. Jackie Robinson, the first black in major-league baseball, had a stormy nature but he suppressed his temper nobly in the face of years of vilification because he was determined to gain acceptance for his race. He was asked how he had survived the abuse from white fans, players and management with such control. He replied, "It's being able to rise up, I guess, when you have to."

Patriotism, or a sense of mission larger than the self, can lift entire nations to a high level of courage. Weston LaBarre, anthropologist and author of *The Human Animal,* wrote that it was morale which enabled the Greeks to win three great battles against the Persians. What the city-states had on their side at Marathon, Thermopylae and Salamis, he noted, was *arete,* manliness and decision, which crumbled the mighty Persian *hubris,* "the overweening arrogance and fatal pride in great power." The same dynamic can be seen when any small nation, such as Vietnam or Afghanistan, fights tenaciously against superior foes.

"If people know—even though it be an illusion—that they fight for freedom and justice, they are able to bear much suffering," wrote Joost Meerloo. "The illusion of fighting for ideals fosters much moral courage." As examples, he gave the struggles for religious freedom, for social justice, for national independence. "A minority gains vitality and strength through its conviction of moral power," he concluded.

The theologian Paul Tillich marveled at the distinctive and resilient courage of Americans. "The typical American," he wrote in *The Courage to Be,* "after he has lost the foundations of his existence, works for new foundations." He saw in American pragmatism, process philosophy, ethics of growth, progressive education and crusading democracy "the courage to be a part in the progress of the group to which one belongs, of his nation, of all mankind."

Sometimes courage is too theatrical for any work of fiction. In 1962, a British major with a swagger stick under his arm was assigned to a Nigerian unit of the United Nations forces in the Congo. Shortly after taking command he was informed that the Congolese had massacred twenty priests but one priest was left alive. He set off unarmed in a light aircraft to effect a rescue. When he landed, the plane was surrounded by eight hundred furious Congolese tribesmen. He approached them briskly, shook hands with the largest, gathered up the priest and departed.

In 1876, after George Custer and the U.S. Cavalry ran into an ambush at the Little Bighorn in which 264 men were killed by the Sioux, Chief Sitting Bull took three thousand Dakota Sioux across the line into Canada. James Walsh of the North West Mounted Police rode into Sitting Bull's camp accompanied only by a scout. He took note of the fresh scalps hanging from the belts of Sioux warriors and the horses wearing the brand of the U.S. Cavalry as he reined in before the chief's lodge. He announced, through the scout interpreter, that the Sioux were to obey the laws of the Great White Mother (Queen Victoria).

He accepted a place to sleep that night in the middle of a camp boiling with enraged Sioux. He was wakened to find his lodge filled with natives in war paint ringed around him in the light from campfires. *What laws?* they wanted to know. He listed a few: no killing, rape, horse stealing, injuring people or property, that sort of thing. Then he went back to sleep. In the morning he had a truce. Sitting Bull marveled, "He comes to my lodge alone and unarmed."

During the Boxer Rebellion in China, a timid missionary from Boston, Mary Morrill, stepped outside the compound wall to confront a howling mob. She asked them to kill her if they wanted a life but to spare the other inhabitants. They dispersed in astonishment but returned the next day to slaughter the colony. Her they beheaded.

Esquire magazine once chronicled "the overreachers," and they made a dashing parade. One was Manolete, the greatest of Spain's matadors, who in 1947 accepted a challenge to fight a vicious Mirua bull when he was past his prime and overdue for retirement. He killed the bull and the bull killed him. In Chile in 1925, the legendary flier Jimmy Doolittle broke both ankles in a fall from a second-story window which occurred when he slipped while walking on his hands on the sill. The next day, in agony, he nevertheless took part in an exhibition dogfight and deliberately scraped his opponent's wings with his wheels.

Fear creates a pool of usable energy which the brave can tap. If the situation requires iron control, that energy must go somewhere, sometime. The mother who calmly gets her injured child to the hospital, giving reassurance all the way that everything will be fine, may afterwards go into shock, or faint, or cry. Stoic sailors from wartime convoys where they endured weeks of watching for torpedoes, would be vicious in barroom fights. People who endure prolonged bombardment never fully recover. Certain sounds will make them cringe for the rest of their lives—for one woman, it was a certain kind of wind that reminded her of shells passing overhead.

The Royal Navy had a famous hero, a man who sipped tea on the bridge of his ship while a lookout gave him bulletins on an approaching dive-bomber. Not until the lookout reported, "Bomb released, sir," did the captain turn his head and in a normal tone of voice give the order, "Hard a-starboard." While the bomb exploded harmlessly a short distance away, he took another sip of tea. When the raid was over, he went into his cabin and wept.

A superhuman effort is required to sustain bravery for long periods. Medgar Evers, an official of the National Association for the Advancement of Colored People (NAACP), who lived in a small Mississippi community during nine years of unrelenting harassment while he was organizing blacks to vote, was capable of such an effort. Eventually he died with an assassin's bullet in his back, a fate he had been expecting daily for all those years. James H. Meredith, the first black to attend the University of Mississippi, is another example. A British newspaper, *The Observer*, suggested that Meredith be granted a medal for heroism because he dared to "incarnate in his own person humanity's struggle against racial oppression and mob fanaticism."

By the same measure, those who function despite poor health are heroic. Some suffer continuous pain or nausea but live productive lives anyway. Herbert Spencer, said to be the founder of English philosophy, had a breakdown which destroyed his health when he was thirty-five. Nevertheless, he commenced his eighteen-volume *Synthetic Philosophy* in the first year of his illness. Though the pains in his head were so severe that he dosed himself heavily with opium to sleep at night, he labored on. Toward the end he could dictate only ten minutes at a time, five times a day. His monumental *Principles of Sociology* was written in that excruciating manner.

Charles Darwin was so ill after he returned from his voyage on the *Beagle* that he never again was able to work more than a few hours a day, but he completed the bulk of his life's work and gained his lasting reputation under those conditions. Robert Louis Stevenson wrote incessantly while dying of tuberculosis; George Orwell hastened his death from tuberculosis by typing the manuscript of *1984* though he knew his lungs were disintegrating.

Beethoven, deaf and ill, cried out, "I will so far as possible defy my fate, though there must be moments when I shall be the most miserable of God's creatures."

A Toronto physician who was the mother of three children discovered in 1959 that she was a victim of multiple sclerosis. Though her right arm and leg became almost useless, she toiled on as a part-time medical examiner in schools and in the summer she operated a camp for girls. She was inspired to keep going, she said, by a line her mother wrote in the family Bible while she was dying of cancer: "I practice the heroism of carrying on."

The jockey-trainer Johnny Passero, recovering from cancer, was advised to take a complete rest. He preferred to keep working and trained his horses at Toronto's Woodbine every morning before driving one hundred miles to Buffalo for his cobalt treatments and driving back to Toronto in time to saddle his horses for the afternoon's racing.

Some people's capacity to bear suffering strains belief. Willpower —the power to not give in—has armored heroes against torture, disease, grief, poverty, cold, imprisonment, failure and betrayal. Marcus Aurelius concluded that "nothing happens to any man which he is not formed by nature to bear."

When people are determined to face danger, the brain's triggers release powerful chemicals to help them do it. Many of these come from the pituitary gland, the so-called gland of courage. Experiments on animals have shown that when the pituitary is removed, they become four-legged cowards. No one is sure why this happens. Adrenaline floods the system, providing strength and agility. In addition, the brain lays down chemicals which will give a measure of hypalgesia, immunity to pain. This is known as the blinkers effect. When people are totally committed to a fight, wounds and fractures are painless. Women who slash themselves in prisons report that they watch the blood spurt with a sense of release. "If it hurts," one explained, "you shouldn't be slashing." The sensation is one of dreamy detachment.

The most remarkable heroism of which humans are capable is so quiet and seemingly ordinary that it is admired chiefly by the cognoscenti. The psychoanalyst Alfred Adler listed three areas of normal living which demand courage to be well met. One was marriage, one was social relations and the third was occupation. Conscious commitment to responsibility requires a day-after-day steadfastness that has much in common with Lord Moran's model of courage, that of sensitive people doing their duty. They hold the line under a bombardment that has no end. Men and women who meet their responsibilities when the flesh shrieks for escape are the truly valiant.

"Our banal everyday life makes banal demands on our patience, our devotedness, endurance, self-sacrifice, and so on," commented the great Carl G. Jung, "which we must fulfill modestly and without any heroic gestures to court applause, and which actually need a heroism which is not seen from without. It does not shine and is not praised . . ."

All growth, all change involve acts of courage. When people give up a prejudice or a long-held set of beliefs, they give up a piece of what they have been as surely as an amputee has been deprived of a limb. Jean Piaget said that all learning is a process of accretion and substitution. People are exposed every day to information new to them, some of which they load into their memory banks because it interests them and much of which they slough off. Substitution, however, demands a conscious decision to give up what was believed and accept something different, even contrary. It is wrenching and disturbing, like a snug household taking in a stranger. Some people move forward eagerly to envelop what is novel and stimulating because they have the confidence of practiced brains, but for many who dearly prefer the comforts of apathy the effort to acquire new vistas requires a great and heroic struggle.

"Each step forward is a step into the unfamiliar and is possibly dangerous," wrote Abraham Maslow. "It also means giving up something familiar and good and satisfying. It frequently means a parting and a separation, even a kind of death prior to a rebirth, with subsequent nostalgia, fear, loneliness and mourning. It also often means giving up a simpler and easier and less effortful life in exchange for a more demanding, more responsible, more difficult life."

He added, "Growth forward is *in spite* of these losses, and therefore requires courage, will choice and strength in the individual, as well as protection, permission and encouragement from the environment, especially for the child."

Parents who support their children's inquisitiveness and powers of invention are teaching courage. A child learning to tie shoelaces is risking ridicule and failure, and therefore is showing a degree of genuine bravery in making the effort. By an effort of patience and sympathy, a parent can assist in a notable victory that will enhance the child's confidence lastingly.

Cautioned Abraham Maslow, "It is necessary in order for children to grow well that adults have enough trust in them."

Lord Moran commented that courage is a moral quality which

must be learned, and not "a chance gift of nature like an aptitude for games."

Paul Tillich once declared that courage means "the acceptance of want, toil, insecurity, pain, possible destruction. Without this self-affirmation, life could not be preserved or increased."

Courage is so subtle that a prizefighter may have little of it, being driven instead by ambition, envy, hatred and despair, while a man who apologizes may have waded a river of personal crocodiles.

The U.S. Navy admiral Bull Halsey made a famous comment on heroes. "There are no great men," he declared, "only great challenges ordinary men are asked to face." Such a moment occurred in August 1962, when a propane plant began to burn near the small Ontario village of Maple. A workman, Herbert C. Joslin, realized he was the only person in the vicinity who knew where the turnoff valves were located. He ran into the building, suffering severe burns to every part of his body except the bottoms of his feet and a small area of his spine.

Such clear-cut challenges are rare in a lifetime. Few people happen to pass a roiling stream and see that a child has fallen in. What is common to all human experience, however, is apprehension at knocking on a door without being certain of welcome, or deciding to confront someone who has been unfair, or applying for a promotion. Courage triumphs inconspicuously when it rises above misery, death, frustration and injustice. Women who keep shabby homes spotless are demonstrating courage in the face of adversity; so are the elderly who enroll in extension courses, prisoners who write poetry, and clergy who march in demonstrations for unpopular causes.

Resolute people, following the high road of principle, sometimes become as legendary as the "man in the water," the hero of the Potomac plane crash. The Irishman Edmund Burke, freshly elected to the House of Commons two hundred years ago as a Whig representative of the prosperous and insular city of Bristol, told his constituents he would not vote on controversial matters as they dictated. A person's "unbiased opinion, his mature judgment, his enlightened conscience, he ought not to sacrifice to you, to any man, or to any set of men living. These he does not derive from your pleasure, they are a trust from providence." At their first opportunity, the citizens of Bristol indignantly turned him out.

George Washington, a wealthy aristocrat whose personal style was to avoid fastidiously all that he found unpleasant, spent six thank-less years as the head of an unruly, sometimes barefoot, usually hungry, frequently cowardly and thieving rabble, deprived for long stretches of the support—financial or moral—of his own Congress. For almost six months, he was virtually without ammunition. He was kept informed of the several plots to have him removed. To all these afflictions he offered the mild complaint that he wished "that the dispute [the revolution] had been left to posterity to determine," but he stuck with it.

Thomas Paine, of the same period, who was fearless in the face of the eighteenth century's religious fanaticism, wrote in *The Age of Reason* that "my own mind is my own church." Amid threats to lynch him, he circulated his pamphlets personally. Abraham Lincoln fought extremists in both the North and the South while he searched for a compromise that would avoid the American Civil War, and was cursed by both camps. Henry David Thoreau, outraged that his country had not abolished slavery, had entered into a bullying war with Mexico and was mistreating its native people, urged Americans to stop paying their taxes. For that, he went to prison. He was unrepentant. He stated that prison was the only place for a just man.

The NAACP chairman in Virginia, the Reverend Francis Griffin, made a noble statement in September 1963, after a summer of violence and bitterness against school desegregation. He informed his congregation, "In this country, there are plenty of things worth going to jail for."

The spirit of Thoreau walked with those Americans who protested against the war in Vietnam and were beaten by the police, thrown into jail and even killed. Griffin's voice is heard wherever people gather to demonstrate against the arms race. Some protesters come for excitement, but many are responding to a genuine call of conscience. In every demonstration, people are putting jobs or status or relationships on the line. That's courage.

The courage of high-mindedness is displayed by the Texan judge William Wayne Justice, who ignores the prejudices of his community and in his years on the bench has desegregated schools and closed harsh juvenile institutions. He received hate mail and obscene phone calls; his friends snubbed him. He refused to ask for armed guards but instead took lessons in Tae Kwon Do, the Korean form of karate, and pronounced it a great way to relieve frustration.

Some tests of courage are not self-selected. An American soldier in World War II, Harold Russell, awakened in a hospital bed to discover that both his hands had been amputated. He later wrote, "In one way or another, each of us must pass through the fires at least once in his lifetime. Each of us must find out for himself that his handicaps, his failures and shortcomings must be conquered or else he must perish."

He concluded with the memorable line: "It is not what you have lost, but what you have left that counts."

The catcher for the Milwaukee Braves, Del Crandall, was asked how he and his wife could bear the pain of raising two retarded sons. He replied, "You start by saying, 'Why did this have to happen to me?' The worst is over when you begin to ask yourself, 'What's the best thing I can do about it?' Another thing: No matter how bad it seems, you can find somebody worse off by looking around, and you don't have to look long or far."

Socrates once complained that humanity had "failed to discover what courage is," a strange comment from a man who possessed so much of it. Philosophers have always defined courage as a quiet flame within everyone, one which may never show, rather than the daring deeds that fill the imagination of screenwriters. They believe courage to be most manifest in those who behave with integrity on issues, though it costs them dearly, and those who risk derision by stepping forward from the crowd.

Courage is the ability to love wholeheartedly, without protecting the self against loss by asking for hostages. It is also the ability to accept love without suspicion. In the summer of 1984 when a gentle and beloved woman, Margaret Frazer, slowly died of cancer, she was tended in her Toronto home by a team of forty friends working in shifts. She had the great grace not to cheapen their gift by protesting or thanking them unduly.

Courage is the personal touch on living. The result is one's own creation rather than a mass-produced gadget full of popular views and marketable charm.

Courage, at bottom, is faith in oneself, in the purpose and dignity of all life; it is a cathedral.

Courage has its own true reasons. It dares to accept limitations on energy and output, so for some committed people it is the sound of their own voice saying "No." Gandhi took one day off every week for silence and prayer, to restore his mental freshness and save himself, as he put it, "from becoming formal, mechanical and devitalized."

Jack Wells, a Winnipeg football reporter given to flights of irrepressible vulgarity, is a funny and endearing man who used to say, "You only come this way once, so you'd better smell the flowers."

For a perfectionist, courage is leaving undone something that ought to be done. For a woman who says she isn't a "woman's libber, but . . ." it is saying she is. For a child, of any age, it is admitting blame. For a person whose parents were negligent, abusive or wrongheaded, it is forgiving them.

The capacity to assume responsibility for a decision is bravery. Wrote psychoanalyst Karen Horney in *Our Inner Conflicts*, the person who can say, "This is my choice, my doing," is demonstrating unusual powers of inner strength and independence.

Benedict Spinoza said courage was "the desire whereby every man strives to preserve his own being in accordance solely with the dictates of reason."

People whose lives have been brave will die courageously.

No act of courage is an island. It enlarges the well of courage within the person and strengthens the courage in everyone who is touched by it. Courage gives the human race hope for itself on a reeling planet. There's a goodness and decency in courage which communicates wordlessly; *everyone* feels more splendid when someone is brave. "Men are like this," Antoine de Saint-Exupéry wrote in *Wind, Sand and Stars*. "Slowly but surely, ordeal fortifies their virtues."

In the citation for the Nobel Prize that was awarded Albert Camus, it was observed that the French humanist philosopher was the defender of "those silent men who, throughout the world, endure the life that has been made for them."

Judge Learned Hand, son and grandson of judges and one of the most venerated of all the U.S. judiciary, once observed, "Man's highest courage is to bet his all on what is no more than the best guess he can make, ask no warranties and distrust all such; face the puzzle of his life without any kit of ready-made answers . . ."

Cicero wrote, "Whoever is brave is a man of great soul." Gary Cooper, the movie star, who died as well as anyone can, echoed that sentiment. He said, "Take for example the courage of certain sick people who have to rearrange their philosophy, their mental processes. Courage or guts originate in the true heart of the machinery, which is the mind."

Real courage, like love, like maturity, is not common. Lord Moran noted sadly, "The honor of our race is in the keeping of but a fraction of her people."

Some days, when the man in the water saves five lives at the cost of his own, it is enough that there is one.

GUILT

GUILT is North America's homeland. Everyone has something to feel guilty about on a personal level, from the big guilts of failing to meet one's own expectations to the familiar small ones of missed anniversaries and unanswered letters.

Class guilt strikes the poor, who feel responsible for their state, and the rich, who may feel their wealth is unearned. Racial minorities feel guilty because they aren't white and whites feel guilty because their breed is racist, with genocidal undertones. Americans have not stopped feeling guilty about Vietnam, and Canadians feel guilty because their country is ineffective.

Men feel guilty because they compromise their ideals, because they don't love their families enough, because they are fearful; childless women feel guilty because they didn't give birth and mothers feel guilty because they didn't give their children enough time, enough thoughtfulness. Children feel guilty because they believe they have disappointed their parents.

Despite the pain it causes, guilt is a poorly informed, not too bright child. People very often feel guilty about the wrong things. A righteous bigot who does his best to see that sinners get what's coming to them will feel guilt the morning after he has had too many drinks. Executives who are shameless about taking credit for work others have done will be upset with themselves when caught in a social gaffe. Murderers would feel remorse if they were not kind to their mothers; swindlers who have bilked thousands of their savings give the victims no thought but would feel lacking in sentiment if they did not donate to funds to build hospital wings or send slum children to summer camp; torturers go home after work with a clean conscience but feel guilty if the garden isn't weeded.

On the other hand, people who lead blameless lives will be mortified with guilt if they masturbate. Devout, good men and women are horrified by their erotic fantasies. Perfectionists are tormented day and night by guilt: nothing has ever been done well enough, soon enough, and if they can't find fault with their performance they can always denigrate themselves anyway because what they did well was done with secret resentment.

Guilt has been measured by a University of Connecticut psychologist, Donald L. Mosher, who developed a widely accepted scale to qualify and quantify guilt. He found three distinct classifications of guilt, which he labeled sex-guilt, hostility-guilt and morality-guilt. When he applied the Mosher scale to prison inmates, he made an interesting discovery. Sex criminals scored low on sex-guilt and those who had committed violent crimes scored low on hostility-guilt, demonstrating that guilt does act to repress aberrant behavior.

Further uses of the measuring system have demonstrated that people with a poor formation of sex-guilt retain less information about birth control or rape than those with higher levels. They simply aren't interested in restricting themselves.

Guilt bears some resemblance to anxiety, as Carroll E. Izard, psychologist at Vanderbilt University, has pointed out, in that "the individual suffers from a wide disparity between the real and ideal self."

"People sometimes have a very moral attitude about stealing, but an immoral one about war, politics or justice," commented the Columbia philosopher and theologian Herbert W. Schneider.

Yet this archfool guilt is indispensable to the development of decency. As biologist and writer Julian Huxley put it, guilt is the embryonic notochord which evolves into ethical backbone. Without a sense of guilt, humans would be as animals are: neither moral nor immoral but simply nonmoral. When there is too little guilt, the spine of ethics is supple and accepts the winds; when there is too much guilt, the rigidity of the structure makes for a ruthless system of values.

Guilt is the emotion that people construct, piece by piece, from the early haze of feelings in their infancies. Some believe that the shame-guilt-humiliation triad is a fundamental emotion which takes its direction from the events in a young child's life.

Five hundred children were examined at the Michigan Guidance Institute, which found three outstanding patterns of personality disturbance, all related to poor guilt formation. One group of children were insecure, inhibited and overly anxious to conform; these were bearing too much guilt. A second group was unsocialized and aggressive, showing too little guilt. The third was characterized as "socialized delinquent," youngsters who were seemingly socialized within the group but, like gangsters, considered the rest of the world fair prey; these had supple guilt which could arrange itself to suit whatever the group wanted.

Of the latter, R. L. Jenkins, Illinois University psychiatrist, once wrote, "The child who is socialized within a delinquent group can commonly be benefited if some adult can reach him and enlarge his conception of those to whom he owes loyalty." Dr. Jenkins's premise is the one on which all street workers operate when dealing with juvenile gangs.

The so-called psychopaths, mass killers who feel no remorse, spring mainly from environments in which they made no attachment to any living thing. In order to begin a guilt system, people have to care about someone enough to regret deeply an offense or imagined offense against that person. All babies make that attachment to the person who cares for them regularly, even if the care isn't of a high order of attentiveness or consideration.

Babies aren't dunces. They can see early on in their lives that they are dependent for survival on a person with a touch, smell, voice that become familiar. Gratitude and appreciation create a bond, so that when the baby senses disapproval in that familiar adult a stew of feelings is generated, in which fear and what becomes guilt are dominant. The more affectionate the care giver has been, the more remorse the baby will feel if the care giver is disapproving. Richly loved but sternly, harshly disciplined children are ripe for a bumper guilt crop.

Babies who have many care givers, as may happen in a family breakup, illness or infant-care center with high staff turnover, may be confused in selecting one person with whom to bond. Some of these hand-me-arounds become affectless, in that they are equally receptive or indifferent to all advances and show no concern when left with strangers. Such children may seem delightfully civil to adults who are unaware of the emotional utility of attachment, but they alarm the experts. By the age of three, when most children are capable of empathy, the affectless ones will lack any sense that other people are even human.

One indicator for the kind of guilt the person will develop is the attitude of the care givers toward a crying baby. Some parents take all crying seriously and will hurry to give sympathy on every occasion but most parents decide to ignore certain kinds of crying. They separate real need, such as hunger, from what is seen as a lesser need for mere cuddling. Infants get the message, as Yale psychiatrist Helen Block Lewis pointed out in *Freud and Modern Psychology*, that there is something shameful and inappropriate about some forms of crying. Dr. Lewis noted that adults also feel shame when they have done something which is considered to be inappropriate. "The implication is that the child could wait but is unwilling to do so," said Dr. Lewis. "Now crying is not only inappropriate but bad or wrong." Thus guilt is hatched.

Dr. Lewis commented that uncertain care givers are humiliated and angry when a baby cries, taking the infant's distress as criticism of their parental skills. The alarming message that the baby receives is that crying is totally wrong. On the other hand, care givers may feel guilty about their anger and resentment of a crying baby and overcompensate by giving the baby an inordinate amount of attention. Accordingly, the babies have no inkling that anything they do is unacceptable, a situation which may mire them in narcissism.

Parents have four alternatives when disciplining children, said David C. McClelland, of Wesleyan University, in *Personality*. They can admonish by saying, in effect, "If you do that I won't love you," which is the conditional-love, shame-arousing formula characteristic of most middle-class upbringing in North America. The second is "If you do that you'll be disapproved, rejected, teased," which results in situational morality and conformity. The third is "If you do that I will punish you (or reward you)." The punishment model of this configuration results in harsh, fearful, paranoiac personalities but reward-for-goodness turns out a well-adjusted person. The last model is based on "If you do that, I will suffer," a superb model for inducing irrational levels of guilt.

Of the latter, Willard Gaylin, a New York psychotherapist, wrote in *Feelings: Our Vital Signs*, "A long-suffering mother who greets a transgression with a sigh rather than a slap is capable of producing a guilt-ridden child who, while not terrified, is just as easily controlled by this kind of intimidation." Dr. Gaylin, however, has considerable admiration for rational guilt, which he calls "the guardian of our goodness."

Guilt grows out of the feelings babies and toddlers experience on being disciplined. It therefore increases as babies begin to crawl and explore the environment, putting themselves on a collision course with adults who want to preserve books and ornaments. Guilt separates itself as a distinct emotion around the age of two, at which time the inquisitiveness and mobility of two-year-olds give ample opportunity for clashes with adults over their behavior. By the age of three, children want to avoid conflict and they have begun to internalize discipline. They give themselves instructions, often the same instructions and in the same tone of voice that the adults use for them. Their play is full of commands to dolls and teddy bears to behave and their language is colored with adult expletives.

For a brief period, North American child-raising techniques embraced what later was called permissiveness. A reaction to the severe parenting of the previous generation, it aimed at an ideal of free-floating untrammeled childhood which would produce creative, independent adults. Instead such children emerged into the world as lost souls, doomed to chronic infantile restlessness and self-preoccupation because they had no introduction to the duties and responsibilities of living in a community.

When there are rules of conduct, a conscience begins to gather in the brain. This is the right code of behavior; this is wrong, wrong, *wrong.* It is someone else's concept of good and evil, but it serves to make life smoother in the child's household. Schools and the games children play present another set of rules which children must acquire to succeed. It never occurs to a small child that the adult rules might be unfair or morally wrong; that's a development that awaits. For young children, the goal is only to learn the system well enough to avoid punishment and get praise. Eventually the process works. The rules become so internalized that even if the misdeed is not discovered the child will punish himself or herself with guilt.

Something else is operating to create guilt: the child is growing more independent. All growth and change means shattering the status quo, old patterns, dependent relationships, as Rollo May observed in *The Meaning of Anxiety.* The refusal to grow makes people feel guilty toward themselves but to accept growth means to move away, perhaps even to betray the expectations of others who are dear, so this also is a carrier of guilt.

Shame and guilt are healthy developments and occur inevitably when children become attached to an adult. Yale's Dr. Lewis wrote that these two are evoked simultaneously over the same transgressions in early childhood. Studies of preschool children show that the happiest and best adjusted of them were treated at home with sympathy and affection but also were given consistent discipline.

Toilet training has a long tradition of influencing the development of shame and guilt. Most parents are well aware of the pitfalls of imposing rigid or too early training for bowel and bladder control, but their own perfectionism or distress may be difficult to suppress. Babies are particularly vulnerable to the implications of rejection if they fail to achieve dry pants in accordance with an adult schedule.

The child of three has the embryo of a homemade conscience. What it contains has been put there by family, school and peer influences, which interact with the child's nature. A sensitive, vulnerable child is more likely to be crushed by a mistake and therefore hatches a severe conscience; an angry, bellicose child may settle for learning what is negotiable and blustering through difficulties, reserving remorse for those occasions when the ship goes down.

Psychologists call this early conscience the authoritarian one; a great many people never develop anything better. Like children, they accept the rules they are given without questioning their logic or fairness. They hold severe views against boat-rockers. So long as they are behaving according to the code of their community, they feel correct. The Bible has a comment on this: "Thou shalt not follow a multitude to do evil." So did the judges at the Nuremberg trials, who were asked to accept as a defense for killing six million people the excuse that the Nazi government ordered it.

"A good conscience, from the authoritarian point of view, depends upon blind submission, mitigated by trust in the love of the superior," wrote Erich Fromm. "It is a withdrawal from the constructive love of self and from human responsibility for the destiny of the race. The dynamic consequence of any variety of reliance on external authority or extrinsic values is impoverishment in the very nature of man."

Righteous parents who admit to no doubts or flaws and a school system rich in punitive controls create such a conscience in malleable children, who form a majority. By not tolerating criticism or variance, authoritarian institutions and families crush children's ability to be spontaneous, to be original. Because minor mistakes are heavily punished, children may grow up to be adults whose guilt begins to whir over an incomplete file. A divergent opinion presents a challenge that the authoritarian conscience cannot accept. To preserve the small, frantic field in which such a conscience lives, everything must be predictable and accepted by the safe majority.

Psychotherapist Otto Rank said unkindly that this straitjacket morality is the domain of the "average man." By making no effort to be individual, such people avoid the conflicts that might stir their guilt. They conform to society in order to spare themselves pain. "It represents the first and easiest solution to the problem set by birth," observed Dr. Rank, the problem being a separate identity.

The art of living is to evolve a sane guilt which will prod ideals and check impulsiveness. People must think and act their way clear of the "crippling burden of good and evil," according to Brock Chisholm, a Canadian psychiatrist who headed the World Health Organization for many years. He said, "The unnecessary and artificially imposed inferiority, guilt and fear, commonly known as sin, produces much of the social maladjustment and unhappiness in the world." He went so far as to state to a conference of his peers that the rock-hard authoritarian conscience, expressed by such groups as the Moral Majority, constitutes the world's greatest danger, threatening the extinction of the human race.

Happily, the natural tendency of a conscience is to move its owner toward goodness. One researcher asked a thousand youngsters in grades six to twelve to list the qualities they admired most in others and the ones they admired least. *Honesty* topped the first list in all age groups and *dishonesty* the second.

When children get something right, it makes a satisfying click in the conscience and reinforces the child's capacity for rightness. Erich Fromm described this as going with one's natural current, trusting in the consequences of doing what feels right. "Conscience is thus a reaction of ourselves to ourselves," he said, "to become what we potentially are."

Nationality, race and religion are all factors in determining the quality of the conscience a person will develop. The Protestant branches of Christianity, for instance, particularly the fundamentalists who rejoice in hell and damnation for sinners, are magnets and incubators for guilt. Cause and effect can be seen in the lives of such founders of religions as John Calvin and Martin Luther, both of whom were abused mercilessly as children and went on to establish punitive faiths. Roman Catholicism and other religions with a confessional element generally produce less tyrannical natures.

Guilt is the rudder by which humans have always steered their course. Most religions and all mythology are preoccupied with guilt and the search for the holy grail of forgiveness. The great legends, from Prometheus to Jesus, have in common a theme of redemptive agony and death in the service of the human race; both suffered cruelly, and both were received back by God. The shape of Christianity, as drawn by Paul, owes much to classic literature in which semi-gods fall from grace and are resurrected in heaven.

Because there is so much misplaced and neurotic guilt in the world, and because so many of its victims wind up on the psychiatric couch, some therapists have developed the strong opinion that guilt is a useless emotion. Others hasten to champion guilt. Helen Block Lewis told Jane E. Brody of the New York *Times* that guilt helps people stay connected. "Guilt is one of the cements that bind us together and keep us human," she said.

The history of guilt is as old as life. Sigmund Freud wrote that guilt is "the most important problem in the evolution of culture," and anthropologist Weston LaBarre noted, "Man's original sin was not so much the eating of the fruit of the tree as in climbing down from it." People are uneasy within the restrictions of the human tribe: domesticity feels confining and wild shores draw; being bipedal means that babies are born in pain. Deep in the caves of the brain, there is an atavistic longing which brings a haunting guilt and regret.

Great literature is saturated with the theme of guilt. José Barchilon, director of the Denver Psychiatric Institute, has written about guilt found in such works as Mark Twain's *Huckleberry Finn* and Albert Camus's *The Fall*. One of the theater's most dramatic portrayals of guilt is the banquet scene in William Shakespeare's *Macbeth* when the ghost of Banquo appears to Macbeth, who gave the order for Banquo to be killed. The ghost, which is Macbeth's guilt, so disturbed the murderer that he is unable to join his guests—that is, guilt makes it impossible for him to be a member of society.

The pervasive theme in the works of playwrights from Aeschylus to such moderns as Eugene O'Neill and Arthur Miller has been guilt and the impossibility of expiating a great wrongdoing. The classic causes of guilt have been death and sex. Sören Kierkegaard, the nineteenth-century Danish philosopher, believed that people feel guilty about sex because it represents individuality, rather than because of its sensuality. According to Rollo May's theory, whatever step people take toward individualization is guilt-laden because it shifts all relationships.

For whatever cause, people rarely enjoy guilt-free sex. They feel guilty about their sex fantasies, feel guilty if they want sex often, feel guilty if they don't want it at all, feel guilty about their erotic dreams, feel guilty when they have a flash of desire for a comely stranger, feel guilty while engaged in sex because someone might overhear, or the sex is stolen, or the performance isn't adequate, or the partner isn't satisfied, or the partner is the wrong sex, or the revealed body is not beautiful.

Middle-class North America is the most guilt-prone of all income groups because this is where success depends on following the rules of decorum. Neither poor nor rich people have such needs for conformity. The idealized personality of the middle class, obsessed with a pleasant exterior, can create demoralizing guilt in people who fail prim ideals of conduct. This kind of merciless, unreasonable guilt became established with the dawn of the industrial age, according to some anthropologists, and is a condition of the development of modern technology.

When anthropologist Margaret Mead was conducting her study of cultures in the Admiralty Islands, she came upon a tribe, the Manus, who resembled the middle class she knew. Children were raised with strictly prescribed puritanical rules and emerged from the discipline, as she described it, as "stone-age people with modern guilt," laden with hysterical sex taboos and devoured by ambition to succeed.

The holocaust is seen by behavioral scientists as owing much to the child-raising practices of middle-class Germans, who were loving of their children but demanded immediate, unquestioned obedience to authority. The product of that model is a confident, assertive person who follows orders without hesitation. The British upper class, dispirited by the chilliness of nannies and harsh public schools, has been marked by a prevalence of listlessness and guilt.

A so-called "moral" upbringing laded with prohibitions is most damaging when the authority figures are righteous, leaving no room for doubt. Jean Piaget wrote extensively about this mirroring effect. Parents who are obsessed with stamping out evil, such as those found in child-whipping cults, almost invariably produce children who either are broken or grow to become severe and punitive themselves.

Similarly, parents who place great value on appearances and material possessions will instill in their children a paralyzing fear of public embarrassment. Highly controlled parents have children who are appalled by a show of anger. If the parents equate virtue with denial, their children will become adults who feel guilty over mild indulgences.

For most people, the conscience is a colossally inefficient instrument for perceiving right and wrong. John Dewey used an interesting test to determine the quality of the moral upbringing in a family. It was based on the parents' response to a fundamental but hypothetical question a child might ask: "Why should I tell the truth?"

Some parents would answer all variations of that query with the flat reply that lying is wrong. Others explain that liars aren't popular and don't have friends. Others would say that liars always get caught and will be ridiculed. The reply that developed the best kind of conscience, a social conscience, is that society would break down if people couldn't trust one another.

"To a marked degree, culture, class membership and their respective prejudices mold both conscience and conduct," psychologist Gordon Allport declared in his 1955 Terry lectures at Yale. "Early fixations in character often leave infantile traces that bind the mind in such a way that democratic relationships in adult life are impossible."

Dr. Allport cited three stages of development in the human conscience. The first is when external sanctions rule, as in the case of young children and authoritarian adults. Conduct is determined on the basis of what might be found out. Whatever can be done without detection is acceptable; being caught is the ultimate evil.

The second stage is the internalization of rules, so that people behave circumspectly even when there are no witnesses. The conscience contains the dicta of parents and other authority figures, such as teachers, police, clergy and media opinion makers, that the parents respect. Most ten-year-olds have this kind of conscience, a great improvement on the crude authoritarian version but still lacking in skepticism and creativity.

The highest development of the human conscience, the third stage described by Dr. Allport, is called the humanistic or social conscience. Those adults who possess this guilt apparatus are self-guided according to their own "experiences of preference and self-respect." Humanistic ethics require social regulations, Erich Fromm explained, "but the distinction is that the authority behind them resides in the man himself."

The person has taken the ultimate step, and is responsible to her or his own self.

Such people are rare. Just as no autopsy has ever discovered a perfect body—and indeed autopsies routinely reveal anomalies that astonish doctors, who marvel that the person could have existed with such an oddity—no one is perfectly mature emotionally. Guilt will warp judgment somewhere, in spite of wisdom and experience. Irrational guilt, which is present in every neurosis, can make perverse even the holy people who have become national treasures.

Looking at the distortions of guilt, psychoanalyst Karen Horney once observed, "In the manifest picture of neuroses, guilt feelings seem to play a paramount role. In some neuroses these feelings are expressed openly and abundantly; in others they are more disguised, but their presence is suggested by behavior, attitudes and ways of thinking and reacting."

The paramount fear of people loaded with guilt is that they will be found out and exposed as the mean and crabbed individuals they believe themselves to be. They feel unworthy, filled with inner ugliness, which they struggle constantly to conceal. Believing themselves unworthy of love or respect, they strive to behave well but can trust neither their own performance nor the rewards that the show brings. They never lose sight of the hideous gap between the person they present to the world and the sour, angry person they really are.

Guilt is lonelier than loneliness and more frightening than fear.

At the Menninger Clinic in Topeka, Kansas, patients with symptoms of guilt did well in a treatment program which required them to perform mean, monotonous or annoyingly difficult tasks. Will C. Menninger explained that the "sunshine and roses treatment" doesn't work on such people because the patient "will only think that you don't understand him. His troubles are burning his soul—he has to expiate in some way. We know it is a mistake to let people go on punishing themselves emotionally, so we get them to punish themselves with menial tasks."

A bank president was put to work scrubbing the splattered walls of the clinic's ceramics studio. A fragile old lady was given a soot-crusted pot, bought in a secondhand store, and asked to make it shine. Others were told to sew buttons on pajamas or put together two-thousand-piece jigsaw puzzles.

An unmarried English woman with a strict Catholic upbringing became ill with guilt after an abortion. She went to a psychiatrist, but he was unable to help and she grew steadily worse. In despair she went to a convent, where the nuns told her she was a wicked, wicked woman and put her to scrubbing floors as penance. It was a balm to her sore conscience and she recovered.

Dr. Horney points out that guilt sometimes is very evident, such as in people who immediately assume blame for whatever goes wrong. They insist that every mishap is really their fault, however far-fetched that might seem to all observers. They have unsecured opinions and will change their mind effortlessly if they encounter someone with an opposite view. They actually feel better and behave more coherently in a disaster. Playing a wounded victim or a martyr is the typecasting for which they have been longing.

As psychiatrists have learned, people rather admire their own guilt and are reluctant to give it up. They see it as the mark of their superiority, a sign of acute sensitivity such as is found in poets. Dr. Horney was among the many therapists who have come to believe that guilt complexes don't rest on a sense of failure so much as on a bedrock of infant narcissism. Guilt-ridden people, it has been observed, protest that they admire constructive criticism but it always seems that criticism aimed at them doesn't fall into this acceptable category. They insist that they aren't worth bothering about, but they require for daily nutrition large amounts of reassurance, praise and attention.

Not all guilt-afflicted people are this blatant. Some are withdrawn, suspicious and secretive about themselves, taking affront at personal questions. They view innocent queries as patent nosiness. A woman was asked idly, as a conversation starter, if she was married. She answered frostily, "I never answer that question."

Many people with a high level of guilt will put out perfection as a way of keeping off the wolves. By fulfilling heavy obligations they have arranged for themselves and being Good Samaritans to the universe, they hope to avoid censure. They are so "loving" that they leave a wake of dazed and confused people, astonished to be singled out so fondly by a near-stranger.

Still others use the tactic of helplessness, courting the ill health latent in themselves in order to avoid wading into real-life situations that they might handle badly, thereby increasing their already impossible guilt. Childish incompetence is a variation of the same theme. Women protest that they can't do math or keep a checkbook straight, while men are pleased to flounder and crash around in the kitchen. They forgive themselves grandly for being so endearingly unable to cope, and by refusing to compete save themselves from the guilt and embarrassment of a poor showing.

Too much guilt is the mark of a dysfunctioning conscience, but so is too little guilt, or none at all. When the conscience is infantile and scarcely formed, people have no sense of the consequences of what they do and therefore break rules with a casual air.

Disastrous experience teaches them nothing. A middle-aged man who let himself drift into dealing drugs and got away with it for ten years was indignant when he was arrested. It was only a soft drug, he protested. It shouldn't be illegal in the first place. In the second place, the judge was biased. In the third place, the police rigged the evidence and the prosecution lied. When last heard from, he was attempting to serve his sentence in a soft prison with an adjoining golf course. At no time did it occur to him that he might have gone into some other line of work.

Such people are alarming to their families and a public nuisance but they are no trouble to themselves. They exist in a safety net of excuses, evasions and contempt. Their mood swings are as sudden, violent and evanescent as a child's. They make superb mates for masochists, whose dreams of hardship and betrayal will be richly realized.

A shortage of guilt is the indicator of a rudimentary personality, one which has not yet embarked on the tedious, discouraging, silent, difficult and noble work of constructing a whole person. Overactive guilt, on the other hand, is a beginning of growth which has become paralyzed along the way. There can be no forward progress until the issue of guilt is addressed. A person with neurotic guilt is tormented by a mistake and will brood for a week in real pain but will change nothing. A healthier person making the same error will also feel wretched but will make whatever amends are possible and will change the conduct which caused the problem.

Montreal's Karl Stern, writer-psychiatrist, said, "Objective guilt can be assuaged. Like debt, to which it is related, it can be paid. Neurotic guilt is insatiable. You cannot appease it. You cannot pay it off."

But the human organism will always move in the direction of health if it can, and guilt-ridden people unconsciously administer their own therapy. When they are sick at heart, men and women find themselves performing some long-neglected task they have been avoiding. In many cases, the chore consists of cleaning, sorting, making something right—all of which carry symbolic meaning for the chaos inside them. When the basement is tidy, the closet rearranged, the car washed, some of the order imposed on the environment works its way into the troubled mind and gives relief. Cleanliness may not be next to godliness, but it sometimes comforts an unpeaceful mind.

An extreme form of the same mild therapy is seen in the curious obsessions about cleanliness of such guilt-ridden people as billionaire Howard Hughes, whose staff wore gloves with which they selected tissues from a box which would be used to cover whatever object he was handed. The gangster Mickey Cohen had a handwashing compulsion, and would shower, shave, shampoo and change his clothes several times a day; so does comedian Jerry Lewis.

Many guilty people try to make a deal with their conscience, operating on the principle that a good deed will counteract an evil one. Philanderers buy expensive gifts for their mates; robber barons head United Way appeal drives; women who don't like children become teachers.

George Bernard Shaw observed dryly, "The more things a man is ashamed of, the more respectable he is."

One of the more common ways of dealing with guilt is the sophistry of "everyone does it." Income-tax cheating and expense-account padding are more guilt-free than is pilfering a ballpoint pen from a receptionist's desk. Cribbing on examinations does not stir much guilt and neither does vilifying a politician. In a police force where accepting bribes is normal, bribed policemen feel little guilt. Honest people who go to work in a bureaucracy riddled with kickbacks and graft are likely in time to accommodate their conscience to the opportunities presented.

Others habitually blame someone else for their own mistakes, converting their own guilt into outrage. Dr. Gaylin called this the "hot-potato syndrome," and gave as an example a man who in the course of doing his wife a favor loses his wallet. He then turns on his wife as the cause of the loss. "It is much easier to feel anger than guilt," Dr. Gaylin observed.

The process is circular. The twists and evasions of guilt avoidance become habitual, until no other response even occurs to the individual. The Bhagavad-Gita says, "Repeated sin impairs the judgment . . . He whose judgment is impaired sins repeatedly."

Other popular ways to trick the conscience and avoid guilt are such justifications as "I've had it happen to me plenty of times," or "They are rotten people who had it coming to them," or "After all, I apologized, didn't I? What more do you want?" or "I never get a fair break, so what can you expect?" or "I did it for the cause." Terrorists who kill innocents employ the latter.

"The cause" is history's greatest gift to those who do remorseless evil. In the name of righteousness, Inquisition priests put people on the rack, Moslems flog sinners, Crusaders speared Saracen babies, the U.S. Cavalry made tobacco pouches out of the breasts of Sioux women, Jesus Christ was crucified, in Belfast Catholics kill Protestant children and Protestants kill Catholic children, the Royal Air Force pulverized the beautiful city of Dresden, Nazis murdered six million people in concentration camps, Marines napalmed Vietnamese civilians, the Soviet Union puts dissenters in psychiatric hospitals where their minds are broken, Benedict Spinoza was excommunicated and Socrates was ordered to drink poison.

Socrates said before he died, "The difficulty, O my judges, is not to escape from death, but from guilt. For guilt is swifter than death and catches up with us more rapidly . . . I have been overtaken by death, but my accusers by wickedness . . . I submit to my punishment, and they to theirs." It is unlikely, however, that the philosopher's executioners suffered the punishment of guilt: like most who murder, torture, imprison and maim, they were acting out of principle.

The infamous torturer Tomás de Torquemada was a pious man whose conscience was not troubled by the death and pain he caused, but on the other extreme are North Americans in the present century whose conscience flails them if they leave the telephone unanswered. Even when they are exhausted, overscheduled or ill, they can't refuse a request for help. They can't abandon for a moment the Augean task of shoveling out the stable of their guilt and discontent. They make poor administrators because they can't chastise, order or fire anyone. They don't complain in restaurants about sloppy service or rotten-tasting food. If they are cheated or exploited, they feel at heart that they deserved no better; they find excuses to avoid complaining.

Unforgiving consciences of this ilk will push men and women to surpass themselves in endurance and production. Overwork serves two purposes: it functions as well-earned punishment and it also staves off the lash of self-criticism. By making a superhuman effort to contribute to society in the arts, or business, or the social field, people hope to silence the guilt-devil that lurks in their minds.

Karen Horney said that the guilty long to get rid of themselves and that exhaustion is one of the techniques they use to numb self-awareness. This search for sedation is also seen in people who require inordinate amounts of sleep, or become addicted to drugs, sickness, insanity, promiscuity or danger. The liquor industry owes much to guilt, as well as causing much guilt; so do manufacturers of tranquilizers and sleeping pills.

Shame is related to guilt but is somewhat different. In guilt, according to Helen Block Lewis, "the thing done or undone is the focus of awareness." In shame, it is the whole self which is mortified. Objective guilt carries with it the possibility of action to put things right; like debt, it can be repaid. The transfusing, depressing and paralyzing emotion of shame or neurotic guilt, however, cannot be appeased.

As Phyllis Chesler pointed out in *Women and Madness,* shame is more common to women and guilt to men. Theories abound for why this is so. Mothers and fathers tend to give daughters an easier upbringing, for one reason, out of the old societal belief that the lives of women will be more protected than those of men. When this happens and discipline is gentle and loving, the detachment of self from parents is slow, and therefore arouses less guilt than a rapidly freestanding male will feel. Helen Block Lewis observed that because men are encouraged to be aggressive, they are compelled more than women are to put themselves in situations which will create guilt for them. Dr. Lewis also noted that little girls do not have to separate themselves from their mothers in order to acquire gender identity, but little boys do. This necessary rejection of mother is also a prime guilt producer.

In recent years, however, women are catching up in the guilt department. The culture's expectation that women will be nurturers and conciliators puts a burden of guilt on women who resist the definition. Women who choose to remain in their careers despite motherhood are devastated by guilt; so are women who do not take on the responsibility of caring for an aged parent, or women who are obliged to be hard-edged in business dealings. The culture is hitting back: separation, especially from children, is more difficult for women than for men.

Echoes of a woman's state are seen in the definition of a shame society, in this case Japan, given by cultural anthropologist Ruth Benedict in *The Chrysanthemum and the Sword:* "Shame cultures rely on external sanctions for good behavior and not, as true guilt cultures do, on an internalized conviction of sin. Shame is a reaction to other people's criticism . . . it requires an audience, or at least a man's fantasy of an audience. Guilt does not."

Women, relying more acutely on relationships and approval for self-definition than men generally do, are therefore more vulnerable to shame. So are certain cultures, such as some Pacific island groups, African and Arabic tribes, India, Jews and many native North American tribes. The Ojibway, cultural kin of the Japanese, will commit suicide out of shame. To preserve the delicate balance that holds such societies together, it is necessary to stress cooperative values and to avoid being in another's debt. The child-raising technique that produces such preoccupation with shame begins with great warmth and closeness with babies and toddlers in order to form a strong attachment bond, after which ridicule keeps younger children in line and banishment is the fate of older ones who don't follow the rules.

Karl Menninger related in *Man Against Himself* the story of the native man, Inepegut, who lived on the White Rocks reservation in Utah and killed his mother accidentally while drunk. He exiled himself for the rest of his life, for thirty years wearing no clothes and living without shelter, eating what little food was given him out of pity. Such self-punishment is not usually so obvious, Dr. Menninger commented, but is present in the ascetic practices of cult diets and the courting of exhaustion by work addicts and joggers.

Shame cultures are marked by very high levels of ambition. As O. Fenichel noted in *The Psychoanalytic Theory of Neurosis,* ambition represents the person's first fight against shame.

Shame is always associated with blushing but no one yet understands that involuntary response. All people blush, even blind people, apparently because the addled brain thinks it is hiding the person behind a curtain of blood as a way of escaping embarrassment. Blushing occurs when there is a sharp sense of being at a disadvantage—when the person is clumsy, for instance, or overpraised, or wrongly accused, or has violated etiquette. Teenagers, in whom poise in social situations is poorly developed, are the most prone to blush of all age groups. Women blush more than men do, since feeling at a disadvantage is systemic in them. Women in menopause blush more than anyone in the world, the so-called hot flushes which are glandular in origin rather than emotional, though women whose lives are stressful will suffer the flushes more intensely and frequently than calmer women do.

Shame and guilt produce a cluster of less evident physiological changes. Guilt causes a sense of congealing which is reflected in a heaviness in the organs. The heart overworks, breathing is labored, digestion is poor, so that guilty people are often constipated.

Despite its problems, a well-ordered guilt is much admired by philosophers and psychiatrists alike. "The function of the feeling of guilt is to redirect the conduct of the individual into a course harmonious with his moral or ethical standards," said University of Illinois psychiatrist R. L. Jenkins. "Feeling guilty about what we have done often leads us to do better."

Adults cannot use the same conscience all their lives. A childhood conscience is bestowed by parents and other influential adults; it may need review and adjustments. As people mature, the conscience built on obedience gives way to what Gordon Allport in *Becoming* called "generic self-guidance."

"In the moral sphere," he wrote, "we may say that becoming depends upon the development of a generic conscience which, in turn, depends upon possession of long-range goals and an ideal self-image." Healthy adults, Dr. Allport said, are influenced as they develop by their sense of values and their goals for themselves, even if they know in their hearts that the goals may never be attained.

A strongly developed conscience is fundamental to the unfolding of integrity and the ability to love, without which life has little point. The philosopher Georg Wilhelm Friedrich Hegel said, "It is the privilege of a man to feel guilty." Carl Jung wrote that even a bad conscience is a gift from heaven because without a conscience there would be no self-criticism, and without self-criticism, people would not attempt to understand their own psychology and improve upon their natures.

"To become foolish is certainly not an art," Dr. Jung observed, "but to draw wisdom out of foolishness is the whole of art. Foolishness is the mother of the wise, but never cleverness." He called conscience "a thorn in the flesh" without which there is no progress and no ascent.

Abraham Maslow held the same view. He described intrinsic guilt as the consequence of the betrayal of one's own inner nature or self, a turning away from the path to self-actualizing, his term for emotional maturity. He added, "It is good, even necessary, for a person's development to have intrinsic guilt when he deserves to. It is not just a symptom to be avoided at any cost but is rather an inner guide for growth toward the actualization of the real self, and of its potentialities."

The poet Robert Frost once described conscience as that which determines "what you can and can't possibly stand." Victor Hugo was in awe of such a conscience. He wrote, "There is a spectacle grander than the ocean, and that is the conscience. There is a spectacle grander than the sky, and it is the interior of the soul."

Like earth and sky, conscience and soul meet.

AMBITION

AMBITION is highly regarded in twentieth-century North America by almost everyone but behavioral scientists, who take the sour view that most of what appears to be admirable drive and motivation is really neurotic. At its purest, ambition represents a search for wholeness and the pleasure of full functioning, but most ambition is more base. It contains large measures of guilt (if I become a success I will stop feeling I'm rotten), or its motivation may be to impress denegrating parents, teachers, mates who deserted, friends who were false, or it may be to compensate for a real or imagined handicap.

Left to its own devices, human nature wants to improve itself—and will. That's ambition in its healthiest form. At its worst, ambition is a lifelong compulsion that can never be satisfied.

The elements that combine to create what society calls a monkey on the back are a certain kind of restless, quick person and a certain kind of upbringing, in which there was enough affection and reward to instill confidence but plenty of indifference, unresponsiveness, error and rejection as well.

The high achievements of people who were wretched as children are written on the firmament, giving rise to the suspicion that a requisite for driven genius is an unhappy childhood. Loving parents have seriously wondered if they were doing their children a favor by being understanding: perhaps, they thought, the motivation for developing aspiration is as much a flight from misery as a search for greatness. If children are content, will they become adults who burn with ambition?

Studies demonstrate that such fears are groundless. Tormented children who achieve greatness are miracles of resilience; for most people, a blighted childhood will club enterprise to a pulp. Children who have the luck to receive affection and habits of independence from their parents are likely to be able to work at a level close to their natural potential, and will do so with enthusiasm and creativity.

"Capacities clamor to be used, and cease their clamor only when they are well used," wrote Abraham Maslow. "Not only it is fun to use our capacities, but it is also necessary for growth. The unused skill or capacity or organ can become a disease center or else atrophy or disappear, thus reducing the person."

North American industry and commerce no longer tolerate many of the old ruthless, dictatorial styles of management. Instead, taking a tip from the collegial approach of Japanese industry, top management is selected on the basis of ability to work collaboratively and create a friendly, enthusiastic spirit in employees. Such skills come more readily to people raised in democratic homes. The move from austere bosses to approachable ones was not the consequence of humanist ideals, or not entirely, but came from careful observation that people work more efficiently when they like one another than when they are under a whip.

The University of Iowa did a classic experiment to illustrate this point when it assigned several groups of five boys to make masks. Some of the groups were supervised by critical, angry, officious instructors and some by relaxed and helpful ones. Some predicted that the casual instructors would get poor results and the perfectionists would turn out the better products, but the reverse was true. Discipline and output dropped under the tyrants and soared under the pleasant leaders.

Other controlled studies were conducted in such settings as a railway, a tractor factory and an insurance company. In every case, the best production came from the team with affable, considerate and cooperative leadership.

A benign environment, in the home or workplace, has been shown repeatedly to facilitate learning and increase effort. People, children and adults alike, think more clearly when their anxiety output is lessened.

Ambition comes in degrees. At the minimal level, it concerns itself with sustenance alone. This bottom gear is not restricted to the poor. People of all income groups spend their lives preoccupied with food, dress and their homes, to the exclusion of almost all else. Next on the scale is the most common form of ambition, which seeks power, prestige and possessions. This ambition contains a high quota of guilt, anger and hatred. Psychoanalyst Karen Horney spoke of it as "moving against people."

The highest form of ambition has a competitive edge but is inward, rather than interpersonal: the person aspires to a better self.

Brooklyn College's department of psychology analyzed mature ambition almost forty years ago and noted that it contained such qualities as loyalty, friendliness, civic consciousness and the desire to excel as mates, parents, teachers and so on. Such people, the report stated, "love mankind the most and tend to be more individual and nonconforming."

Far from being passive blobs, soaking in the sun like a bed of sweet peas, adults with a mature level of ambition appear to be a yeasty lot, passionate about integrity and capable of courage and good judgment. Stanford University's vast *Studies of Genius*, published in the late twenties, observed, "Youths who achieve eminence are characterized not only by high intellectual traits but also by persistence of motion and effort, confidence in their abilities and great strength and force of character."

In the early sixties, the schools of Prince Edward County in Virginia were closed for four years to avoid desegregation. Black children had no formal education, though some were drilled by their parents. With the quiet help of John Kennedy, then President of the United States, and a generous Ford Foundation grant, a privately financed school system was established in the county seat, Farmville. Teachers gathered there from all over America, prepared for a difficult task of catching children up to their grade level. Instead they found a good many of the youngsters had simply continued to learn reading and arithmetic on their own and were not nearly as badly off as predicted.

One of the teacher volunteers, a woman in her seventies who had taught school all her adult life, explained, "All children love to learn," she said. "You can hardly keep them from learning."

Everyone is born curious and avid for knowledge. The species could not have survived if its young were not greedy to understand their environment and master it. Curiosity levels vary: some newborns have a look of astonishing interest and perception in their eyes; others seem inner-preoccupied. Parents who present their infants with a stimulating environment, such as Burton White's red mittens for newborns or the simple addition of bells to the booties, obviously perk up this natural interest. However the capacity to be curious and seek information doesn't entirely shut down even if the surroundings are bland or—an equal disaster—if the environment bombards the baby with so much activity and change that the infant shuts down in self-defense.

The brain is taking in data, storing it in the prodigious memory banks; it is also learning how to learn; most important, it is learning that it can learn. The approach that the future adult will take to novelty is being established. The variety of experience and the freedom and the safety provided for inquisitive babies determine how confident they will forever be in their ability to master something new.

The early American psychologist William McDougall speculated early in the century that natural curiosity is a kind of muscle. Neuropsychology has confirmed that hunch. With repetition, the brain develops highways that facilitate the travel of emotions and thought. Like a muscle, when the curiosity-integration pathways are much used they are more supple and flexible. The result is called confidence and motivation. When natural curiosity is thwarted and understimulated, the inexperienced brain produces quantities of uncertainty.

The venerable pediatrician Benjamin Spock once recommended that a home should not have more than 25 percent of its contents off-limits to an exploring child. He computed that a toddler could tolerate being frustrated a quarter of the time, but more than that would not be good for an inquiring mind.

Overindulgence is almost as drastic an error as treating a child coldly. A child's ability to reason requires practice at working out a problem, enduring a certain amount of frustration and surmounting adversity. Coping with difficulties is a nourishing activity and the child who encounters no roadblocks is underfed. When children can triumph over what seemed hopeless, they learn to be dauntless.

Laboratory animals have been put through thousands of experiments in incentive-conscious North America in order to demonstrate this dynamic. When animals have an edge of hunger or are otherwise slightly deprived, they work vigorously. Like most humans, however, they quit trying altogether when the deprivation exceeds the limit of their tolerance.

People with the highest levels of tolerance for difficulties are those with a realistic view of their abilities. Children will usually test the outside of the envelope, as space pilots put it, attempting to extend the boundaries of their world, their selves. If the support they receive from adults is sensible and stable, they will go as far as they can reach, and then a bit farther, alert to the feel of ground giving way.

Children must power themselves, or else it doesn't work. A child who is pushed can become frantic. In Montreal, a survey conducted by McGill University found that tough, aggressive parents who bully their way into positions of affluence and power are very likely to produce emotionally disturbed sons. "Fathers go for the jugular," commented one of the researchers. Yale's Richard C. Carroll made the same observation. "Somehow," he reflected sadly, "in striving for brighter students—and getting them—we have increased the incidence of emotional instability."

One significant achievement test with encouraging implications for overburdened single parents found that many successful young people were children of parents who expected them at an early age to be self-reliant. Because the parent or parents had their hands full or were philosophically committed to making their offspring independent, the children were required to find their own way around the community, prepare their own lunches, take responsibility for getting themselves up in the morning, find friends by themselves.

David C. McClelland, psychologist at Wesleyan University, pointed out that this training for self-reliance didn't include what he called "caretaking" items, such as children putting themselves to bed. He said that there was no rejection involved "but rather a positive interest in the child's independence, growth and development."

Another achievement test of outstandingly able children demonstrated that they had in common a measure of independence gained before they were eight. In addition, the child-raising technique in their households was based on the reward system. Long before the women's movement succeeded in giving women permission to be uppity, Abraham Maslow examined the background of women in college whose personalities were unusual: they were vigorous, independent and ambitious. He found what they had in common was a childhood in which they were expected to be competent and responsible.

Inherent intelligence can be high or low, but one thing certain is that IQ interacts with the environment. Children tested at the age of six and again when they are twelve have varied as much as fifty points, up or down, in the intervening years. Great stress, for instance, will reduce a child's ability to learn or react well on a test. A Fels Research Institute project at Antioch discovered that children whose intelligence increases with age generally come from stable, democratic homes that place a high value on education. Those whose intelligence diminished suffered serious uprooting or else were being raised by autocratic, demanding parents whose standard of achievement was social status.

Most of the ability to learn is established in a child before formal schooling begins. Adequately staffed day-care centers provide a rich environment for a toddler and so do parents who take time to read to young children from babyhood, take them on outings to zoos, parks and museums and restrict television viewing to selected shows of a picture-book character, such as *Sesame Street.*

In 1910 a German chemist, Wilhelm Ostwald, listed the ten leading characteristics of successful scientists. Early training headed the list. A study of one thousand scientists, only thirty-two of whom were women, was done fifty years ago by J. McKeen Cattell. He reported that those who received the earliest education were among the most distinguished and accomplished of the group; those whose education began later were lower in both respects.

The world over, highly industrialized nations take care to send children to school early. When anthropologist Margaret Mead revisited the South Seas twenty-five years after her original study of tribal culture, she found one of them, the Manus, had changed drastically. Because there was a U.S. Army base nearby, Manus children were going to school and young Manus adults had become hustlers who could operate complicated machinery, set up small businesses and establish a democratic form of government. Dr. Mead concluded that what was responsible for the easy adaptation of the Manus people was the fact that their children were prepared for learning by their rigorous early training. Since Manus villages consisted of houses on stilts over water, all Manus children learn to swim as soon as they can crawl and even toddlers can handle canoes.

People who encourage children at an early age to master their environment seem also to be people who revere achievement myths.

People who see the world as fearful and mythologize danger will crib and confine their young.

Anthropologist Ashley Montagu declared, "Where human beings tend to receive little or no assistance from their environment in the development of their potentialities, there will be little or no development of them. Where individuals tend to receive a mediocre or moderate kind of assistance from their environment, their potentialities will tend to be correspondingly developed. Where humans beings receive a high degree of assistance from their environment, their potentialities will tend to be most highly realized."

Intelligent parents are likely to produce intelligent children for two reasons. One is the genetic factor which contributes to the brain's acuity; the other is that adults with high IQs have a wide range of interests, exposing their children at an early age to books, science, current events, the arts. Intelligence is inherent to some unknown degree and certainly is also elastic.

For instance, though scientists form only 3 percent of the population, more than half the scientists in the United States were raised in homes where at least one parent was a scientist. As a cultural group, Jewish adults are twice as likely to be employed in upper-income occupations as are non-Jewish people. It is also significant that most of the most prominent women in human history have lived in this century, which is the first to expect and allow more from women than sex, housekeeping and motherhood.

"The old idea that genius will out despite any handicaps or restrictions is no longer tenable," wrote Norma V. Scheidemann of the University of Southern California in *Psychology of Exceptional Children.* "All indications are to the contrary. Environment is the great factor in releasing or hemming in innate ability."

Some nursery school children were surveyed by David C. McClelland of Wesleyan University, who found that those with the highest intelligence, as demonstrated by their originality, playfulness and fancifulness, came from what psychologists described as "acceptant" homes. The most quarrelsome children were being raised in rejectant homes, the behaviorists reported, and the most despondent tots had indifferent parents.

In *Personality,* Dr. McClelland reported on a famous study of identical twins, Johnny and Jimmy, who were raised separately. One twin was raised in a stimulating environment where he was encouraged to learn a variety of complicated skills, while the other was raised in a home with no interest in extracurricular activities. This twin eventually caught up to his brother in such areas as skating but the two had widely disparate attitudes as adults. The accelerated brother was vastly more confident than his twin, more receptive to change, more intrigued to acquire knowledge and new experiences.

Such findings have created a recent craze for teaching children to read when they are little more than babies, as a technique for zapping their intelligence quotient. Scientists have grave concerns that such early force-feeding of the intellect can have a backlash effect, creating resistance and exhaustion in overstimulated youngsters. Retaliatory idleness is a common consequence of parental pressure to keep busy. Children need assimilation time as well as acquisition time; daydreaming children are working on their creativity and a child bent over a chessboard is learning anticipation and strategy.

A significant number of writers and artists had childhoods which permitted them solitude. Some had long illnesses, some lived in country villages where children roamed free, some had the luck to be raised in quirky old houses with nooks where a child could curl up out of the way of domestic traffic.

For some children, isolation is social and not of their choosing. For reasons of race, color, income, family behavior or religion, they don't fit into the neighborhood. They are forced on their own resources, a loneliness which makes some of them readers. As Marshall McLuhan feared, the present generation of isolated children more often turns to television, deafening music and electronic combat, which suggests to some alarmed adults that their creativity is being converted to disengagement.

Dissension in the home causes children to flee, some to the streets and shopping plazas, some to the inside of their heads. Carl G. Jung made a thoughtful observation about people who turn their unhappiness as children into careers in the creative arts. He wrote that their intensity toward the work they do can result in the work outgrowing them, so that the work becomes fully realized and profound while the creator remains a child, petulant and fearful.

"The lives of artists," he mused, "are as a rule so highly unsatisfactory—not to say tragic—because of their inferiority on the human and personal side."

This displacement of creative self-realization into creative work-realization creates serious emotional problems for anyone who uses it as a technique for coping with unhappiness. It appears that artists, writers and poets are thirty-five times more likely to seek treatment for mood disorders than are people outside the arts. A psychiatrist at the University of California at Los Angeles, Kay Jamison, conducted a study of creative people and concluded that the incidence of manic-depressive disorders is twice as high in novelists, playwrights, poets and sculptors as in the general population.

Career choice follows the line of self-evident talent, parental influence and serendipity, with the latter often the most significant factor. Placement in the family also plays a role in the selection of a vocation. Eldest children are most likely to follow the career line of one of the parents, while younger children usually select something so different as to appear willfully frivolous.

A 1984 study of American adolescents, led by Francis A. J. Ianni of Teachers College of Columbia University, came to the conclusion after eight years of examining teenagers that adolescent values are taken more from the adults in their lives than from their peers, as had been commonly believed. Though parents very often have a sense that their teenaged children are out of their control, most children of this age are only playacting a separation from parental mores. The daughter who colors her hair green and the son who wears an earring are having a superficial fling. Beneath the gaudy exterior, the research shows, their standards and goals are not much different from those of the dominant adults in their lives.

Because adults invariably ask children what they plan to be when they grow up, children become adroit at giving an answer. Any answer will do, but their options are limited by their experience. If they have been ill a good deal, they want to be doctors or nurses. If they travel, they want to fly a plane or be a member of the airline crew. A group of high school teachers was asked what their childhood ambitions were and all confessed that teaching was low on the list. Their first choices were professional athletics, medicine, music and film star.

Some children are so clearly endowed with a particular gift that their career path is never in doubt. Michelangelo was the despair of his father because he was always drawing instead of attending to schoolwork. Rembrandt, Murillo, Raphael and Leonardo da Vinci all drew compulsively from an early age. Tennyson, Southey, Goethe and Emerson wrote acceptable poetry before they were ten. At the age of fourteen, Honoré de Balzac told his sister, "You shall see; I am going to be a great man."

Not all brilliant people demonstrate their promise when young. Winston Churchill, for instance, was an indifferent student. One of the teachers of Oliver Goldsmith later complained that the comic playwright was one of the dullest pupils in her experience. Napoleon stood forty-second in his class. The philosopher Georg Hegel was judged "especially deficient in philosophy" by his tutors at university. U.S. President Woodrow Wilson, father of the concept of a world peacekeeping body, didn't do well at Princeton.

One explanation psychiatrists find for such late bloomers is that their energy as children and adolescents was consumed by emotional difficulties. As they matured and came to terms with their difficulties, their creative powers were released to pursue other achievements.

Carl Jung viewed energy as a finite resource, something like a bank account. He wrote that everyone is born with a certain capital of energy resource which can be invested as the person desires. Some put it all into career accomplishment, leaving nothing left over for the work of emotional growth and relationships. Overachievers with underdeveloped personalities are a common sight at country clubs and marinas.

Psychoanalyst Alfred Adler was the earliest proponent of the theory that such people are compensating for a handicap, whether it is visible or not. He believed that helplessness of any kind is so difficult to endure that people are driven from infancy to overcome the disadvantage of being weak and vulnerable. As Dr. Adler was fond of pointing out, Napoleon was very short (so was Dr. Adler). In corroboration of this, Mildred G. Goertzel and Victor Goertzel studied four hundred famous people and in their book *So They Had Problems Too* declared that all four hundred were raised by fierce, competitive mothers who made them feel inadequate and unwanted.

"Most of the greatest efforts I ever made in life were to escape inferiority and mediocrity," commented the U.S. pioneer in psychology, G. Stanley Hall.

Demosthenes, the Greek orator who overcame a frightful stammer, is another favorite example that Dr. Adler gives for his theory of overcompensation. So is Annette Kellerman, who was physically frail as a child but swam the treacherous and frigid English Channel. As well, there are the great Finnish runner Paavo Nurmi, who was lame, and the weakling boy Eugene Sandow, who became known as the world's strongest man and could support thirty-three men on his back. The American actress Julie Harris once observed that she would not have needed to be such a good actress if her breasts had been bigger.

Noting that individual well-being depends on a sense of being secure, Rollo May wrote in his second edition of *The Meaning of Anxiety* that the high level of competitiveness in North American society leads to pervasive feelings of depression, melancholy, skepticism and anxiety which some people handle by being zealous about their careers or tennis games. Many human tribes manage to remain intact despite the intense competitiveness of their individual members, but Americans and Canadians suffer from a sense of being isolated and unbound.

In the famous study of a midwestern rural village by Abram Kardiner, researchers found the residents struggling for prestige and self-validation which they sought to achieve by competitive work. The lack of support in society for aggressive, ambitious women can result in their need for self-validation, turning inward to become self-directed hostility and shame.

Ambition and aggression are not the same. Aggression is not a natural, innate, instinctive emotion in the sense that hate and joy are. Aggression is a culturally determined reaction to provocation. Most behavioral scientists believe it is strongly influenced by identification with the same-sex parent. Because of sexual stereotyping, aggression, like ambition, is encouraged more in boys than in girls. People develop aggression, it appears, in accordance with the expectations and tolerance of their environment.

Magda B. Arnold, in *Emotion and Personality*, wrote that aggression floats in the personality. If it can't be channeled into literature or public works, it may submerge and pop into view as enthusiasm for the peace movement. Such displacement, she said, does not make aggression go away or drain it; the strong feelings merely have been channeled into a socially accepted activity. "People who are aggressive in one direction," she observed, "are aggressive in others."

The element of envy in aggression and ambition is only beginning to attract professional curiosity. Envy was one of Dante's seven deadly sins; in his *Inferno,* the eyelids of the envious were sewn together. Leslie H. Farber wrote in *Lying, Despair, Jealousy, Envy, Sex, Suicide, Drugs and the Good Life* that envy "arises from the person's apprehension of another's superiority and consequent critical evaluation of himself." Envy is a limp and unhappy response to someone else's physical attractiveness or success, a tactic which is the person's attempt to redress the imbalance without making any effort at personal development that would reduce the perceived superiority.

Envy flourishes in childhood because all children are surrounded by people who have superior skills. When it is stimulated by parents or other adults who make invidious comments, disparaging the child while praising some other child, the habit of envy can become rooted and the child will become an adult who makes little effort to diet away fat, for instance, or excel in any endeavor. When children are not overwhelmed with hopelessness and believe that they can improve their state, envy converts into ambition to improve and it makes a fine stimulant.

Whatever the level of ambition, studies agree that for most people the golden period of their careers comes when they are in their thirties. People write the most books, publish the most articles and make the most discoveries in their thirties, though John P. Zubec noted, in *Human Development,* that industrialists, prime ministers, cabinet members, presidents of republics and religious leaders generally are older when they make their major contributions.

Harvey C. Lehman spent twenty years studying the lives of gifted people. He found that down through the ages writers, scientists, mathematicians, astronomers, artists, actors, philosophers, explorers, inventors, singers, composers, psychologists, doctors, educators and geologists achieved what turned out to be in retrospect their finest hour when they were in their thirties.

By his analysis of the finest hour, which he took some pains to establish in each profession, orators, architects and best-selling authors tended to be older, and university presidents, not surprisingly, were older still when they produced their personal best. Poets have two good periods: one is in the twenties, when their bellies are full of fire, and the other is when they are in their forties and confront existential mysteries. Politicians, ambassadors and judges are at their peak between fifty-five and sixty; generals, bishops and heads of government are rarely younger than sixty and accordingly do their finest work between that age and retirement.

Dr. Lehman noted that people rarely made their largest income in the years when they produced their best work. Though their thirties were highest for achievement, the cash rewards generally were found to come as long as thirty years later.

The world abounds, however, in people whose genius remained aflame into old age. Galileo made important contributions to astronomy at the age of seventy-four; Goethe wrote the second part of *Faust* in what he called his "golden period," his eighties; Samuel Johnson wrote his ten-volume *Life of the English Poets* at seventy; William Pitcairn was seventy-seven when he connected rheumatic fever with heart disease; Verdi wrote *Otello* when he was seventy-three. As well, there are the young phenomenons: Jane Austen, who wrote *Pride and Prejudice* when she was twenty; John Milton, whose hymns composed when he was fifteen still enrich liturgical repertoires; William Pitt, who was Prime Minister of Britain at the age of twenty-four; John Paul Jones, who commanded a fleet when he was twenty-eight; Edmund Halley, for whom the comet is named, who made his first significant astronomical observation when he was eighteen; the redoubtable Mozart played the clavier at the age of three and wrote his first sonata at seven.

Few people, however, ever enjoy the exhilaration of working at the top of their ability. Athletes who run or swim against the clock know exactly how well they are doing, a satisfaction denied those whose occupations have no definable edges, but even athletes cannot know for certain if their minds and bodies could yield more. Harvard's William James once commented that a spur of some kind is needed to produce flat-out effort. Sometimes the spur is positive, as when a surgeon spends eight hours bent over a youth's wrecked body in a fight for the boy's life, and sometimes it is negative, as when people are carried into brilliant careers by anger against the unfairness of their childhoods. Wrote Wayland F. Vaughan in *The Lure of Superiority*, "Derogatory opinion is a fertile seed for ambition."

Men and women hurl themselves into careers at a velocity largely determined by their passion to escape from an odious state. In middle age, the crisis some endure is the discovery that they have not left the unloved self behind after all. That child who felt betrayed and abused thirty years ago is within; it has been waiting for a pause in the hubbub of career building in order to say, in effect, "Now deal with me. It's my time."

The fundamental issue may be one of control. Children suffer acutely from their lack of control over their lives. Personality construction in large measure concerns itself with vulnerability. One tactic is to use weakness as a defensive tool, as wolves signal surrender in a fight by exposing their throats. Another tactic is to conquer the known world, an Alexander the Great ruling the household, impressing the neighbors, taking command in the office.

"Domination springs from impotence," psychoanalyst Erich Fromm claimed. He said that a person infatuated with power often acts "under the illusion that his actions benefit his self-interest, though he actually serves everything else *but* the interests of his real self." The power aggressive people acquire eventually corrupts; they dominate associates and family without qualifying themselves by personal worth to do so.

Many of the world's most famous people are addicted to triumph and are considered to be no more emotionally sound than any other addict. When they are exhausted and become aware of their loneliness, the obsessively ambitious come very close to mental illness.

"Men are a thousand times more intent on becoming rich than on acquiring culture," observed the morose Arthur Schopenhauer, "though it is quite certain that what a man *is* contributes more to his happiness than what he *has.*"

The philosopher Benedict Spinoza declared, "If the greedy person thinks only of money and possessions, and the ambitious one only of fame, one does not think of them as insane . . . but, factually, greediness, ambition, lust, and so forth are but species of madness, although they are not enumerated among the diseases." Friedrich Nietzsche called ambition "the evil breath" and commented bitterly, "See how they climb, these swift apes! They climb over one another, and thus drag themselves in the mud and depths." Judge Learned Hand, one of the greatest of the American judiciary, called ambition "Satan's apple."

When North Americans meet for the first time, they commonly locate their relative status by asking, "What do you do?" Women with no paid job shrink from the inquiry and only recently trained themselves to stop answering, "I'm *just* a housewife." When people make their occupation the primary identification of themselves and their worth, the experts worry. "To look for a personality beyond this shell would be fruitless," Carl Jung wrote pessimistically. "The opening up would be a massive undertaking, but inside it we would find only a pitiable little man."

A kinder view of ambition is that it is love-seeking. The Scottish psychiatrist Ian D. Suttie was a leading exponent of this perspective. He stated, "The quest for admiration is one of the earliest adopted of all the false starts or blind alleys of social development."

An obvious example of what Dr. Suttie is getting at can be seen in children clamoring for their parents to watch them jump into the deep end, or ride their bicycle no hands. In adults it is a large part of the magnetism of sports and show business; performers and athletes often are eloquent on the subject of riding the wave of love that comes to them from an audience. The tragedy for them is that they are sustained primarily by the admiration of ticket holders; when that fails, few of them have taken the precaution to build a support to take its place.

Montreal psychiatrist Karl Stern, noting a prevalence of stomach problems, particularly peptic ulcers, among those who practice the high art of achievement, drew the thoughtful conclusion that there was a correlation between food-intake difficulties and an immature love-intake system.

He wrote, "Deep down, such people have a great need to receive; they are people whose hard spartan shell covers a yearning to be mothered."

The results of such yearning, if this is the case, are impressive. Asked how he was able to discover his mechanical explanation for the universe, Isaac Newton replied, *"Nocte dieque incubando"*—"By thinking about it day and night." Abraham Lincoln's advice to young lawyers was: "Work, work, work . . . your own resolution to succeed is more important than any other one thing." And Charles Darwin observed, "It's doggedness that does it."

No list of the world's greatest figures would be complete without those three names but none was emotionally sound. Lincoln suffered so acutely from melancholy that he sank several times to the edge of insanity. Newton sulked like a teenager because he was passed over for a state appointment. Darwin was so fearful of his father's disapproval that he put off publishing his world-shaking theory of evolution for twenty-six years.

"We wholly overlook the essential fact that the achievements which society rewards are won at the cost of the diminution of personality," Carl Jung observed.

North Americans have been slow to realize that the most successful individuals are those who manage to balance a career and lasting relationships, accepting that neither will occur without substantial effort. A beloved Canadian obstetrician, Marion Hilliard of Toronto, used to describe it as "paying the rent on a good house," by which she meant that people who plan to have more than what Shakespeare called "mouth honor" in their autumn years are obliged in the period when they are rejoicing in careers to keep up the payments on relationships with family and friends.

In his famed Terry lectures at Yale in 1955, Gordon W. Allport described "propriate striving," the labors of emotionally mature people. "Propriate striving," he explained, "distinguishes itself from other forms of motivation in that, however beset by conflicts, it makes for the unification of the personality."

As Dr. Allport saw it, those who strive propriately are capable of taking career risks without really jeopardizing safety, since they are moored in themselves. It makes for spontaneous and flexible behavior, since a mistake puts nothing essential in danger. The safe, conventional route is not necessarily compelling; if they fall off a mountain, they are their own safety net.

He offered consolation to those who feel themselves a long remove from the Allport vision. No one should abandon hope of improvement, he said. "Personality is less a finished product than a transitive process."

Failure to develop inner resources has a dismal outcome, no matter how impressive the batting average. Carl Jung called maturity "inner spaciousness."

He wrote, "Without the inner breadth, we are never related to the size of our object. It is therefore right to say that a man grows with the size of his task. But he must have within him the ability to grow, otherwise the most difficult task will be of no use to him; at the most he will break himself upon it."

Henry David Thoreau was full to the brim with inner breadth. He wrote in *Walden*, "If the day and the night are such that you greet them with joy, and life emits a fragrance like flowers and sweet-scented herbs, is more elastic, more starry, more immortal—that is your success."

DEPRESSION

DEPRESSION, the most severe of all emotional suffering, is an affliction peculiar to human beings and some apes and so destructive that babies can die of it, willingly, and adults become insane or suicidal. A thick, gray limbo that floats in and out of every normal existence, it is more prevalent than the common cold and the most desolating feeling on earth.

In its mildest states—discouragement, discontent, the blues—it is unpleasant but can goad people into good works or a reviving change of scene. At its most surprising, it is an irrational calamity that bewilders new mothers, embarrasses middle-aged executives and dismays newlyweds.

Depression can last an afternoon when it rains on the day of a picnic or it can begin soon after birth and stay for a wretched lifetime. It is demi-death, a black hole in the human psyche which eats light and swallows up the senses. It happens to everyone. Estimates are that more than ten million North Americans suffer from severe depression. The U.S. National Institute of Mental Health once listed typical early warnings: feeling of sadness and hopelessness ("I will never be better"); loss of the ability to enjoy anything; loss of interest in sex; loss of appetite (or overeating); insomnia (or sleeping too much); anxious or restless behavior (or apathy); difficulty in concentrating, in remembering things and in making decisions; becoming upset by small things; feeling of worthlessness ("I'm no good"); withdrawal from friends and relatives.

People in such a state lose contact with their friends and alienate their families, who may suspect them of putting on an act and urge them impatiently to "snap out of it." This isolation is what the sickness craves, but it is the enemy of a return to health. A Montreal psychiatrist once said he started to worry about the possibility of suicide at the point where his patient said that she or he no longer knew a single person who really cared what happened.

The content of depression is disappointment. An infant whose life is uninteresting and lacking in tenderness will become quiet and vacant; an adult whose gifts go unnoticed retreats from contact with others in order to protect the too small flame of self. Depression is a background sound, one of the dark notes in the brain that ring for all disasters from losing a good-luck piece to hearing that a twenty-year-old son has been killed by a drunk driver. Most people recover from the worst effects of depressions that are caused by outside forces in about six months but few people ever free themselves entirely from depressions which have been internalized since childhood.

Depression ages. No matter how young the victim, the consequences to the body are funereal. Even infants have dry, withered skin if they are depressed.

In some people an underlying quality of sorrow creates a personality marked by softness and sympathetic understanding which can make their lives a gift to the world. Aristotle noted twenty-three hundred years ago that poets, philosophers, politicians and artists "appear to be all of a melancholic temperament." Jesus Christ emerges in the scriptures as a grave, sad man. Abraham Lincoln's depression verged on psychosis. In the days when it was known as "the English malady," Charles Dickens was almost crushed by despair and his mood permeates his books. Anton Chekhov, the Russian playwright who suffered from depression all his life, wore a pendant on his watch chain which was inscribed, "For the lonely man, the desert is everywhere."

Sorrow gives soul to poetry and philosophy. It is probably indispensable to the development of humanity in an individual. If teenagers did not feel depressed, they might not learn to be kind. Melancholia is the common thread in all existence; those who have touched the bottomland of depression are never strangers to one another.

Because so many people believe themselves unworthy, depression often follows good news. A surprise party given by a hundred jubilant friends can leave the guest of honor flattened for days. Sunlight is an antidepressant but the aftermath of a glorious afternoon is often wistfulness. Depression accompanies all illnesses, even the sniffles, and such other setbacks as a failed job interview or a social blunder. Babies are particularly susceptible to depression because their ego systems are so weak that they are easily discouraged. Old people are vulnerable for much the same reason.

Despite the fact that the clinical details of depression were outlined as long ago as 400 B.C. by Hippocrates, the father of medicine, scientists only recently began to understand why some people are sadder than others.

A prevailing mood of depression is established by the setting in which the newborn human is raised and how it impacts on the infant's own self-preserving style. All babies who are severely neglected and understimulated will become depressed, but some will be pathologically passive while others, rescued by innate and feisty anger, will protest valiantly. The classic pattern in chronic depression is to have been loved and approved as a baby but subjected to a cold bath of stiff standards and unrelenting pressure in childhood. All primal depressions share the characteristic of early disappointment in love, at the point where the toddler's narcissism isn't strong enough to handle the blow.

Parents who demand perfection of their children, imposing frightful discipline and fixing hard rules, are governed by a frantic hope for their own redemption. By their eviction of the toddler from a paradisiacal babyhood, they convey a message that the child suddenly has become worthless. Some children will rebel, but others strive to recover the bliss of the happier state by trying to fulfill parental expectations. The perfection the parents seek is impossible, of course; the parents are increasingly upset and the child grows more morose. The inescapable conclusion for the child is that he or she is not lovable.

This mutilation is most common in the middle class where parents compete with one another by means of their children's accomplishments. Firstborns are standard-bearers in most families and accordingly are most exposed to depression. Depression also is endemic among the poor. Poverty-stricken children are affected around the age of nine or ten, when they first perceive that their futures are uncertain or hopeless.

People who emigrate from their homelands are likely candidates for depression because they have reproduced the infant's fall from Eden. Where once they lived in the warm knowable sea of their own kind, they find themselves an ethnic minority required to meet impossible standards which are never clearly articulated.

"A key predictor of moderate isolation from mankind is low social status," said Letitia Anne Peplau and Daniel Perlman in *Loneliness*. The researchers said that depression wasn't particularly associated with old age as much as with social status; they also found that the age group from eighteen to twenty-five rated very high on loneliness scores, and teenagers higher still. Adolescence is a long, uneven preparation for nest-leaving, another exodus from safety, and is experienced as grief for the loss of childhood.

The shocking rise in the suicide rate among adolescents has prompted considerable research. Among the warning symptoms are extreme fluctuations in interest—the adolescent apathetic at one moment and riveted by something trivial the next—and overwhelming fatigue out of proportion to the activities engaged in. Depressed teenagers seek perpetual distraction or else they withdraw into headphones. They hate to be alone or else they demand privacy; or, they may demand both at the same time.

The glandular changes of adolescence, like the changes women experience during menses and pregnancy and immediately after childbirth, also increase depression. The body mourns that it is not its former self.

Some old people collapse into permanent melancholia which converts to testiness against those who would rouse them. They cannot be reconciled to the loss of physical well-being, to their wrinkled faces and diminished mobility. No one is really ready to be old; it always dismays. Distractions work only briefly and are followed by a slump into gloom.

When people give up their dreams, something of them dies. The brain sorrows for the departed. A person needs time to grieve when ideals prove to be vanity and ambitions absurd. Goethe commented sympathetically on youth "that hurls itself madly against windmills and evils of the world, and sadly sheds it utopias and ideals with every year."

The middle years are fertile ones for the growth of depression because hopes must be abandoned and the summer soldiers are coming home on their shields. Men and women who staked all on romance no longer have the right currency—naivety and a slim young body—to go shopping. Those who wanted success in business or career are confronted with their limitations and past errors of judgment which can't be reversed. Both sexes have a menopause marked by thickening bodies, wistfulness and discouragement.

One woman's lassitude was so deep that one morning she put the breakfast dishes in the sink to soak and wandered to a window to stare at the rain. She was startled out of her mood by the sight of her children, tilted against the wind, returning home from school for their lunch. She discovered by a glance at the kitchen clock and the cold, congealed dishwater, that she had been brooding by the window for more than three hours.

An insurance salesman became alarmed about himself when he realized that for months whenever he drove his car at high speeds he would consider longingly the attractiveness of turning the wheel only a bit in order to ram into a concrete abutment or an oncoming truck. A professional musician, exhausted by touring, couldn't sleep more than two or three hours at a stretch. He would come brittle-awake, hours before dawn, and lie taut and wide-eyed imagining illnesses.

Depressed people are among the most ingratiating in society. Since their own ill opinion of themselves is already more than they can tolerate, they go to great pains to ensure that they will not incur further criticism. Depressed women are soothers and mediators, while depressed men are sensitive and observant. They set high standards for themselves, longing as they do for rescue from mortification, but there is a merciless edge to their martyrdom. They require that everyone be as thoughtful and reliable as they are and can be demoralized by being left out of a dinner party.

Fastidious, punctual, conscientious and charitable, they carry a needy, insatiable child within who perpetually yearns against the window of a locked toy store.

Almost two thousand years ago the scientist Aretaeus described the melancholy as guilt-ridden, religious and sacrificing. The formulation has changed very little over time. Robert O. Jones, Dalhousie University psychiatrist, once observed that the Scottish Calvinists in his part of Nova Scotia produce a bumper crop of depressives. Depression is rife among followers of stern religions and punitive governments; it is a component in the character of those who admire superhuman conduct and cannot believe that second prize is any prize at all.

Silvan S. Tomkins, Rutgers psychologist, wrote that depression has three parts: distress, evinced by tears and sad expressions; contempt or disgust, the sour-faced who appear to have smelled decomposing skunks; and shame, where the head hangs down and eyes evade contact. If the depression is agitated, a prevalent form, there is an admixture of fear as well. Comments Dr. Tomkins, "It can get to be quite a complicated thing . . . Some have more of one component than another."

Researchers are intrigued by the amount of anger that underlies many depressions, particularly those of women who are culturally discouraged from displaying anger. When anger is smothered for the sake of appearances, its chemistry somehow converts to depression. While a recognized treatment for depression is to provoke the sufferer to unleash the anger inside, this tactic is not effective with most women. If they are pushed to explode the rage they have contained, they are likely to be overcome by guilt.

Despair is often a tangle of emotions, only one of which is anger. Self-contempt and self-hatred, found in those who believe that they are unlovable, also fuel depressions. So do the fear of rejection, guilt over the human failure to behave perfectly, greed for approval without end, and envy of everyone who seems happy or healthy or attractive or young. The chronically depressed yearn to believe that they are good people, but they cannot.

Depression, like anxiety, is present in most neuroses. The American psychologist O. Fenichel commented that depressed people either lack any self-esteem of their own and therefore must rely on an uncertain community to provide it all, or else they are diffused with guilt that requires constant assurances. Depressed people depend on others, which may account for the prevalence of depression among women. Men who commit suicide, studies show, tend to be dependent people rather than self-reliant.

Gross overdevelopment of the conscience is so typical of depressed people that an English psychiatrist, Edward Glover, gave the condition the pedantic label of "chronic hyperplasia [overgrowth] of the superego [conscience]." Freud found depression so distasteful that he described it as a kind of greed for love. However the scientists come at it, the state represents a total or partial loss of self-esteem—seen most profoundly in babies who find they cannot please their parents.

Toddlers are vulnerable to any slur on their importance. If the adults around them are loyal and friendly, they can make the leap from narcissism to sociability confident of their own unique worth. If the adults are indifferent, or tyrannical, or if their faces keep changing before the child can get adjusted to their expectations, toddlers conclude they aren't worth much. They become discouraged and droop, physically and emotionally. René Spitz, who studied twenty-one depressed babies in institutional settings, noted their apathy and silence, their intelligence reduced to the level of morons. At the age of three, only five could walk unassisted and eight could not even stand alone.

The pessimist philosopher Arthur Schopenhauer had a dreadful relationship with his mother, whose unfaithfulness had caused his father's suicide. She disliked him so much that once she pushed him down the stairs. An angry, suspicious man who always slept with a loaded pistol under his pillow and would not allow a barber to shave him, he wrote one of the gloomiest sentences in literature: "The only honest wish man can have is that of absolute annihilation." And Lord Byron's mother doted on him excessively one moment and beat him the next, which contributed to the poet's acute ear for sorrow.

Children who reach the age of three or four without experiencing such rejection will likely be free of neurotic depression for the rest of their lives. Studies of small children in hospitals are illuminating in this regard. Well-loved children younger than three suffer severely from separation if their parents cannot visit them regularly. They become withdrawn and dazed; they sleep poorly and lose weight in spite of all efforts to tempt their appetites. When parents visit, the children may turn their heads away in utter misery. But well-loved children older than three are able to tolerate hospitalization without such exaggerated signs of grief. Their self-esteem is sufficiently developed so that they don't believe their parents have abandoned them.

"The feeling of not being independent and not being loved can contribute to the primary feeling of helplessness," wrote E. Bibring. Depression, Dr. Bibring said, is powerlessness and people fasten themselves to one of three solutions. One is what Freud called love addiction and S. Rado "a cry for love"—the longing to be loved; the second is the wish to be strong and secure, which draws depressed people to power and influence; and the third is the wish to be good and loving, which makes depressed people considerate and generous.

Depression is broader than loneliness; loneliness can be relieved by a visit but the depressed feel forlorn and empty at a party. Lonely people may become so fatigued in coping with their state that they collapse into apathy, but if they have energy at all they put it into good works such as instigating the office collection for a newlywed, or lining up a lunch date, or being the bright person at the health club. Depressed people, on the other hand, find conviviality oppressive and cannot sustain for long the appearance of being interested in others.

The entertainment business is a magnet for depressed people because it offers love (the audience), importance and an opportunity to seem loving, providing the need to simulate cheer is not tested too long. Comedians and clowns are notoriously depressed people who use laughter to stay alive, as a diabetic does insulin. Paul Tillich tells the story of a doctor who was treating a melancholic man. "You need amusement," he told his patient. "Go and hear Grimaldi. He will make you laugh and that will be better for you than any drugs." The patient was horrified. "My God," he cried, "but *I* am Grimaldi!"

Jack Benny, Danny Kaye and Red Skelton, among the greatest of American comics, were seriously depressed all their lives; so were Mark Twain, Molière, and Jonathan Swift, all renowned as wits. In this they resemble the cheeriness of depressed teenagers and the "smiling depressions" that frighten psychiatrists. Being jolly is a common cover-up for depression, as people try to divert themselves from the blackness within. The technique is dangerous because it consumes precious energy, of which depressed people have pitifully little; when the performance is over, the sufferer may be too exhausted to combat thoughts of suicide.

Nietzsche took a positive view of suicide. He wrote, "The thought of suicide is a great consolation: by means of it one gets successfully through many a bad night."

Studies of people who have attempted suicide, or appear at risk of committing suicide, have shown that the strongest element in their makeup is their sense of hopelessness. The University of Pennsylvania recently published a report on 207 people who were hospitalized for suicidal depression and were followed for five to seven years after their release. Of the fourteen who killed themselves in that period, all but one had rated among the highest in the group on the hopelessness scale, as measured by the Beck Depression Inventory, which is considered a reliable tool for psychological assessment.

The study created wide interest because it seemed to point to a way for doctors to identify which suicidal patients are most at risk. The cause of the fatal levels of hopelessness, however, was not part of the research.

Depression belongs to one of two families: either it is innate, or endogenous, arising from the child's experience of being rudely snatched from heaven, and therefore has become a lifelong emotional tone; or it is exogenous, caused by circumstances outside the brain's patterning, such as a death in the family, or a loss of prestige, or a serious illness. Either kind has a full range of effects on the body and behavior, from the free-floating rues which make clouds a poignant parade to the gut-wretching howls of a bereaved parent.

The difference between a depression that is a certifiable mental illness and one that is bittersweet and rather comforting is solely one of degree. In either case, the symptoms are the same—loss of appetite, sleeplessness, inability to concentrate. In states of sadness, dejection or defeat, as Vanderbilt University's Carroll E. Izard explains in *Patterns of Emotions,* the parasympathetic nervous system predominates. Weeping, Dr. Izard wrote, is a parasympathetic function activated by an increase of norepinephrine, which is the neurochemical transmitter which attempts to decrease depression.

Therapists are grateful that human evolution has reached the point at last where strong men are not ashamed to weep. There are times in a life when weeping is beneficial. A woman who had lost her mother and her son within two years explained to her psychiatrist that she cried a lot. "I figure I have to cry about two buckets for my mother, who was seventy-five when she died, and fifty for my son, who was only twenty, so I see crying as getting on with my quota." "Good," he replied. "That's exactly right."

The chemical imbalances of sorrowing interfere with digestion. The blood vessels serving the alimentary system are dilated, contracting the entire tract so that it is less willing to function. More insulin is produced, lowering blood sugar and diminishing energy. Muscles are slack, the heart rate slower, blood pressure is down and reactions are sluggish. The poor flow of blood results in headaches, constipation, tiredness, backache, inability to sleep more than a few hours at a stretch, giddiness and sour digestion. The Danish physiologist Carl Lange commented, "There can be little doubt that continuous sorrow may have an atrophying effect upon the internal organs. Sorrowful persons have the appearance of senility."

A peculiarity of the emotion is its weight. People move heavily and clumsily. Holding themselves erect takes great effort; sitting is easier than standing and lying down is the best of all positions. Depressed people lean against walls for support; depressed babies rock monotonously, thudding their heads against their cribs.

No one is certain how the antidepressant drugs work to relieve these symptoms when they become extreme, but they do. By firing another chemical transmitter into the brain's message bank, doctors can restore the body to an almost normal level and the patient becomes receptive to efforts to help.

Grief is not well understood and is the subject of controversy among professionals because doctors rarely see pure grief, and have few tools to relieve it when they do. When grief has a strong component of remorse, as when a loved one commits suicide, or narcissism, as when a parent was living through the dead child, or ambivalence, as when the deceased relative or spouse was disliked when alive, therapists can assist only with the other elements.

Most people can regain their perspective with time, but in some the grief seems to increase rather than abate. Specialists think of this as a double grief, a mourning for the lost person and a mourning for the self who was invested in that person. People whose sense of personal worth and accomplishment is based on the achievements of a mate or child will suffer the equivalent of two deaths, a dreadful burden indeed.

Grief is loss; it can follow a burglary, a fire, the death of a pet, destruction of a garden, the removal of position. Frail people can be shattered by a change of status. Investigations of the suicides which followed the 1929 stock market crash revealed that the men who threw themselves out of windows were distant from their families; they related most to their money and the sense of power wealth gave them. When their fortunes were gone, they were emotionally bankrupt as well.

Guilt is a common factor in the grief of bereavement: no relationship is unflawed. When there has been real hatred of parents mixed with love, mourning for them is complicated by remorse. The death of parents is always perceived as a death of self, the shattering of the only record of one's self as a child, the removal of the generation that formed the barrier against one's own mortality. Middle-aged people weep for their parents because they have been orphaned as surely as if they were still children.

Lifelong wakes, such as Queen Victoria's conspicuous mourning for her consort Albert or Dickens's Miss Havisham grieving into her old age for the man who jilted her in her youth, are not the testaments to steadfast devotion that they appeared to be. The experts call such behavior neurotic. People who continue to flaunt their grief aren't showing a superior ability to love but, rather, a superior self-attachment.

Normal grief moves on its own inexorable timetable and can't be hurried or distracted. Denial doesn't make it go away. It lasts forever but, gradually, only hurts occasionally.

The significant difference between grief and depression is that there is no loss of self-esteem in the former. As Freudians put it, the world has become poorer, not the self.

Grief bears some resemblance to injury, a sharp blow. Disbelief and shock provide a merciful anaesthetic in the earliest stage, following which there may be a period of unnatural energy in which funeral arrangements can be made, relatives housed and fed, thank-you notes written. The grief that awaits is so terrible that the system seizes on distractions for as long as strength lasts. Later, grieving people have only hazy memories of that early period.

The long, hard grief that follows is marked by loss of sleep, taste, energy; people go through the motions of their routines without interest. There is enduring wisdom in the old Jewish injunction "Do not hasten to rid a friend of his grief." The National Academy of Science recently concluded that rituals such as Irish wakes and Jewish shivahs are psychologically sound in that they dramatize mourning, giving grief acknowledgment and a place to stand.

The work of grief, whether screaming, crying or cleaning out the dead one's closets, is restorative. Once it was believed that weeping should not be provoked, but modern hospitals now allow bereaved parents to hold their dead baby for as long as they need.

The first anniversary of a loss is traumatic, but the second is less so. Times *does* heal, though not perfectly; after a while, memories are sweet with nostalgia.

Once it was believed that mourning follows a pattern that begins with denial, passes through obsession with thoughts of the dead person and ends in a certain time frame with peaceful acceptance. Psychologists now see that normal grieving does not follow a predictable course and that the agony of the loss can return years later, out of nothingness, to cause fresh tears.

The National Academy of Science believes that some 10 to 20 percent of widows suffer grief to such a degree that they slip from the category of normal into the pathological. The proportion of bereaved parents whose mourning is pathological is believed to be much greater. The emotional upheaval following a child's death puts such a strain on relationships that experts believe as many as 80 percent of marriages are destroyed or severely impaired.

Grief must out, in one form or another. Psychiatrist Erich Lendermann of the Harvard School of Medicine once commented, "The duration of a grief reaction seems to depend upon the success with which a person does the grief work, namely emancipation from the bondage to the deceased, readjustment to the environment in which the deceased is missing, and the formation of new relationships. One of the big obstacles to this work seems to be the fact that many patients try to avoid the immense distress connected with the grief experience and to avoid the expression of emotion necessary for it."

The grief of a woman for her mother is felt with special poignancy, according to studies. Mardi Horowitz, a psychiatrist at the University of California Medical School in San Francisco, believes that the relationship of adults to their mothers, as the "original primary source of warmth and sustenance," makes the mother's death a loss of the primary caretaker. Said actress Kate Reid when her mother died, "No one, ever, will care so much for me again."

The pain that follows the death of a child is simply not bearable, though it is borne. Perhaps the most difficult of all mourning follows the death of a relative who was not loved enough. When grief is tangled with regret, self-hatred, relief or guilt, mourning may never be completed.

Paul Clayton, a psychiatrist at the University of Minnesota, feels that the apathy and numbness after a bereavement that once were seen as alarming are in fact a useful cushion against the reality of the loss, so long as the hibernation is not too intense or prolonged. Mourners need to review their relationship with the dead person, going over and over scenes of disagreement, lighting gladly on the good times. The process is rich in self-discovery, offering to the bereaved a possibility of insight and growth that might otherwise have never occurred.

Every year in North America almost nine million people suffer the loss of a close relative. A National Academy of Science report in 1984 described the link between a death in the family and the onset of serious illness in the survivors. Men younger than seventy-five run an increased risk of death from accidents, cardiovascular disease and some infectious diseases after the death of someone dear to them. The suicide rate among older widowers and single men who lose their mothers is high in the first year after the death. Women are more likely to kill themselves in the second year after a death. In them a serious health hazard is cirrhosis.

Women more often seek professional help than do men. This is not an indicator that women suffer more but that they suffer differently, allowing themselves to know their pain.

Sorrow, even a mild one, inhibits the muscles and generates a feeling of lassitude. The head droops and its weight curves the spine. Facial muscles sag, giving the expression a heavy-lidded droop. The voice becomes weak and thin. Because of the impoverished blood supply, there is pallor and shivering; mourning people feel cold. Sometimes the chest muscles are so constricted that there is a sensation of smothering, which victims relieve by taking irregular deep breaths. Sighs sound like moans, *are* moans. Dull-wittedness is common and there is an irresistible urge to sleep. The unconscious self wishes to stop time and hold the pain at a distance.

Jean-Paul Sartre, the existentialist philosopher, had a theory that all emotions are attempts to change the world. The fainting induced by fear, for example, is seen by him as a device to avoid the knowledge of danger. By "lowering the flame of life to a pinpoint," as grief does, the French intellectual believed, the person achieves a state of nonliving which allows postponement of the moment when the life must be rearranged.

Nature tends to be impatient of the vacuum in which the melancholy linger. Eventually appetite reasserts itself; interest is caught by a task or diversion and sustained for hours, with the sorrow gone from mind. Finally, even curiosity and enthusiasm are restored. The grieving person mourns another death, the loss of grief, and wonders guiltily if the lost person is being dismissed. "We go on," a husband said to his wife, weeping forlornly two years after their son was killed. "What else can we do? Tell me, do we have a reasonable alternative?"

They don't. So on they go.

Religion is a comfort for many at a time of grief but affords little solace for those who suffer chronic depression. The irony is that the love and forgiveness which religions promise are what depressed people feel unworthy to receive. The central image of the Judeo-Christian faith is the casting of two sinners out of paradise, the replica of what the melancholic suffered when they emerged from euphoric infancy to the imposing of grim standards.

Christmas is an emotional catastrophe for many people. The "Merry Christmas," "Happy Chanukah," joy-to-the-world time of the year brings some to consider suicide, divorce, murder or some other form of escape. Newspapers are filled with domestic violence and there are arguments under the mistletoe.

Few do not flinch from the strident jolliness, the driven consumerism, the ritual laboring in kitchens, the debts. Ghosts of Christmases Past haunt everyone; the season provides a comparison study by which to measure what has been lost and to reopen old wounds. The main symptoms of what is called the Christmas neurosis are depression and anger.

Many feel more acutely than at any other time of the year that life has cheated them. They don't have the perfect family around the holiday hearth, or they don't have a family at all, let alone a hearth. The idealized sweetness and love of the season have passed them by —have always passed them by. They are amazed at relatives or friends who fling themselves with what seems to be genuine pleasure into the Christmas-Chanukah spirit; the obvious conclusion is that something is lacking in themselves.

"Not being joyous during the Christmas season is much more common than most of us realize," reported four psychiatrists at the University of Utah who studied psychological complaints associated with Christmas. "There are few spontaneous exclamations about how wonderful it all is," agreed Montreal psychiatrist Alastair MacLeod. "There seems to be a great deal of hostility and anger over being impelled into something distasteful."

The psychoanalyst Ernest Jones said that Christmas represents psychologically "the ideal of resolving all family discord in happy reunion," an illusion that is born on the outer edge of reality where insanity begins. When the dream fails, as fail it must, disappointment is painful. The heavy drinking, overeating and sullen moods of the Christmas season are a testament to the enormity of the despair.

All holidays have a tendency to be less than they promised. Even an idle Sunday afternoon can bring about a mood that feels like homesickness. Those who depend on work routines and established play rituals to give their lives meaning will be unsettled and vaguely alarmed by unstructured time. Such people prefer organized tours when they travel.

Sandor Ferenczi, the Hungarian psychoanalyst, was interested in holiday depressions. He noted that loosening of external and internal restrictions leads to heightened sexual appetites and an interest in experimentation but leaves people feeling restless and ill. L. Bruce Boyer, an American psychoanalyst, wrote, "It is to be expected that the degree of neurotic response to such an intense holiday release would be frequent and severe."

The American psychoanalyst J. P. Cattell called this the holiday syndrome and observed that its most severe form occurs in the month of December, lasting until a few days after New Year's. He reported to the American Psychoanalytic Association that the characteristics of the disorder are "diffuse anxiety, numerous regressive phenomena including marked feelings of helplessness, possessiveness and increased irritability, nostalgic or bitter rumination about holiday experiences of youth, depressive effect and a wish for magical resolution of problems."

Christmas and Chanukah bear some resemblance to the potlatch ceremonies of some Pacific coast Indians, who destroy their enemies by loading them with gifts and food. Some gifts are indicators of guilt: the more lavish the present for one's mother, the greater the guilt at resenting her. By going into debt for one's family, there is satisfying punishment for a year of neglect.

Not all the blame for the emotional debacle can be laid at the doorstep of religious mania. The shorter days of winter, the waning of the sun, have caused a prevailing mood of depression since the age of primeval cave people. The primitive fear of the sun's disappearing altogether, of their own lives ending, still grips the unconscious mind. The early Christians chose December 25 as the birth date of Jesus, despite most thinking that he was likely born in April, because they could piggyback on the existing pagan festivals that focused on the winter solstice. On that day, people believed, the old sun died and a new one was born. To celebrate their relief at the renewal of life, the Romans ornamented their homes with wreaths and exchanged gifts; the Druids gathered mistletoe and the Saxons holly and ivy.

Similarly, the Jewish ceremonial lighting of candles at Chanukah bears some resemblance to the Roman saturnalia, a festival of goodwill and celebration which lasted seven days beginning December 19.

Of late, researchers have been saying that the "holiday blues" are a figment of journalistic imagination. The fact is, they say, that people who eat more, drink more and sleep less are bound to have their emotions intensified. In an article, "Christmas Depression," published in 1982 in the *Journal of the American Medical Association,* John Buckman, a psychiatrist at the University of Virginia, wrote, "On balance, [the Christmas season] is more positive than negative. Even those of us who like Christmas grumble about its negative side. But that doesn't mean we don't enjoy it. It's a positive, essential, health-giving experience."

Dr. Buckman studied the literature on Christmas depression and came to the cheerful conclusion that it is overrated. The closer family spirit of Christmas gives people hope, he said, and can be seen as good for mental health, rather than the reverse.

A genuine state of depression, however, converts gradually into a genuine illness. Depression can result in physical breakdown in such forms as asthma, colitis, diabetes and tuberculosis. Karl Menninger said of the latter, "It is, after all, a graceful way to destroy oneself."

The body's immune system seems to buckle under the weight of sorrow and grief. Cancer patients very frequently have had some serious loss or setback in the year or two previous to the illness. Similar patterns of loss of a job or mate appear in the history of people who become ill with environmental allergies.

The ultimate breakdown is suicide. Every few minutes in North America, someone kills herself or himself. The real total is higher than even the horrendous statistics show because many so-called accidental deaths by drowning, car crashes and other mishaps are in truth suicides. In some cases, suicidal people first kill their entire families, but these are more rare than media attention would suggest. Young mothers in postpartum depression, however, are very likely to kill their infants because their separation from the newborn isn't complete, and men in rage and grief over a betrayal will kill in vengeance before taking their own lives.

Spectacular suicides have a hypnotic effect on people who have been brooding about suicide but haven't fastened on a method. A suicide at Niagara Falls, for instance, puts guards on the alert for imitators. A Japanese woman who in 1933 leaped to her death into a volcano, Mihara-yama, created a tourist attraction on the site. The following year, three hundred and fifty people followed her into the lava and more than a thousand were restrained from doing so.

Men are more likely to die in suicide attempts than are women, in part because men use irreversible techniques such as guns and jumping from bridges, while women prefer such methods as drug overdoses and wrist slashing. On the other hand, more women suffer from depression than do men. It is almost the feminine neurosis and psychosis; it is so genteel, so *respectable.* Depression becomes an unconscious technique to force others to provide the attention and love for which the women long. But women shrink back from being dead.

"By simple mathematics," explained Lillian E. Smith and Paula Snelling, "the sex that has to spend nine months in the begetting of each human being would have less time to devote to the service of death, were it equally inclined, than has the sex of whom nine seconds are required."

Some people have rhythmic depressions which signal arrival with a snappish mood and inexplicable fatigue. Despite the tiredness, sleep is difficult. The person wakens in the darkness hours before dawn and reviews a merciless parade of grievances, failures and fears. Self-dislike is so acute that it has the taste of aloe. The despair may ease as the day progresses and the person plunges into familiar routine. If the victim is on a structureless vacation, there is less likelihood of this common cure; holiday blues and irascibility are a familiar and baffling phenomenon.

Often melancholia wears off in a few weeks as mysteriously and causelessly as it began. There is almost no discernible edge: one day the person wakens gloomy, the next day is normal. What happened? For one thing, the brain gave up its production of the chemicals of blues because it had other fish to fry; places to go, people to see. For another, and this comes first, the patterning for depression wasn't stable and the brain could switch comfortably to something else.

The longer depression lasts, the longer it is likely to last. Physical complaints will arrive to compound the problem—a litany of headaches, sexual impotency, nausea, menstrual difficulties, blotched complexion, dry bad-breathed mouth, chilly hands and feet, fatigue. The person is a bomb with an unsteady detonator. There is almost no tolerance of criticism or stress and requests for extra services will be resented furiously.

The penalties for unsocial behavior are sickening. The person needs affection and self-approval more than ever before but has rarely deserved it less. Guilt and self-condemnation make the night-time wakings a hell. Wild fears enter the imagination: poverty, unemployment, illness, a mate's infidelity.

It is perhaps time to see a doctor. Depression is the easiest of all emotional malfunctions to treat. Though electroshock therapy is controversial, in some cases of deep melancholia it produces dramatic improvement. A former model, in a terrible state because her marriage had fallen apart and her face was aging, attempted suicide and was taken to a psychiatric hospital. Six weeks later, she was back at work, shaky but coping.

More commonly, treatment consists of antidepressant medication in conjunction with a course of therapy based on evaluation of the patient's personality and attitudes, with the aim of introducing reality and forgiveness that will allow self-esteem to flower.

The heart of melancholia is the absence of safety. If a feeling of being at risk has taken root, the usual efforts that humans make in order to feel nested will be fruitless and self-defeating. A relationship, however loving it appears, will not be comforting because the person can't believe it will last. Praise doesn't help because compliments are not truly deserved. Honors are empty because they weren't earned and won't endure.

The world is seen as unredeemably bleak and cold, so the person can be excused from combat. He or she is too sensitive, too weak to make a difference. Jean-Paul Sartre said, "The emotion of sadness is the magical playacting of impotence."

Recovery from depression and grief caused by something external is inevitable in a well person; healing a depression that began before the person could speak is exceedingly difficult. The processes for each, however, have much in common. Like recovery from a fall down the stairs, it begins with flexing first one limb and then another. There may be soreness, but nothing is really broken; the person is essentially intact. The thing to do is to get up and walk. Lying at the foot of the stairs in a heap cannot be justified.

The Chinese have a story about a woman who asked Buddha to restore her dead child to life. He agreed, if in return she would bring him some grains of mustard seed from a plant growing in the garden of a home to which death had never come. Years later the woman returned to Buddha empty-handed and chastened.

Cicero said, "There is no grief which time does not lessen and soften." The grieving for the loss of one's self-esteem responds to time only if there is conscious effort to stop undermining the self. It was once believed that people couldn't overcome the effects of early loss of self-respect, but examples abound of people who succeeded. They gave up believing that the devices of popularity, success or praise would help and concentrated instead on less spectacular, deeper, winning ways such as inner honesty, sympathy, forgiveness of themselves, easing their merciless perfectionism.

People who don't like themselves imagine that no one else really likes them either. The projection feeds the negative view of self and can be reversed by determination to stop looking for proof of rejection. The necessary first step is to accept that a compliment was truly meant and that a slight was not really intended. When depressed people can begin to believe that they are valued for what they are and not for what they do, they are relieved of the burden of their perfectionism and can function more naturally. Their goodness is real; it doesn't have to make chicken soup every day to prove itself.

Growing oneself out of a depression is uphill work, a private act of courage, but it yields a lasting victory over loneliness.

The case of John Stuart Mill, the nineteenth-century reformer, is illustrative. Mill was raised by his father, John Mill, who ruthlessly crammed the child with knowledge, so that among his accomplishments was the ability to read Latin and Greek at the age of three. The child's intelligence flourished but his emotional deprivation was severe and he grew to become an exceedingly depressed adult.

He cured himself, almost magically. "I was reading accidentally Marmontel's 'Memories' and came to a passage which relates to his father's death, the distressed position of the family, and the sudden inspiration by which he then a mere boy felt and made them feel that he would be everything to them—would supply the place of all that they had lost. A vivid conception of the scene and its feelings came over me, and I was moved to tears. From this moment my burden grew lighter . . . I was no longer hopeless . . . thus the cloud gradually drew off and I again enjoyed life."

Marian Engel, the Canadian novelist, once wrote of her battles with depression, and spoke of four and five o'clock in the afternoon as the time "when dusk and craziness fall." She spoke of the solace of meetings of the Writers' Union of Canada, of which she was the first chairman, and of going to restaurants because there people talked to one another.

"When I was young I thought my father's insistence that everyone have a hobby was corny," she added. "I was intolerant of amateurism. Now, I'm a chaotic gardener, a bad pianist, and a jigsaw puzzle fanatic. You have to outfox the failing day, the lapsed timetable, and if you're a writer, the terrible need to put the smallest experience in sentences. Be kind to people who talk to themselves on the street."

Everyone who acknowledges depression and isolation is richer for it. The philosopher Immanuel Kant believed that no one who had not been profoundly sad at some point could be counted as mature. A person who has known depression, he said, "values himself and regards every human being as a creature who merits respect." William James said the same. He suffered a physical breakdown and a long depression in his thirties and later wrote, "No man is psychologically complete unless he has at least once in his lifetime meditated on self-destruction."

The Soviet poet Yevgeny Yevtushenko agreed. "People who see danger in sadness are themselves immensely dangerous to mankind," he wrote. "Artificial optimism doesn't make people advance, it makes them mark time. A clean, honest, unsentimental melancholy, for all its air of helplessness, urges us forward, creating with its fragile hands the greatest spiritual treasures of mankind."

ANXIETY

ANXIETY begins in human beings before they are born. It is regarded by many behavioral and medical scientists as a basic and essential condition of human existence but there is no agreement on what it is, how it grows, how it can be measured or why it incapacitates some people and to others gives an edge that sharpens their senses, pushes them to learn and makes them amusing.

W. H. Auden called this the "age of anxiety," anticipating not only the increased stress under which all sensate beings are living as the ecology falls apart and the heavens fill with floating gunships, but also that anxiety would be studied more than any other emotional state. Charles D. Spielberger, who edited *Anxiety: Current Trends in Theory and Research,* counted some five thousand articles and books on anxiety and four thousand studies in medical journals in the twenty-year period from 1950 to 1970.

Scientists approach the study of anxiety in the spirit of partying with an old friend. There is almost nothing they learn about anxiety, bad or good, that really surprises them—they have been living with anxiety all their lives—and they are certain they won't be bored. The goal of the research is to get a handle on anxiety so it can be subdued without turning the brain into warm soup.

An eleventh-century Arab philosopher, Ibn Hazm, tried to identify those aspects of human existence which everyone would agree had merit and were sought by all. He concluded there was universal agreement on only one: escaping anxiety.

He wrote, "Not only have I discovered that all humanity considers this good and desirable, but also that . . . no one is moved to act or moved to speak a single word who does not hope by means of this action to release anxiety from his spirit."

Wrote Rollo May, whose *The Meaning of Anxiety* is regarded as a contemporary authority on the subject, "Our knowledge has increased but we have not learned how to deal with anxiety."

Because anxiety is related to suicide, divorce, addiction, heart disease, strokes and mental illness, it was regarded for a long time as pathological in humans, something that healthy people avoided like herpes. Sigmund Freud viewed anxiety as a neurosis and the key to personality—a "modal point, linking up all kinds of most important questions: a riddle of which the solution must cast a flood of light upon our whole mental life."

Upon reflection, scientists now agree that anxiety is normal—that is, *normal* anxiety is normal. Dr. May welcomes the shift of viewpoint but doesn't think that people have yet abandoned entirely the illogical belief that the definition of mental health is to be without anxiety. He wrote, "Anxiety has meaning . . . it is essential to the human condition." For a start, he notes approvingly, anxiety got primitive people away from predators and required them to learn to think. Contemporary efforts to avoid anxiety direct people to find diversions, acquire skills, seek company—to go forward. The psychoanalyst Karen Horney took a tranquil view of anxiety. She said it merely indicated the presence of a problem which needs to be solved.

It was Sören Kierkegaard, the Dane whose examination of anxiety illuminated the subject in the nineteenth century, who said, "Anxiety is always to be understood as oriented toward freedom." In every experience where people move ahead, Dr. May wrote, there is anxiety. Healthy people advance despite their anxiety; neurotic people give up their freedom and creativity because they are fettered by their anxieties.

Howard Liddell wrote that the capacity to experience anxiety and the capacity to plan are two sides of the same coin. O. Hobart Mowrer conducted experiments which demonstrated that rats learned best when acquisition of skills reduced their anxiety, a not uncommon motivation for humans.

The study of anxiety was given impetus in North America when psychologists seized on this notion that anxiety creates drive. Admiring ambition and hustle as the society as a whole does, researchers inevitably focused their attention on the search for the neurogenerator of anxiety that could be distilled and fed to dreamers and layabouts.

Until an accident flooded the laboratory where Ivan Petrovich

Pavlov was conducting his conditioned-response experiments on dogs, it had been assumed that animals could not feel anxiety. One of Pavlov's most intelligent dogs was almost drowned and afterwards had what could only be described as an emotional collapse. When scientists realized that animals could have nervous breakdowns, they proceeded briskly to the task of creating conditions that would make laboratory animals exceedingly anxious.

A tiny white rat, separated from its kin in a solid-walled cage, became insane in two weeks. Rats were punished with shocks when they didn't jump a barrier and punished with shocks when they did, until they became frantic. Sheep and goats, broken down when they were lambs and kids by shocks given ten seconds apart, or by continuous darkness, or by monotony, remained neurotic animals all their lives. A man at Cornell University spent twenty-two years of his life engrossed in giving animals anxiety attacks. Others devote themselves to human subjects—university students who volunteer for situations in which they are advised that, in the course of the next twenty minutes, they will receive a severe electric shock.

The results have been interesting in themselves but not of much practical use. At Northwestern University, psychologist Janet A. Taylor developed a method of measuring anxiety in individuals which was called the Taylor Anxiety Scale (TAS). It consisted of two hundred and seventy-five statements, fifty of which were deemed to be clues to the presence of high anxiety.

These included: I am often sick to my stomach; I worry quite a bit over possible troubles; I wish I could be as happy as others; life is often a strain for me; I certainly feel useless at times; I feel hungry almost all the time; I have nightmares every few nights; I am easily embarrassed; I have been afraid of things or people that I know could not hurt me.

A 1984 study of social anxiety, conducted by Warren Jones at the University of Tulsa and Dan Russell at the University of Ohio College of Medicine, found fear of attending a party with strangers to be at the top of the list of anxiety-producers. Three-quarters of all the people surveyed said they were acutely uncomfortable in that situation. Next alarming were giving a speech, or when asked a personal question in public, or meeting a date's parents, or on the first day in a new job, or when made the victim of a practical joke or when talking to someone in authority.

A low level of anxiety is said to tone up the system, making eating and sex more pleasurable. High levels lead to impotence and obesity. The physical changes of a mild state of anxiety give energy but as the system moves toward nameless terror the body shivers and sweats, breathing becomes rapid and uneven, sugar floods into the bloodstream for energy and the cerebral cortex, the thinking brain, starts to work on a solution.

If none presents itself, the body's state of preparedness for action will remain, grinding its wheels ineffectively and destructively. The extra sugar the liver has released can result in diabetes and the abnormal pressure on the thumping heart can cause heart disease. Frequency of urination, also associated with anxiety, can emerge in middle life as incontinence. The acidic stomachs of anxious people predispose them to ulcers. Rollo May wrote that anorexia nervosa, which is a fear of the consequences of eating, and bulimia, fear of the consequences of overeating, are also associated with anxiety, as are less dramatic obsessions about food.

Doctors suspect that anxiety underlies *all* physical illness. It is known to be a strong factor in hyperthyroidism, epilepsy, asthma, chronic diarrhea, profuse sweating, peptic ulcer, hypertension. It causes fatigue, irritability, inability to concentrate, nausea, flashes of panic, aching muscles, restlessness, tension. Robert B. Malmo of McGill University in Montreal reported that aching legs may be associated with anxiety about sex and pains in the arms and shoulders with unconscious hostility.

Anxiety makes noncontagious conditions catching. If a friend suffers a heart attack, an anxious person may feel chest pains that are real enough. Though cardiograms can't confirm any difficulty, the stress remains until the prophecy is fulfilled and the heart breaks down.

Migraine headaches are believed by some to be influenced by anxiety and blocked anger, and susceptibility to migraine is anxiety-producing in itself. Harold G. Wolff, of Cornell's department of neurology and psychiatry, more than thirty years ago told the Mooseheart Symposium on Feelings and Emotions that his analysis of migraine had led him to conclude that sufferers are likely to be people who exhibit perfectionism, overalertness, tension, search for approval and a habit of postponing decisions—all indicators of anxiety. He declared that study of the childhood causes of too much anxiety should be "the prime medical responsibility of our day." Doctors are still rising up before symposia and colloquia to make the same pronouncement.

The most careful dissection of anxiety suggests that it is inevitable because it accompanies all change in the human condition. It is found as early as fetal life, rising in the mind of an unborn child whenever the mother's state of mind is strikingly altered. Two months before they are born, babies have an increased heartbeat at the sound of a doorbell. During birth, as babies are extruded violently from the mother's body by the contracting walls of their uterus home, their hearts beat faster and they have respiratory difficulties, both of which are also symptoms of anxiety in adults.

Anxiety accompanies the decisions made at each of life's crossroads, from a job move to the profoundly existentialist crises of self-awareness. The earliest and most painful psychic ordeal—so stressful that it is shoved under the rug of the subconscious—comes when children as young as two first realize that they are essentially alone: that their parents do not truly know them and never will. Dr. May said that children make a conscious choice at this point to move toward being individuals, desolating as it is to confront the truth of their basic isolation. Sören Kierkegaard called it "the alarming possibility of being able."

Literature, art and religion are saturated with the theme of anxiety as a force that shapes destiny. Franz Kafka and Albert Camus fashioned characters whose entire beings radiated anxiety. Paul Tillich held the belief that anxiety is aroused by the threat of nonbeing, which Sören Kierkegaard expressed as "fear of nothingness." What the psychologists call "separation anxiety," which is experienced first by babies when their parents aren't in view, is to philosophers and theologians the separation of people from their own goodness or from their God.

Dr. Tillich was apprehensive that the flight from the anxiety of no-God would lead to such excesses as the "born again" movement and other forms of evangelical fervor. He believed that extremism could not be a lasting solution to emptiness. "A spiritual center," he warned, "cannot be produced intentionally, and the attempt to produce it only produces deeper anxiety."

The instability of most of society's institutions compels uncertain people to seek cults and other forms of authoritarian security to give them the safety of order. Erich Fromm wrote of what he called "the escape from freedom," and declared that the shattering of primary ties to family, state, church, tradition, social order—whatever—can only be endured by the development of self-strength. All other imitations of a secure vessel run the risk of having false bottoms that will plunge the person into isolation and helplessness.

Anxiety also results from emotional overload, occurring when people have too many conflicting feelings. Normal anxiety, for instance, accompanies such life-shattering decisions as divorce, job moves and submitting to mutilating surgery, all situations full of conflicting pulls.

Carroll E. Izard, one of the leaders in recent research on anxiety, maintained that it is a complex which contains at least two fundamental emotions. He proposed that one of these emotions is always fear but the others could be shame, distress, shyness, guilt, anger or what he termed the positive emotion of interest-excitement.

Anxiety differs from fear in that it doesn't know what it is afraid of, whereas fear sees the threat distinctly. Four-month-old infants show what psychologists call "negative effect," a tenseness in strange situations. "Eight-month anxiety," which most often begins in the seventh month and continues until the child is one year old, is demonstrated by the baby's apprehension when the mother or other regular care giver is absent. If something unusual happens while the mother is away, the baby will be much more upset than if it occurred in her presence. A familiar kind of early anxiety is the distress babies show at the approach of people they don't know, an aversion to aliens that grandmothers call "making strange" and anthroplogists see as the human animal's protective reflex against an unknown and possibly carnivorous enemy.

People who fear strangers operate on a vague apprehension of peril, which is the essential quality of anxiety. While unable to pinpoint the source of danger, they nevertheless have a real sensation of being in jeopardy. Such undifferentiated alarm is unbearable and must find something on which to fasten. For instance, a baby placed in a crib in an unfamiliar room might be in a state of high anxiety, in which mood a flapping blind or a black thread on the pillow will trigger panic. Anxious adults look for a cause, something palpable to fear, and tailor a phobia to suit that need.

A survival technique for anxious people of all ages is to be so agreeable that they won't be abandoned to face their fears alone. Babies and children, when they are worried, will run through a small repertoire of tricks, wailing, clinging, or, later, being beguiling, to keep the caretakers in attendance. Harry Stack Sullivan believed that everyone constructs their personalities on the basis of whatever works best to relieve anxiety.

Everyone is anxious; that's normal. It is provoked on all occasions where there is a risk of being rejected, embarrassed or hurt, and lifts when the crisis is over. Disproportionate or neurotic anxiety can last a lifetime and has its genesis in infancy, when the baby's anxiety was unrelieved for such a protracted length of time that it penetrated the subconscious.

Alterations in circumstances are dislocating to everyone; those with normal levels of anxiety will fret but those with neurotic levels may panic. Change produces a sense of vulnerability in both animals and people. This century's technological revolutions are amply unsettling, but people must also deal with economic insecurity and paranoid world diplomacy. Morals are fluid and faith self-defined; women sit in executive offices and terrorists board the subways; the environment is killing people; ancestor destruction has unsettled a sense of comforting continuity. Humans, feeling small and betrayed, crawl on the floor of a poisoned ocean and seek what humans have always sought: love, purpose, the absence of anxiety.

Though the stresses are the same for everyone, not everyone feels them the same. Some people are so anxious that everything alarms them. Two psychologists, A. E. Wessman and D. F. Ricks, call this "the A trait," a state of more or less constant anxiety with fluctuating levels. Its hallmark is an excessive fear of failure.

Others, more fortunate, exist in a state of anxiety-preparedness something like background music. It doesn't interfere with their attitudes or actions but is on hand to mobilize their glandular-visceral, cardiovascular and respiratory systems when required, such as when called to make a speech. People with low levels of anxiety are not immune to the vagaries of human disaster. Everyone has a breaking point, *everyone*. When the limit of endurance of stress is reached, anxiety will swamp even the most stable.

Highly anxious people will perform below the level of their competence when circumstances are threatening or competitive. Curiously, when the element of hostile competition is removed and all participants are assured of success or recognition, they excel beyond the performance of people with more orderly natures. Using the TAS measurement, researchers have established that highly anxious people do well in situations which require mastery of routines but fall apart as soon as there is competition or a demand for flexibility.

In essence, as Florida State's Dr. Charles D. Spielberger pointed out, test-anxious people are characterized by "acquired habits and attitudes that involve negative self-perceptions and expectations."

Beeman N. Phillips, psychologist at the University of Texas, has devised two strategies to help anxious students. A first step is to identify the source of the stress in the school environment and the next is to change the learning situation to eliminate what has been determined to be intolerable.

Scientists believe that differences in individual levels of anxiety lie in a mix of constitutional factors and early environment. All primate babies can be startled by sudden noises or something moving abruptly in the periphery of their vision, but some are decidedly more jumpy than others. Some sleep deeply while ghetto-blasters pass under their window and others will waken at a door squeak. It is one of the oddities of the startle reaction that it occurs before the brain figures out what is happening. Nevertheless, if the people who care for the jittery baby are calm and reassuring, the child may become relaxed in time; if they are inattentive and irritable, or if the home is marked with upheaval, even a calm baby will become chronically alarmed.

The direct result of every unpleasant family situation is an increased load of anxiety on the children. Karen Horney once listed some of the common causes of childhood anxiety. She wrote, "A wide range of adverse factors in the environment can produce this insecurity in a child: direct or indirect domination, indifference, erratic behavior, lack of respect for the child's individual needs, lack of real guidance, disparaging attitude, too much admiration or the absence of it, lack of reliable warmth, having to take sides in parental disagreements, isolation from other children, injustice, discrimination, unkept promises, hostile atmosphere . . ."

Studies of anxiety in children have demonstrated that the lowest levels are found in those whose parents are affectionate and stable and whose family life is disciplined. When the rules change unpredictably, children are more anxious; children who are overdisciplined and treated with a general tone of hostility register highest on anxiety measurements. Such children may become bigoted adults, obsessed by the threats they imagine to surround them and putting high stock in an authoritarian solution to their fears.

Even children who are cushioned by thoughtful parenting will not be able to avoid anxiety. A new baby makes the other children in the household anxious; all children are anxious over starting school, changing schools, a family quarrel, taking examinations, illness, moving to a new neighborhood, adolescence and, especially, separation or divorce of the parents and the remarriage of either.

Children whose environment has helped to strengthen their confidence obviously will be better equipped to face the normal vicissitudes of family life and will recover better from disasters, while children already operating at the edge of their resources may crumble under even minor stress. Since acute anxiety is painful, they devise a technique to displace it. Bullying others is one way of discharging anxiety; being infantile is another.

The hurdle that overanxious children are least likely to manage is puberty. Some balk and won't go forward into the uncertainty of sexuality. They choose to remain childish. "It is impossible for anyone to mature fully without coming to grips with the sex drive," said Harry Stack Sullivan. He wrote that anxiety can prevent the development of genuine love.

The relationship between anxiety and sex is a curious one. Anxious people are usually lonely and yearn for unifying sex, but anxiety is a powerful inhibitor of sexual performance. As a result, wretched people who most need the tranquilizing completeness of mutual consummation are exactly those least likely to achieve it. For many who do climax, the peace and release of tension are fleeting, followed by a wave of horror and refreshed anxiety.

Anxiety is part of every neurosis; it is the bedrock of them all. If mental health is "deeply felt happiness," as Dr. Dallas Pratt put it, then mental illness is deeply felt anxiety.

In the emotional rainbow shyness lies between fear and anxiety. Only one person in five claims that he or she has never experienced shyness. According to Daniel Goleman, New York *Times* science writer, the symptoms include failure to make eye contact when talking with someone and subterfuges to avoid conversation altogether. Jonathan Cheek, a psychologist at Wellesley College, who is fascinated with the subject of social anxiety, said, "Shy people are their own worst critics."

The negativeness of shy people defies all challenges. They live in perpetual expectation that they will make fools of themselves, that they are conspicuous on social occasions for their gaucherie, that all their failures are their fault and all their successes are due to someone else's efforts. Worse, they remember distinctly, long into the night, every social blunder, however undetectable to anyone else.

Shyness is one of the persistent traits of a lifetime. Shy children are very likely to become shy adults. Jerome Kagan, Harvard University psychologist, studied infants to record their spontaneity and confidence and checked back four years later to see how they were developing. None of the children who were outgoing as babies showed any timidity in kindergarten, but two-thirds of those who had clung to their mothers when they were toddlers were still quiet and reticent at the age of five.

"Those children who had become less timid by kindergarten seem to have had parents who put gentle pressure on them to be more outgoing," Dr. Kagan said.

In recent years Dr. Kagan's fierce defense of the health and resiliency of children has been cheering to parents and is gaining acceptance with his peers. In his view, no child is condemned to eternal shyness because of early physiological and environmental factors. Shyness is somewhat more difficult to combat than some other temperamental traits, he conceded, but "no human quality is beyond change."

Dr. Raymond B. Cattell, research psychologist at the University of Illinois, studied anxiety for twenty-five years and once described it as "a lack of confidence, a sense of guilt and worthlessness, a dependency, a readiness to become fatigued, irritable and discouraged, an uncertainty about oneself and a suspicion of others, and a general tenseness." Blaise Pascal in the seventeenth century was speaking of anxiety when he commented on the "perpetual restlessness in which men pass their lives."

More recently scientists have been using such descriptions as "acutely unpleasant state of diffuse arousal following the perception of threat." Anxiety is the outcome of three basic conditions: first, that the person is anxiety-prone; second, that the event is outside what is familiar and safe; and, third, that no effective response seems available. As many have noted, the difference between fear and anxiety is whether something appropriate can be done; indecision produces vast quantities of anxiety. Anxiety itself is anxiety-producing; as panic rises in the mind and all the escape doors are locked, what begins to make people most anxious is that anxiety is about to go out of control.

Because anxiety is objectless, it can last a very long time. A celebrated study of black students at Jackson State College in Mississippi following a police raid showed high levels of anxiety still present long after the raid was over. Newcomers to the United States from Latin America also demonstrated elevated states of anxiety even though the events leading to emigration and a difficult resettlement were very distant.

The tardy recognition of the influence of anxiety on happiness and health is due in part to the tendency to call anxiety fear whenever it shows itself and depression when it doesn't.

The most accepted theory of the root of anxiety is the one loosely labeled "separation." The first experience of anxiety is separation from the caring adult and the others are variations on that theme, all involving separation from what is familiar. Anxiety also is associated with fear of death, the ultimate separation from the known.

Otto Rank, the Austrian psychoanalyst who was one of Freud's first disciples, thought that the central problem in human development is individualism, and that anxiety therefore is concomitant to all growth. "Anxiety has a purpose," Rollo May wrote, and Sören Kierkegaard said that anxiety was a better teacher than reality: those who move through anxious experiences are strengthened to meet the next one. Those who avoid that which makes them anxious will succeed only in making themselves more anxious next time.

Karen Horney compared the anxious neurotic to a soldier in a trench under constant shellfire. The trench can be made quite comfortable and homey, but the outer danger remains paramount in the mind. People who feel under siege will adopt whatever survival technique worked for them in childhood. Dr. Horney identified three styles: *moving toward people,* which involves becoming an ingratiating person, overappreciative and oversolicitous, with insatiable needs for appreciation and praise while reacting almost hysterically to criticism; *moving against people,* which results in emotional inhibitions, efforts to control others and a keen eye for self-advantage; and *moving away from people,* the technique which produces secretive, uncertain, withdrawn behavior to keep the world at a safe distance.

Another common defense against anxiety is to show it plainly so that people will be obligated to behave more considerately than they otherwise might.

The language of anxiety is "I'm all wound up inside." K. Goldstein wrote in 1951 that anxiety, "the catastrophic reaction," is the person's sense of being unable to react adequately. Karen Horney described basic anxiety as "the feeling of being small, insignificant, helpless, deserted, endangered, in a world that is out to abuse, cheat, attack, humiliate, betray, envy."

In order to survive in such a world, people must imagine themselves powerful and right. This posture is not really believed and therefore must be defended vigorously. Arm waving bluster is intended more to convince the self than critics. The armor of perfection is futile and exhausting to maintain. People collapse eventually and yield to despair. As Dr. Horney said, they lose the capacity "to wish for anything wholeheartedly."

Anxiety sometimes fixes on whatever parents identified as threatening. For instance, parents who were frightened of disease and flew into panic over injuries can instill a lifelong anxiety about infections. Judson S. Brown, psychologist at the State University of Iowa, told the first Nebraska Symposium on Motivation that anxiety about money is conditioned in families where finances were a burning issue. A family obsession with neatness is difficult to shake: sloppiness is the obverse of the same compulsion. Children who are overcautioned about strangers, as many "street-proofed" children are today, may become adults so profoundly uneasy in an unfamiliar environment that they cannot travel at all.

Parents who are hostile to one another but behave politely in front of the children create whole oceans of anxiety in their confused offspring. The children can sense the anger but they can't hear it, can't see evidence of it. Erich Fromm thought that this particular kind of anxiety would be so distressing that the baffled child would likely withdraw into daydreams of violence in order to give the rage in the family an outlet. He thought that when they grow into adulthood, their fantasies and their social and sexual preferences might have a masochistic tone.

Parents who demand perfect goodness from their children some-times create adults who live with a sword of Damocles suspended over their heads. Their sense of imminent punishment is so powerful that nothing makes them so unhappy as success—the greater the success, the more fearful the retribution that can be expected. Such people are drawn to authority to help them contain the miasma of feelings they dare not express. Wanting boundaries for themselves, they believe in to solving unrest with police enforcement and the military.

Paul Tillich listed three forms of anxiety: anxiety about death, anxiety over meaninglessness and the anxiety about condemnation. Anxiety about death is particularly acute in people whose lives have disappointed them. Propelled by routines and duty, they function without pleasure and feel their gifts have never been used. At whatever age they become debilitated, they see themselves as dying without ever having lived.

The anxiety of meaninglessness is a recognition of the absurdity of the human condition and its self-importance. Like Albert Camus's prosperous smug man who one evening heard a mocking laugh behind him, people sometimes have a sudden view of their own insignificance. As Blaise Pascal put it, "When I consider the brief span of my life, swallowed up in the eternity before and behind it, the small space that I fill, or even see, engulfed in the infinite immensity of spaces which I know not, and which know not me, I am afraid."

The anxiety of condemnation, commonly experienced by people with a stern sense of responsibility, consists of expectation of failure and punishment. Dr. Sullivan called this form of anxiety "an unpleasant state brought on by the apprehension of disapproval in interpersonal relations," a common character malaise marked by certainty that friends and associates secretly hold the person in contempt.

Anxiety thrives in a culture which conspicuously rewards winners while exacting a high emotional price for the rewards of achievement. Executives live with the fear of falling and middle management with the fear of being crushed. Creative people carry within their yearning hearts the specter of talent dying before they do. Women feel as uneasy in boardrooms as immigrants deplaning in a new land. On assembly lines, workers watch the advance of robots.

Plato disapproved of anxiety altogether. He wrote, "Nothing in human affairs is worth any great anxiety."

The cure for anxiety is what Erich Fromm called self-strength. Developing self-strength is hard work and most people duck it. Some handle their anxiety by becoming ill, and can become exceedingly good at getting sick and staying sick. As doctors have noted in countless medical papers, it is almost impossible to treat someone who has resolved to stay in a nice warm disability rather than walk around in the chilly air of indefinite dangers.

Some anxious people become addicted to such jeopardy as gambling for high stakes or mountain climbing. They seek sharply defined and genuine peril, which they experience as comparable to sexual climaxes, rather than endure being always vaguely afraid. Some psychologists greatly admire this spectacular adaptation to anxiety, which is like circus high-wire artists working without a net. Wrote J. Gray in *The Psychology of Fear and Stress*, "This represents in itself a successful way of coping with anxiety."

Others perform temporary frontal lobotomies on themselves by getting drunk, snorting cocaine, shooting up with barbiturates or down with tranquilizers, hanging out in singles bars, going on food binges, reading junk books, sitting for numbed hours before a sedating television set. Anything is better than experiencing aloneness.

Giving birth is often seen by women, and sometimes by men, as a glorious way to defeat anxiety. There are magnificent moments when it even works, but these often are outweighed by the uncertainties and frustrations of actual parenting, a far more difficult venture than television commercials showing adorable babies romping on white fur rugs would suggest.

Human communication is an effective barrier against separation anxiety, which is why strangers strike up conversations on trains. The attraction of health clubs is not entirely fitness: there are *people* in the gyms, the locker rooms, the saunas. Women still go to restaurant bathrooms in pairs, a relic of a Victorian past when women tried their best to give the impression that they never needed a toilet but only an opportunity to chat alone.

People watch polls to confirm that their views are mainstream; divergence is acceptable only if a substantial number of people share it. Vote switching is influenced by a mood in the electorate that vote switching is happening and the opportunity to participate in an approved activity should not be missed. People seek a tribal view of censorship or peace marches and will defend their opinions with vigor not only because they are the result of thoughtful analysis but also because they represent a membership card.

Quite frequently, adults have the illusion that they have cured themselves of being anxious. The severe panic attacks that once embarrassed them in elevators or while standing in line at a supermarket have been absent for a long while. They go unconcerned to dinner parties where they may know only the host. It has been years since they last wakened at five in the morning, sweating that their faults would be found out by nightfall. They go jauntily into a meeting and—pow—anxiety sweeps in with them. Something in the air suddenly catapults them backward into their old uncertain selves.

A woman who was certain she was over her fear of heights found she could not work in a high-rise office with window walls. A man who had forgotten how terrified he used to be as a child when his parents left him alone in the house was just as frightened thirty years later when he found himself alone for a few hours in a hunting cabin. It is a shock to find that the vulnerable child hasn't been outgrown but only suppressed.

People truly move ahead out of anxiety when there is more to be gained by doing so than will be lost. Timothy Findley, award-winning Canadian novelist, overcame his anxiety about flying when it became too inconvenient to continue to travel by car. Others give up the defense of telling everyone how anxious they are because they no longer can find anyone who believes it, or cares.

The first step, always the hardest, is honesty. People start defeating anxiety when they stop assuring themselves that their worries are not exaggerated but are perfectly proportioned and justified. By the time adults reach their thirties and forties, they usually have the time and inner space to make assessments that can lead to the conclusion that the source of anxiety is not outside the person but within. All external explanations, however valid, cannot be blamed for the wretchedness of slopping about in a sea of anxiety.

The bleak truth to be faced is that everyone is essentially alone. Carl G. Jung wrote, "Neither family, nor society, nor position can save him from it, nor the most successful adaptation to actual surroundings, nor yet the most frictionless fitting in with them. The development of personality is a favor that must be paid for dearly."

Immunizing oneself against anxiety is a process not unlike being vaccinated. Small amounts of anxiety must be waded through, again and again, to kill all the demons. People must accept what makes them anxious and then ignore the distress and do it. The heartening aspect of this torment is that each successful contest with anxiety improves confidence and makes the next confrontation somewhat easier. That's not Pollyanna talk: it's a simple fact. The clue that the path is the right one is that it is painful. The heart thuds, the mouth dries, speech tumbles out in a babble of idiocy and the nerve fibers shriek: *Run!*

The only sane approach is to stand still and see it through.

Since neurotic anxiety is defined as fear without danger, with the victim imaging there is a tiger in the bush, the solution, as psychoanalyst Karl Stern saw it in *The Third Revolution,* is to accept that the tiger exists and set out to find it.

Karen Horney observed that the first and best prize for such heroism is the discovery that the real self is more capable than the artifice who was running the operation in the past. With this discovery comes a twinge of self-admiration, always a good thing when it is deserved, and with self-admiration comes the beginning of the pathways in the impressionable cerebellum that eventually will produce confidence more readily than anxiety.

Confident people don't fear to expose themselves; they see no reason to be vigilant and suspicious. They perceive the harmony and commonality of the human race. Out of acceptance of isolation comes relief, a lessened sense of isolation. What is also jettisoned is the compulsion to fight for territory, manipulate, avoid contact or seduce. When self-contempt wanes, women stop accepting abusive mates and men won't tolerate being humiliated. People become wholehearted; they take consequences, drop pretenses, respect others and accept their own mortality.

Anxiety requires an astonishing amount of energy. When people free themselves from chronic anxiety, or even some of it, the first and overwhelming benefit is zest.

A tool of anxiety therapy is to impel victims into their nightmares, where they must bear their most unbearable fears. A woman described by H. J. Eysenck, psychologist at Maudsley Hospital in London, was afraid to go outside her home alone. She was taken on long walks and drives with an attendant and then, heavily tranquilized, was sent a short distance over the same route unaccompanied. Gradually the medication was decreased and the distances grew farther until she was free of her phobia.

Similarly, people with other fears were requested to imagine their worst horror. While they held the picture in their minds, they were hypnotized into a state of relaxation. In time they could contemplate the object on which they had fixed their anxiety without a tremble. Dr. Eysenck's team had the same happy result with children, exposing them to what they feared while holding them tenderly, speaking lovingly and, for good measure, feeding them treats.

Leo Rangell, a psychiatrist, made a suggestion at an American Psychiatric Association convention that anxious people should decide every morning that they will not be anxious for the rest of the day. Simplistic as it sounds, he had been obtaining good outcomes with patients who planted the autohypnotic suggestion in their brains. Anxious people reported to him that for a few seconds after awakening each morning they felt fine. In a moment or two, they would "remember" and be engulfed by anxiety.

"Perhaps this is the crucial moment in determining which agencies or principles are to gain ascendancy in mental life for the day," Dr. Rangell suggested. He told an illustrative story about a 102-year-old man whose secret of longevity was that he considered every morning that he could feel either good all day or bad. The old man grinned and said, "I decide, 'Oh, what the hell,' and I decide to feel good. That's how I live so long."

The morning self-reminder may be in the category of a trick, like a string around the finger. Rollo May's prescription for dealing with anxiety acknowledges that the essential ingredient is self-esteem, but takes the realistic approach that some people will never succeed in liking themselves. He therefore suggests work as a positive outlet for anxiety, and he notes, without comment, that people who believe in their leaders or have strong religious faith are relieved of anxiety.

Walter Lippmann also recommended a form of surrender for dealing with anxiety. He advised that people accept their fate: everything changes and everything ends. In *A Preface to Morals,* he wrote, "An adult has to break his attachment to persons and things. He must learn to hold on to things which do not slip away and change, to hold on by not grasping them but by understanding them and remembering them. Then he is wholly an adult."

HAPPINESS

HAPPINESS is the rarest of all human conditions, and the most prized. Balm of toilers and weepers, the heart's hope, eternal reward for piety, happiness is elusive.

Chinese gift shops offer a choice of good-luck pendants. One translates Long Life and the other Happiness.

Take your pick.

Happy New Year. Happy anniversary. Happy bat mitzvah. Happy retirement. Happy birthday to you. Blow out the candles and wish. Here's a toast to the bride and groom: *happiness!*

The wish for happiness is not for the small change of a good time at the party in progress. That's soon spent. After a picnic day that lived up to the hope that it would not rain, that the children would not cry, that the parents would not argue, what have you got? Leftovers in the fridge and sunburn, mixed with residual good feeling and wistfulness.

Happiness isn't the absence of anxiety. It isn't finding a missing wallet or even a lost relative. It isn't rescue, fine as it is, like the cavalry coming over the hill, or when a mistake gets fixed. And it isn't the creature pleasures of a foamy bath, an oriental rug, a car that has élan.

When happiness depends on something external—a mate, a baby, a position, an address—the holder becomes a worried jailor. Fate or burglars can snatch it away.

> *And there is even happiness*
> *That makes the heart afraid.*
> —Thomas Hood

This is a person-on-the-street interview, and we're stopping people at random. You, madam, what do you want out of life?

Why, happiness, of course. Irreducible happiness.

Lasting happiness is what's inside the person. It comes out of self-approval and self-knowledge, which can't be gained without some experience with unhappiness, desperation, loneliness, guilt, envy and meanness. It is bound up with the capacity to be useful and to love unconditionally, to be curious and spontaneous, to possess a well-stocked mind, to hold certain faiths. Happiness is also the ability to be untroubled by idleness or solitude. It has a discriminating eye for folly, especially that of its copyright owner, and courage, and a sense of humor, which is the hallmark of humanity. Most of all, happiness is openness.

"When people have happiness within themselves," wrote George Bernard Shaw, "all the earthquakes, all the floods, all the prisons in the world can't make them really unhappy."

People can be truly, bone-deep happy at any adult age past the turbulence of youth. Children know joy in wholehearted degrees such as adults rarely experience but they are never in a state of real happiness. Their helplessness and vulnerability preclude the sense of ease and confidence which are integral to mature happiness. "Dependent as a slave," William Lyon Phelps said of being a child.

When a thousand elderly people were questioned by researchers, they reported that the happiest years of their lives had been between the ages of twenty-five and forty-five. People in that age group were astonished and dismayed at the news. Young adults often assure their relatives and friends that they are happy, a serviceable way to protect privacy, but those years most often are too fast-paced for much self-delving or smelling the flowers. Nursing grievances and guilt, they laugh and smile a good deal but feel hollow. They talk a lot, but say little; they play, they work, they breathe, they wait. For happiness.

The American writer Morton M. Hunt flew solitary reconnaissance with the Eighth Air Force during World War II. When the war ended, he suffered emotional collapse. For weeks, his nights were full of fitful, terrifying dreams. When awake, he moved like a robot, a man going through the motions of eating, responding when addressed, walking carefully to make sure his disassociated feet kept in contact with the floor.

One day he was aware that the tension was loosening. His handwriting began to look like his own instead of an arthritic old man's.

One afternoon he happened to hear a bit of Mozart that he had long loved. Suddenly he was flooded with a warm feeling so intense that he was dizzy. "I had the eerie sensation that all at once I was in the presence of a long-lost friend—myself." It's me, he thought, I'm back.

All over the world, people ease toward the same realization that they are whole. The click is not usually so audible as it was for a battle-worn pilot, but the sense of homeostasis they enjoy is a soft form of ecstasy. One middle-aged woman described it as a hum; her feeling of being united, mind and body, felt like background music. Somewhere in the fretting and frustrations of marriage, career, debt and children she had managed to turn a corner she hadn't noticed. She was transfixed by the realization that she was happy.

Nothing had changed, but everything was different.

Happiness is unmistakable. People who wonder if they are really happy, aren't. One woman explained that it's like a labor pain. "When you're carrying your first baby," she said, "you keep wondering what labor will be like. Every time you have a cramp or even a twinge, you wonder if this is it. Then, eventually, you are *really* in labor and there's no question about it."

Philosophers and psychologists are baffled by happiness. They crowd around it, the unseen heat source. Thomas Jefferson, influenced by the eighteenth-century utilitarian philosopher Jeremy Bentham who thought that legislation should promote "the greatest happiness of the greatest number," believed that any state which granted equality to its citizens could also guarantee happiness, and therefore wrote the right to pursue happiness into the Declaration of Independence. Americans are the only people on earth with an astonishing constitutional right to happiness, though the judiciary has been unsympathetic to the numerous bandits who have attempted to use that provision of the founding document to justify holding up the stagecoach.

Surveys of what makes people happy abound, and there are even Gallup polls on the subject. These have not been particularly convincing. For many reasons, hope and self-delusion being only two, people tend to report on questionnaires that they are happy. Also, happiness, like dread, is in the eye of the beholder. Some fifty years ago a network radio series was devoted to the topic of human happiness. It elicited a mountain of mail from listeners who had been burning, it seemed, to describe their own happiness or unhappiness.

The most striking feature of the correspondence was that some people reported themselves happy in almost exactly the same circumstances as were creating misery for others—poverty, disability, isolation. Precisely the same lowly job had one man ready to kill himself but left another pleased that he could do the simple chore unthinkingly, leaving his mind free to contemplate the universe. One couple spoke of despair at raising a handicapped child; another couple was rejoicing that the child had taught them so much that was precious.

Everyone wants happiness: the bluebird, the holy grail, free fall, oceanic bliss, weightlessness. Robert Louis Stevenson wrote, "The habit of being happy enables one to be freed, or largely freed, from the domination of outward conditions."

The happiness industry is booming. Happiness is sold by the bottle in the form of booze and pills. Much of what passes for sex is happiness-seeking. New clothes are better than no happiness at all.

Happy people have no edges. They don't envy, worry about their hair, expect the worst, hold grudges or wake up at four every morning wishing they were dead. Happy people get love because they are so friendly and kind. This makes them even happier, which in turn renders them more lovable, and so on, and so on. Happy people get asked to everything.

Nathaniel Hawthorne once cautioned that happiness is a butterfly. If you chase it diligently, the butterfly will elude you. But if you sit very still under an open sky, the butterfly will light in your hand.

The trail of the shy butterfly begins with Aristotle, who lived twenty-three hundred years ago. The Greek philosopher is the voice of eudaemonia, the theory that happiness is the goal of existence and springs from conducting one's life on the basis of reason. Plato disagreed, so move on to Epicurus, who wrote, "True pleasure consists in serenity of mind and absence of fear."

The Stoics offer no help. They believed that only the virtuous are happy, whereas it is the other way around. Sophocles, Augustine and Kant are definitely out: they believed no one was happy until dead.

Aquinas said happiness came from an active moral life. Horace and Disraeli believed that the basis of happiness is good health. Thoreau, Marcus Aurelius and George Bernard Shaw thought that happiness is *doing.* "This is the true joy of life," declared GBS, ". . . being thoroughly worn out before you are thrown on the scrap heap."

Cicero, Edmund Burke, Bertrand Russell, Henrik Ibsen and Buddha had a theory that happiness was inseparable from tranquillity. "Happy indeed," sang Buddha, "we live unanxious among the anxious."

Conn Smythe, a cantankerous man who owned the Toronto Maple Leafs hockey team, said in his eighties that happiness consisted of keeping one's bowels clear and having sex twice a week. Another old man, hearing this, declared that Mr. Smythe was a liar.

William Lyon Phelps said the happiest person is the one who thinks the most interesting thoughts. Lin Yutang wrote cryptically, "The man who knows what he wants is a happy man."

Ted Twetie, interviewed in Vancouver on the occasion of his one hundredth birthday, announced that he owed his state of happiness to the following: "Always have a strong notion for smoking cigarettes, drinking rum, chewing Irish twist and spitting up against the wind."

What becomes apparent from this catalogue is that they are all, *all,* from Aristotle to Twetie, speaking about themselves. The wise ones, the intellectuals, the fools have each given an analysis based on projection. They put on a billboard their own prescription for happiness, based on whatever wisdom, insight and misapprehension they have managed to acquire. They are Linus the Philosopher King, recommending security blankets.

Psychologists have been slow to study happiness. They viewed the emotion with embarrassment and mistrust, believing it a frivolous subject when compared with anxiety (trendy) or guilt (bottomless) or prejudice (hopeless). Most of them doubt that happiness really exists. They can accept euphoria in small doses but happiness as a steady state makes them suspicious that they are being tricked.

Lately they have been putting together some retrospective studies of what kind of childhoods happy people had, and they are also looking at their old favorite, toddlers in day-care centers, with special attention to the cheerful, agreeable ones who were formerly neglected by researchers keen to understand violence or thumb-sucking.

They find that the qualities that form the unit of happiness are present in large amounts in babies. Infants seem to be born good-natured or not, a reflection maybe of genetic material together with the chemical environment of the wombs from which they were hatched. Babies have to live with whoever decides to raise them, no choice being allowed them, and accordingly some get adults who are friendly, sympathetic and interested in them, while others get a raw deal. The level of happiness potential, understandably, is much higher in the former group than the latter. Research has proved what common sense knew all along.

Babies begin with a capacity to feel pleasure at a level not much above mere absence of distress. When they are warm and well fed, babies are quiescent and contented. By the third month they connect to other people and will smile at anyone who talks softly, cooingly. Babies who are contented most of their waking time are laying down patterns of confidence; their brains are gearing up for happiness.

The responsive smiles of babies, a human being's first demonstration of a state of happiness, have attracted copious attention from behavioral scientists. They began with the undifferentiated smiles of the three-month-old, the evidence of the race's instinctive sociability. They learned that babies will smile even at a hideous horror mask so long as the teeth are bared, there are two eyes, the forehead is smooth and the head nods.

They will never smile at a face with one eye or with the eyes covered. They won't smile at a profile. They soon stop smiling if the mask doesn't move.

One baby girl studied by René Spitz was smiling at the researchers when she was only twenty-five days old. She promptly became a favorite, which, of course, made her feel well attended and resulted in her becoming ever more sociable, so that on her first birthday she was a full four months ahead of her chronological age in development. Dr. Spitz failed to make any connection between this baby's vaulting growth and the fact that his researchers adored her. He reported in a medical paper that the only reason for the child's good nature was her "unusually pleasant and devoted mother."

Children at play are growing an ability to be happy. Ian D. Suttie, in *Origins of Love and Hate*, wrote, "Necessity is not the mother of invention; play is." The play of children is serious business. It consolidates group esteem, without which the human tribe would not function, self-esteem, without which the human person would crumble, and commonality, without which compassion and empathy would not exist. Locomotion almost always pleases babies: to be rocked, to be carried, to be driven gives them bliss. Adult pleasure, interestingly, is also associated with bodies moving through space, such as when dancing, skating, skiing, jogging, flying, driving, swimming.

"There seems to be a general idea that recreation is all right if one doesn't take it too seriously," wrote Karl Menninger. "My belief is that the much greater danger lies in not taking it seriously enough."

Love-starved babies don't smile back at smiling adults; this is the most readily detected symptom of their unhappiness. Dr. Spitz concluded that such babies have been unable to reach even an elementary stage of social development. Like newborns, they are narcissistic and capable of no higher pleasure than quiescence. He had serious doubts that they could ever become adults who would associate happiness with anything other than self-gratification and material possessions.

According to Erich Fromm, happiness is the result of inner productiveness, which he ranked among the great achievements. "It is not a gift of the gods," he said. People succeed at becoming happy in the same way they succeed at learning to love: by building a liking for themselves, by filling in their centers. Hollow people, who don't believe they are worth much, have nothing real to give. Though they transact what appears to be their share of a loving relationship or a friendship, they deal with counterfeit currency. Sooner or later, someone bites the coin and finds it isn't gold.

Their counterparts, the self-flatterers, live in hunger. Their own self-involvement isn't enough to fill their need for admiration, so they seek to coax, wheedle, purchase with charm and tricks all the admiration they can get. For them, there is never enough praise. The fact is, they don't really believe they are worthy of praise.

Norman M. Bradburn, social scientist at the University of Chicago, spent years studying happiness. Some two thousand people in four different American communities were asked a range of sly questions about their lives, the salient one being: "Taken together, how would you say things are these days—would you say you are very happy, pretty happy, or not too happy?"

The results appeared in *The Structure of Psychological Well-Being*, and almost duplicated a less sophisticated Gallup poll in 1952, which asked a similar question, which in turn was almost a replica of a cruder Gallup poll in 1946. In all three studies, approximately 35 percent of Americans said they were very happy; 54 percent called themselves pretty happy; only 11 percent reported themselves unhappy.

Those were impressive findings, but human pride makes the figures suspect. When a stranger asks, "How's it going?" even someone plotting suicide will reply, "Just fine."

In Dr. Bradburn's study the highest percentage of self-described unhappy people was found among unemployed black men in a Chicago ghetto. He expected that the highest percentage of happy people would be in a neighborhood that was the opposite, a prosperous, white suburb of Washington, D.C., but this group was the second-happiest. The happiest group, according to his poll, lived in a stable, all-white, working-class neighborhood in Detroit.

Weather, religion, age, gender, marital status and education weren't indicators of happiness. Studying his charts, the researcher could see only one element that happy people had in common: social mobility. The happier people were dining out, meeting new people, joining clubs, traveling on vacations.

Dr. Bradburn concluded that poverty's social stagnation—its drabness, monotony and limited options—reduced the likelihood of happiness. No one fainted with surprise. He concluded that the Romans were right to provide bread and circuses to keep the masses content.

The relationship between happiness and activity has been noted many times. Aristotle believed that happiness was another word for self-sufficiency. Benedict Spinoza put the same thought in loftier language when he wrote, "Happiness consists in this: that man can preserve his own being."

A much-quoted observation by Timothy Dwight when he was president of Yale University is: "The happiest person is the person who thinks the most interesting thoughts." William Lyon Phelps took this a step further. He said, "The principle of happiness is like the principle of virtue. It is not dependent on things, but on personality."

He added a caution that happiness could not be expected to be unbroken. "You will have days and nights of anguish, caused by ill health or worry or losses or the death of your friends, but you will not remain in the Slough of Despond, you will rise above the depression and disaster because you will have in your mind the invincible happiness that comes from thinking interesting thoughts."

One of the most respected of the early psychologists, William Mc-Dougall, had a similar observation. "The richer, the more highly developed, the more completely unified or integrated is the personality, the more capable it is of sustained happiness, in spite of intercurrent pains of all sorts."

Recent studies of women have shown that the happiest among them are those who combine the exhausting dual jobs of working in a paid job and running a household complete with husband and children. Some years ago, Harry Maas of the School of Social Work at the University of British Columbia discovered much the same when he spent seven years studying old age. He found that the happiest old women were those who had worked outside their homes or else had spent enormous quantities of time in volunteer activities. In *Human Development,* John P. Zubec, a University of Manitoba psychologist, cited a number of research projects which supported the view that happiness in old age is associated with a lifelong and persisting busy schedule.

Voltaire said, "The further I advance in age, the more I find work necessary. It becomes, in the long run, the greatest of pleasures." Nietzsche said the same thing, only backwards: "I do not want happiness; I want to do my work."

"To live is to function," cried Oliver Wendell Holmes, the nineteenth-century American author who lived to his eighties. "That's all there is to living."

Old age is viewed by most people as the decline of the body and the ebbing away of happiness but there are plenty of old people who staunchly stand that foreboding on its head. Bertrand Russell at the age of ninety claimed that he grew happier every year.

He gave his prescription for a happy life in the prologue of his autobiography. He said, "Three passions, simple but overwhelmingly strong, have governed my life: the longing for love, the search for knowledge, and unbearable pity for the suffering of mankind. . . . This has been my life. I have found it worth living, and would gladly live it again if the chance were offered me."

The poet Heinrich Heine took a more pragmatic approach. He defined happiness this way: "My wishes are a humble dwelling with a thatched roof, a good bed, good food, flowers at my windows, and some fine tall trees before my door. And if the good God wants to make me completely happy he will grant me the joy of seeing six or seven of my enemies hanging from the trees."

Joseph H. Choate, a nineteenth-century American diplomat, insisted that the happiest time of life falls between the ages of seventy and eighty. He told an audience, "I advise you all to hurry and get there as soon as you can." On his ninety-fifth birthday, the Canadian educator Sir William Mulock said serenely, "I am still at work, with my hand to the plow and my face to the future. . . . The first of May is still an enchanted day to me."

Philosophers, many of whom lived long lives, held the same view, though the reflections of some seem tinged with the bitterness of resignation. Plato thought of youth as a troubled time and old age the best "because at last a man is freed from the animal passion which has hitherto never ceased to disquiet him"—a comment that says more about Plato's youthful sexual follies than it does about old age being blessed.

Studies of the aged, a fast-increasing element in North American society, give substance to the theory that to be busy is to be happy, or vice versa. Old people with family ties, numerous friendships, pen pals, hobbies, volunteer activities and chores to do are among the happiest. One survey of a thousand people between the ages of sixty and the century mark reported that they were happiest in their middle sixties, when they felt most useful, and less happy as infirmity began to restrict them.

As a tool for *getting* happiness, though, activity is suspect. Unhappy people very often immerse themselves in compulsive work or play, or both, with little discernible improvement in their emotional state. What seems more likely is that happy people are busy as a consequence of being happy. Released from the emotional drain of anxiety, self-dislike and depression, all their natural energy can be directed to whatever fills their desk diary. Because they are lively and confident, and because they are alert to the feelings of others, they are more likely to be in demand. They find themselves involved in stimulating experiences, which of course enhances their own self-esteem and, yes, happiness.

Them as has, gets. Butterflies land all over them.

Two followers of Dr. Bradburn's survey, Philip Shaver and Jonathan Freedman of Columbia University's psychology department, designed a happiness survey of their own which was printed in the October 1975 issue of *Psychology Today*. Under the heading "What Makes You Happy?" were 123 multiple-choice questions which readers were invited to answer.

The response all but lamed the computer: fifty-two thousand subscribers replied. One of them wanted to know, as soon as possible, if his score indicated he was happy.

Admittedly *Psychology Today* readers are not exactly a cross section of the population. They tend to be educated well above the American norm; they are upper middle class in income level, relatively successful in their careers and familiar with the jargon of psychologists. The sampling of this group, however, was taken to have application for others. The respondents with the highest incomes were shown to be significantly happier than those with the lowest incomes. Working women are happier than housewives; single women are happier than single men; married men are happier than single men. However, gay men and lesbians are as happy as heterosexuals, and atheists are as happy as the devout.

As Jerome Kagan of Harvard was later to insist, happy people don't necessarily come from happy childhoods. Plenty of them were unhappy as children.

The findings leave the familiar questions about cause and effect. Are single men unhappy because they are single, or is it the case that unhappy men are more likely to be single? Are women happier because they work, or is it that women with a capacity for self-realization will gravitate to paid employment?

The survey was full of disquieting contradictions. For instance, seven out of ten respondents reported they had been happy over the previous six months, but eight out of ten said they thought about happiness a lot, on a weekly or even daily basis, which doesn't suggest that they were having a wonderful time. Forty percent of the respondents reported they often felt lonely, one-third experienced "constant worry and anxiety," 13 percent of the men and 32 percent of the women had frequent headaches, which doctors often associate with tension, and 18 percent of the men and 30 percent of the women reported that they sometimes felt so low they thought they couldn't go on.

Happiness should be made of sterner stuff.

Happiness is distinct from pleasure, a transitory state, or joy, a euphoric state which can come from alcohol or drugs, or ecstasy, which people often experience as tumescence and release. In her book *Ecstasy*, Marghanita Laski reported on a survey of sixty-three people who were asked if they had ever known ecstasy, and if so in what circumstances. Sixty reported affirmatively. For them ecstasy was triggered by a variety of vistas and events: natural scenery or objects; sexual love; childbirth; exercise movement; religion; art; scientific or exact knowledge; poetry; creative work; recollection; introspection; "beauty"; music.

Ecstasy, they reported, gave them a sense of unity, timelessness, release, salvation, heaven, ideal place, glory, perfection, a new life.

Such findings reinforce the popular notion that happiness is something that people can hunt down. For most, it is whatever they don't have. For a person in a wheelchair, it is mobility; for teenagers it is the absence of acne; for the poor it is a better address; for the childless, a baby; for parents of newborn twins, a night's sleep.

George Bernard Shaw wrote, "The man with a toothache thinks everyone happy whose teeth are sound."

The unhappy become drunk in order to dull their desolation—"temporary suicide," Bertrand Russell called it, "making life bearable by being less alive." The unhappy seek sexual novelty because it promises the temporary suspension of dark thought. The sadistic and unhappy strive to dominate others because superiority makes them feel safer; masochistic and unhappy people cling to others because dependency makes them feel safer. Fearful people, greedy people, envious people think happiness is wealth or fame.

Unhappy people rarely blame themselves for their condition. Their jobs are at fault, or their appearance, or their families, or the spiteful fates. The real cause is not persecution or a life that is being lived wrongly but a life that isn't being lived at all. Miserable, angry, apathetic or confused, the unhappy have no warmth. They wait for the arrival of the Fairy Godmother to grant the wish: *happiness!*

"The typical unhappy man," said Bertrand Russell, who was desperately unhappy as a child, "is one who, having been deprived in his youth of some normal satisfaction more than any other, has given to his life a one-sided direction with a quite undue emphasis on the achievement, as opposed to the activity associated with it."

The world over, faces in a crowd are rarely happy. Travelers, shoppers, idlers pass one another looking distracted or listless, buttoned to the eyes in spiny Keep-Off overcoats. In social groups and at work, men and women tend to smile almost constantly. They laugh a good deal, their mirth concealing the progress of their ulcers and the decision to break up the marriage.

Most people have had a small stretch of happiness, or what appears in the glow of nostalgia to have been a perfect time. Factors which came together—a romance, glorious weather, physical well-being, the cry of a loon in the evenings—don't seem capable of replicating themselves. The poignancy of such enhanced days, weeks, an hour, makes people wistful. To have known happiness briefly sometimes seems worse than never knowing it at all.

Others know how to make themselves a patch of happiness. Old women bake pies; some sit by the sea; some tend the garden; some tidy a closet; some practice the flute. There are also what Erich Fromm called the lower pleasures of satisfying a physical need, such as eating, sleeping, elimination, sex and exercise. The higher pleasures, he explained, were those derived from usefulness, self-possession and the growth of insight.

Charles Darwin found happiness, he said, in domestic affection and the study of nature. Oliver Wendell Holmes delighted in contact with well-stored minds. Socrates and Thomas Jefferson believed that happiness comes from intellect. So did Benjamin Franklin, who said, "What is without us has no connection with happiness. Happiness springs immediately from the mind." Francis of Assisi, on the other hand, thought happiness was the absence of comfort.

Laughter is a different entity than happiness and normally exists without it. Behavioral scientists believe that laughter was evolved for the release of tension and therefore can accompany any emotion, including anger. While people laugh easily when they are comfortable and tend to chuckle when they are feeling good, they also titter when they are nervous. Bigots, full of rage and hate, laugh uproariously at racist jokes. Losers laugh to show that they are good sports. When people say something boastful, they laugh to indicate they didn't really mean it. Sad people are attracted to the ridiculous and there is a line of jokes, called black humor, practiced by people on death row, in foxholes and in ghettos.

Depression often wears a merry mask. Abraham Lincoln, who suffered from long bouts of deep melancholia but was a humorous man, explained, "If I did not laugh, I should die." Voltaire, the happiest of all philosophers, said that he laughed in order to avoid madness.

George Orwell thought that dirty jokes were "a sort of mental rebellion." All jokes, he said, center on qualities society cannot afford to encourage and so must relish vicariously in humor.

Sigmund Freud maintained that humor conceals repressed hatred. He cited as an example Will Rogers, who used to declare he never met a man he didn't like but whose humor was lethal. People lacking the outlet of humor appear grim and rigid. Humor is so effective in siphoning off malice that the playwright Eugene Ionesco wrote, "Where there is no humor, concentration camps arise, and where there is no laughter, we see anger and hate."

Stephen Leacock, Canada's most celebrated humorist, suggested that laughter served another function. He believed that it must have begun as a primitive shout of triumph over an adversary and has become only marginally humane. Society laughs hardest at the misfortunes of others, he pointed out. All sight gags rely for their reception on the pleasure people take in feeling superior to those who seem clumsy, incompetent and dull-witted.

The first laughter of a baby is at what psychologists call "expected surprise," such as when they drop a rattle and laugh when it hits the floor. The same form of joke, Robert S. Woodworth of Columbia University noted, can be found in adult humor. "We learn what to laugh at," he wrote in *Psychology*, "in the same way we learn what to fear." Writing in *Maclean's* magazine thirty years ago, Wendy Michener observed that humor wears an ideological hat. The Russian clown Popov, she wrote, is a good scout who smiles and sings under difficulties as befits a Communist society, while capitalist clowns, such as Chaplin, are sad, full of misfortunes and bewildered by society.

Writer and editor Norman Cousins believed himself cured of an incapacitating illness by laughter. Writing in the *Journal of the American Medical Association* in December 1984, Donald W. Black, an Iowa psychiatrist, agreed cautiously that there are clinical possibilities for laughter therapy. "In an era of increasing demand for 'natural healing,' laughter's potential has yet to be tapped," he said.

Happiness, curiously, is more associated with smiling than with laughter. The smiles of healthy people, wrote Geoffrey Leytham in *World*, "are not based on hostility, aggression or superiority. Their jokes are like parables, they teach as well as amuse, and rarely hurt anybody. If they poke fun at others or themselves it is not due to sadism or masochism but as a way of keeping things in their true perspective."

Tears are as poor an indicator of sadness as laughter is of happiness. People weep when they grieve, but also when they are terrified, angry beyond words, choked by hate or full of joy. When Penelope sighted her husband Ulysses after twenty years of faithful weaving, the poet wrote that "from her eyelids quick tears did start."

James Thurber observed that the perfect tribute to perfection in comedy is not immediate laughter but "a curious and instantaneous tendency of the eyes to fill."

Temple University's Frederick H. Lund believed that tears give pleasure because they release tension. When emotions are mixed and thwart one another in a tangle, weeping is particularly useful for draining away confusion and giving the brain room to think. The weeping at graduations and weddings is a good example; the emotion people feel at such rites of passage is too complex for analysis—the solution is to cry.

The calm of truly happy people does not often require nervous outlets such as laughing or crying (Lord Chesterton, in any case, thought both bad form for the gentry). Goethe, a craftsman at the art of happiness, explained that happiness is not transitory joy but a longevity of secret power.

Walter Lippmann wrote in 1929 in *A Preface to Morals* that happiness was inner harmony.

"In the womb and for a few years of his childhood," he said, "happiness was the gratification of the person's naïve desires. His family arranged the world to suit his wishes. . . . As he grows up, he can no longer hope that the world will be adjusted to his wishes, and he is compelled by a long and difficult process of learning and training to adjust his wishes to the world. If he succeeds, he is mature. If he is mature, he is once again harmonious with the nature of things. He has virtue. And he is happy."

Nothing on earth renders happiness less likely than a determined effort to get it. Historian Will Durant described how he looked for happiness in knowledge and found only disillusionment. He then sought happiness in travel and found weariness; in wealth and found discord and worry. He looked for happiness in his writing but was only fatigued.

One day he saw a woman waiting in a tiny car with a sleeping child in her arms. A man descended from a commuter train and bent over to kiss the woman and then the baby, very gently. When the family drove away Dr. Durant had a sensation of happiness that left him stunned. He said he realized in that moment of observation that "every normal function of life holds some delight."

A man once said to a morose teenager, "Didn't you see anything wonderful today? A weed in flower? Two people holding hands? A good-looking lamppost?"

A Frenchman once wrote that wise men are happy with trifles, but nothing pleases fools. The actor James Stewart said, "I'm never bored. I'm grateful for every moment, every experience."

When Admiral Richard E. Byrd believed himself to be dying on the ice of the Ross Barrier, he wrote some thoughts on the nature of happiness. "I realized how wrong my sense of values had been and how I failed to see that the simple, homely, unpretentious things of life are the most important. . . . When a man achieves a fair measure of harmony within himself and his family circle, he achieves peace. . . . At the end, only two things really matter to a man, regardless of who he is: they are the affection and understanding of his family."

The rasping Frenchman La Rochefoucauld declared, "When we cannot find contentment in ourselves, it is useless to seek it elsewhere."

Abraham Maslow was one of the first psychologists to examine the mystery of wellness. He was engrossed and rapt most of his long and distinguished career before the mystery and beauty of people making themselves whole, which he once described as "functioning easily, perfectly, at the peak of one's powers—in overdrive, so to speak."

He estimated that perhaps only 1 to 3 percent of adults attain full maturity, which he equated with permanent access to happiness. These happy few, he said, "make full use and exploitation of talents, capacities, potentialities."

They are fulfilled. They consistently do the best they are capable of doing. In *Man for Himself,* Erich Fromm spoke of the "inner productiveness" of these self-actualizers.

A woman who became a happy person at the age of thirty-six, for no reason she could ever put her finger on, was startled by what Dr. Maslow termed "peak experiences," moments of intensity when all her faculties seemed sharpened. Blades of grass stood out distinctly from one another, trees were full of separate leaves, each one lovely, and she saw the tiny, unique objects that float in rain puddles. These moments, which came spontaneously and naturally at times when she felt especially glad to be alive, are similar to those people experience under the effect of hallucinogens.

The Maslow peak experience—which he described as "an episode, or a spurt in which the powers of the organism come together in a particularly efficient and intensely enjoyable way" in which people are more integrated, more creative, more humorous, more fully functioning, more fully themselves—is an exalting experience which appears to have come from nowhere and, in that sense, is not entirely one's own.

Leo Tolstoi recorded the same phenomenon in *Anna Karenina* when the hero, Levin, steps into the street after his love has promised to marry him. He encounters a more vivid sky than he has ever seen, faces in the streets seem full of nobility and kindness, a textured clarity to ordinary noises. The Irish-Canadian novelist Brian Moore, in *The Luck of Ginger Coffey,* described Coffey's rapture at being found innocent of a sordid crime. It took the form of an inspired sense of oneness with the world, a good world; he felt himself blend into infinity.

Norman Mailer described a boxer, beyond fatigue, no longer caring whether he won or lost, who had "lifted into flight, something in himself has come up free of the muck."

Peak experiences, Dr. Maslow wrote, can change people's view of themselves permanently. Life seems more worthwhile and they themselves seem worthier. Seneca, the Roman statesman and Stoic, urged his compatriot Lucillus to "learn how to feel joy."

The most common physical sensation associated with happiness is lightness. In 1775 a physician solemnly declared that happiness causes an actual decrease in body weight. The facts are somewhat different. Happy people feel lighter because their circulation is better. Muscles and brain have an enriched supply of blood which causes both to become supple, vital and buoyant. This improved circulation accounts for the better health, longer life and slower aging process in happy people. They have warmer color, glossier skins and more erect carriage than their contemporaries who suffer the graying of anxiety and depression. Happiness in children causes them to jump and dance; in adults it shows itself in alertness and coordination.

"Increased circulation brightens the eye," enthused Charles Darwin. "Color rises, lively ideas pass rapidly through the mind, affections are warmed." He listed other benefits: lifted head, straight back, improved digestion, smooth brow, arched eyebrows, wide-open eyes.

Physicians agree. Elizabeth Bagshaw, a notable family doctor in Hamilton, Ontario, who continued to care for her doting patients until she was past eighty, was interviewed while curling one day and told the reporter, "People who are happy usually have a better degree of health than people who worry."

A psychologist who questioned five hundred young men confirmed her view. The group he identified as most happy were also ill less often, recovered from illness more quickly, even had bones and tissues that knit more rapidly after an injury.

From such physiological evidence that humans were meant to be happy, schools of philosophical thought have flourished for thousands of years on the premise that prudent people should avoid whatever makes them uncomfortable and embrace only whatever gives them pleasure. The most visible modern proponents of therapeutic hedonism are the advertising industry and such publications as *Playboy*.

Epicurus, an abstemious Greek whose name has come to stand for indulgences he deplored, noted the misery and dissatisfaction of drunks, opportunists, misers and rakes, from which he concluded that too much pleasure is harmful. The corollary, that a small degree of anxiety, guilt, depression and anger enhances a well-ordered personality, leads to the conclusion that dottiness is the only happiness which is undiluted by pain.

As a recipe for becoming happy, Cicero advised that people count their blessings. Contemporary therapists even ask their patients to make a list of their assets, a humbling experience for whiners. Before anything in the universe can change direction, it must first stop. People need pauses in which to consolidate their gains and eyeball stale grudges.

Nietzsche cried, "Become what thou art!" And Schopenhauer put the same sentiment this way in *The Wisdom of Life:* "What one human being can be to another is not a very great deal; in the end everyone stands alone. . . . The happiness in which a man lives shapes itself chiefly by the way in which he looks at it. . . . What a man has in himself is the chief element in happiness."

A few years ago, the agony column of the London *Times* ran a question, "Do you wish to know the secret of happiness?" Everyone who replied received two verses from St. Matthew: "Ask, and it shall be given you; seek, and ye shall find; knock, and he that seeketh, findeth; and to him it shall be opened."

St. Theresa offered something else. Her advice was: All things are passing.

Happiness depends on what lies between the soles of the feet and the crown of the head, said Honoré de Balzac: "all happiness depends on courage and work."

Happiness takes practice. Most people need to start small. A seashell will do. All seashells are miracles. So are the following: babies, clouds, wind on water, legs that can walk, ears that can hear, eyes that can see, absence of pain, and, also, insects that lay their eggs next to the food supply their young will eat, the silvery double helix in the genes and the luminous velvety blue color everything becomes at twilight. Albert Einstein spoke of his "intoxicated amazement at the beauty and grandeur of this world."

André Maurois spoke of happiness "whenever we catch a fleeting glimpse of the extraordinary unity of the universe; when the motionless hills, the rustling trees, the swallows darting across the sky, and the insect crawling upon the windowpane suddenly become a part of our life . . ."

In March 1963, Mackey Brown, who described herself as a forty-five-year-old mother, wrote in *The Saturday Evening Post* that she was happy. "I wake in the morning alive with anticipation. . . . Most of my mistakes are in the irrevocable past. . . . I don't spend precious time damning myself. . . . I will never be beautiful, rich or Café Society, but I have planted forget-me-nots, nursed a baby, seen the sun rise and the stars fall, lain with my love. And now I have reached the age of self-discovery."

Human nature tends to improve itself, if left to it, as surely as flowers lift themselves to the sun. Abraham Maslow explored the

instinct for inner development which is within all and came to believe that everyone contains an indomitable essence ready to rally,
eager to win dominion over unhappiness. Given a certain hierarchic,
interdependent order which pyramids in the mind as the result of a
secure, orderly childhood, happiness takes no great effort; but it is
abundantly clear that profoundly unhappy, even disturbed children
have this same essence intact.

The basic needs to be met in the climb, Dr. Maslow said, are first
the physiological ones of hunger and thirst. Then follow safety
needs: the absence of threat. After that in ascending order come the
love and belongingness needs: for affection and a place in the group,
followed by esteem needs: to be liked, to be respected deservedly
and to respect oneself. At the top is the need for self-actualization,
"to become what one is, potentially."

Erich Fromm made a similar distinction between the "lower" pleasures of satisfying a need and the "higher" pleasures of production,
creation and the growth of insight. The first provides the pleasure of
relief from tension; the second, ecstasy and serenity. Spinoza also
believed that pleasure was a passageway by which the person could
pass to a higher stage of perfection.

"I have faith in a process," wrote Rebecca West in *Living Philosophies.*
"I find an ultimate value in the efforts of human beings to do more
than merely exist, to choose and analyze their experiences and by the
findings of that analysis to help themselves to experiences which are
of a more pleasurable kind." Her ladder of pleasure began with food
and wine, exercise and the physical act of lovemaking, and rose to
the practice of a beloved craft or art or science, a happy marriage and
"the service of valid ideas."

Another family of needs relies upon freedom. For growth, people
must have the freedom to speak, which entails the freedom to follow
their own inclinations so long as no harm is done to others, the
freedom to express themselves, the freedom to investigate and seek
information, the freedom to defend themselves, and also justice, fairness, honesty and order.

"I have always done exactly as I pleased," said the actor Katharine
Hepburn crisply, "and paid the price."

Dr. Maslow listed the historic notables who may have achieved
happiness. In the *fairly sure* category, he put Thomas Jefferson and
Lincoln, in his last years; *highly probable,* Einstein, Eleanor Roosevelt,

William James, Jane Addams, Albert Schweitzer, Aldous Huxley and Spinoza; *possibles*, Eugene V. Debs, Goethe, Pablo Casals, Martin Buber, Sholem Aleichem, Robert Browning, Renoir, Thomas More, Benjamin Franklin, Walt Whitman, Harriet Tubman.

What they all had in common, the great psychologist decided, was that they had stopped expecting perfection. He explained, "If the imperfect is defined as evil, then everything becomes evil, since everything is imperfect."

People who are happy have all their faculties in play. They relish life, quirks and all. "In a word," Dr. Maslow added, "they are capable of gratitude."

Further, he continued, "the blessedness of their blessings remains conscious. Miracles remain miracles even though occurring again and again. The awareness of undeserved good luck, of gratuitous grace, guarantees for them that life remains precious and never grows stale."

He also wrote, in the second edition of *Motivation and Personality*, that permanent happiness isn't possible. What people must strive to attain instead is the permanent ability to return to happiness after periods of stress or grief. This capacity is the distinguishing feature of self-realized, full-grown adults.

In any case, as GBS once grumbled, "A lifetime of happiness! No man alive could bear it; it would be hell on earth."

Maslow's self-realization plan paid little attention to the role of the person's environment, possibly because the great man felt it was self-evident that people who learn to live with themselves will invariably be the same people who can live with others without the need for deceit or turmoil. Humans are herd animals and need their tribe. The first smile of a baby isn't for food or a toy: it is for another human face.

Nothing is more useful to the development of personal worth than people. "And the wider the circle, the greater the gain," commented V. J. McGill, in *The Idea of Happiness*.

The element of will and determination in the process of making oneself a happier, better person was expressed by the American novelist Bernard Malamud, whose character Levin reflects, "Any act of good is a diminution of evil in the world. . . . You stopped doing what was wrong and did what was right. It is not easy, but it is a free choice you might make, and the beauty was in the making, in the rightness of it."

True happiness renders people "kind and sensible," wrote Montesquieu, the eighteenth-century French jurist and philosopher.

If people were happier, they would be kinder. If they were kinder, more people would be happy. If more people were happy, the world would be kinder. If the world was kinder, it might survive.

MATURING

No RESEARCHER can weave through the thicket of conflicting opinion, opposing theories and studies which come to diametrically different conclusions on the nature of human emotions without picking a team to support to the exclusion of all others. The selection is supposed to be based on scientific evidence and detached analysis, but instead owes more to the researcher's own foibles, prejudices and background than it does to laboratory reports.

This book has followed the yellow brick road of the humanists and the yea-sayers. The other path is trod by Freud and similar believers in the doctrine of original sin and in the intrinsic evil of human nature. But how can a newborn baby be bad? Babies are pure goodness.

People, even scientists, are pulled and repelled through a firmament of twinkling stars, searching for the home galaxy. Only occasionally does the texture of spatial debate show clear. A current controversy, for instance, rages over Harvard psychologist Jerome Kagan's conclusions, as expressed pungently in *The Nature of the Child,* that early childhood experiences are not life-determining. Since it has taken psychologists and other behavioral scientists almost fifty years to try to get across the idea that babies need, as Anna Freud put it, "affection, stimulation and continuity" in order to grow into sound adults, Dr. Kagan's dismissal of the importance of early environment has outraged his colleagues.

In addressing the old nature versus nurture debate, Dr. Kagan swung away from nurture as a determinant of personality and appeared to have landed solidly back on nature, which has been used for thousands of years to justify bigotry. In his eagerness to salute the strength and courage of adults who outgrow despair, Dr. Kagan came perilously close to suggesting that all can recover from disastrous childhoods. If human destiny was entirely decided by the genes, wolves could be nannies.

Reviewing Dr. Kagan's book in the New York *Times Book Review* of November 18, 1984, *Times* science writer Daniel Goleman agreed that the psychologist had proven his point that "the misfortunes of childhood do not doom adulthood," but he was concerned that Dr. Kagan had skipped merrily by the fact that a troubled childhood is not likely to produce an untroubled adult.

Backtracking in subsequent interviews, Dr. Kagan kept explaining that he didn't mean that a loving childhood was no better than a neglected one. He was attempting to redress the balance which of late has swung so heavily on the side of nurture that parents of children who are constitutionally hyperactive take the blame for broken windows; parents of autistic children feel guilty; parents of children who steal go to a psychiatrist.

It is his view, supported by clinical observation every minute of every day, that children are more resilient than anyone believed a few years ago. He and others who work with disturbed children for long periods have seen marvels of regeneration. Children *do* bounce back from desolating experiences. In retrospective study of the backgrounds of violent or depressed or highly anxious people, it is almost always found that they were the products of certain kinds of harsh or neglectful treatment when they were babies. In recent years, however, a body of research has been growing out of follow-up studies of children raised by battering or indifferent parents, with the dramatic observation that a good many of them grow to become functioning, stable adults, despite the ominous predictions.

Dr. Kagan's concept of the basic needs of a child does not differ greatly from Anna Freud's classic formulation. He lists "food, protection from physical harm, and regular affectionate play with adults and other children." Unlike that of his colleague and tennis partner, Dr. Burton White, who in *The First Three Years of Life* strongly advised three years of continuous one-to-one bonding between child and care giver as essential for the child's development, Dr. Kagan's perspective supports nursery schools. Agreeing with Dr. Kagan, Quentin Rae-Grant, chief of psychiatry at Toronto's famous Hospital for Sick Children, observed in a newspaper interview about the controversy, "Newborns are not just an empty blackboard. They have a great influence on how their parents react. The truly fortunate babies are the ones who make the right choice of parents."

For a long time scientists have been skeptical of all prediction models for human behavior. Infallible people come apart under what seems a minor distress and people who seemed destined for society's garbage heaps veer off and become stable. Harvard's Gordon W. Allport concluded years ago that a dismal childhood was not necessarily a life sentence to maladjustment. A child well fortified by interested, fond parents does not hold the only ticket to maturity.

The good news is that adults can regrow themselves. By acts of will and wisdom, people can rearrange their own stars and attain emotional maturity. An element of luck is often present: at a time when the person was most receptive or most desperate, or both together, someone said or did the right thing; or, out of nowhere, a teacher, therapist, relative or stranger offered support.

"Man has the capacity, as well as the desire, to develop his potentialities and become a decent human being," Karen Horney has written. "Man can change and go on changing as long as he lives."

It's a process no one can explain. People who mature themselves "have so much to teach us that sometimes they seem almost like a different breed of human beings," commented Abraham Maslow admiringly.

Emotional maturity has been called the "master concept of our time" and the most important psychiatry has to make. In his book *Emotional Maturity,* University of Pennsylvania psychiatrist Leon J. Saul commented that therapists have paid little attention to "everyday people." It has been a revelation to the profession that people whose childhoods were as stressful as that of emotionally disturbed people nevertheless function well. Dr. Saul wrote that there is "a tragic amount of emotional tension and disturbance in almost everyone." As evidence, he cites statistics from the U.S. Selective Service of World War II, which screened out one and a half million Americans as too neurotic to be accepted into the armed forces.

He listed some definitions of maturity: the ability to keep functioning even in the face of great frustration; a capacity for responsibility and productivity and decreased receptor needs; relative freedom from inferiority feelings, egoism and competitiveness; standards and ideals which operate unconsciously and automatically in harmony with conscience; integrated sexuality; aggressiveness, anger, hate and belligerence appropriate to the situation; parental and creative; firm sense of reality—not just intellectually but also the emotional outlook; flexible and adaptable.

Maturity is a cottage industry. People must make their own.

For those who worry excessively, or whose visions of revenge trouble sleep, or who feel heavy with depression, the recent analysis of brain function which compares it to a computer holds much hope. Data in, data out. The human mind is circuitry and emotion is a software program. The apparatus has practiced negative feelings until it is perfect; it can deliver resentment, for instance, without notice. However, the brain will accept a new program. It is educable. There is no reason why it can't learn a new trick: for instance, self-esteem.

For the first fifty years of this century, the scientific view of human nature was constricted by Sigmund Freud's belief that people could not alter the character formed in their childhoods. He accepted that later events might modify behavior and the outer personality could change, but he maintained that the core of dark emotions which he thought inherent in all beings could not be reshaped.

Some years ago, when researchers were moved to study healthy flourishing adults instead of the neurotics and psychotics who came into treatment, they discovered that among these mature and productive people were some whose childhoods were just as terrible as or worse than those of disturbed patients.

Indeed, many of them had suffered emotional breakdowns of considerable duration. An experience on bottomland can unearth resources. Albert Camus reflected, "In order to become aware of our eternity, we need to be forced into our last bastion." Depression and guilt seem particularly well suited as scaffolding on which to construct an improved model. Melancholy may be one of the transient stages of maturity. Geoffrey Leytham wrote that people progress by means of a depression when they "become aware of the futility of chasing material possessions but as yet have no substitute outlook on life, living in a philosophical vacuum which is accompanied by feelings of worthlessness and depression . . . a form of divine discontent, a preparation for living, a hunger for something better."

The study of what seems to be limitless possibilities for emotional growth is still new and tortuous, though Carl Jung noted half a century ago that "man is the most educable form of life in the universe." Dr. Maslow, who pioneered research on emotional maturity, said, "It has involved for me the continuous destruction of cherished axioms, the perpetual coping with seeming paradoxes, contradictions and vagueness, and the occasional collapse around my ears of long established, firmly believed in and seemingly unassailable laws of psychology."

His investigation of mature people began somewhat timidly in 1940. What he discovered was so at variance with his training that he didn't begin to publish until ten years later. What exasperated him most was that he could find little consistency. Moreover, his stable adults fluctuated without concern for his doctoral need to put a pin through the specimens and fasten them to the wall. In time he came to realize that human development proceeds irregularly. As Dr. Saul put it, many elements tug the person forward while others pull the person back. The picture is one of disorder and constant change, since everyone contains "dependent and regressive tendencies" which assert themselves unexpectedly, but most commonly when the person becomes childlike because of fatigue or hunger or some other deprivation.

Adults who are most mature will be less vulnerable to such regression. "At high levels of human maturation," said Dr. Maslow, "many dichotomies, polarities and conflicts are fused and resolved. Self-actualizing people are simultaneously selfish and unselfish, rational and irrational. They tolerate their own inconsistencies and contradictions and see a kind of wisdom in conflicts."

The commonality he found in mature people was moderation and independence. They were unemotional but not lacking emotion. Comfortable, sensible, humorous, unpretentious, they seemed, well, ordinary—except for the fact that they were freestanding. Their moral standards, for example, were set by themselves and not by society; the dominant theme was respect for life. Bernard Malamud described this morality as "love of life, anybody's life." He went on, "Morality was a way of giving value to other lives through asserting human rights. As you valued men's lives, yours received value. You earned what you sold, you got what you gave."

Among the other characteristics of mature people described by Abraham Maslow were: superior perception of reality, increased acceptance of self, of others and of nature, increased spontaneity, increase in problem-centering, increased detachment and desire for privacy, increased autonomy, greater freshness of appreciation and richness of emotional reaction, increased identification with the human species, more democratic character structure, greatly increased creativeness, improved interpersonal relations, improvements in the value system.

Dr. Maslow found no one mature by his reckoning who was not older than thirty-five. The explanation most often offered is that people in their teens and twenties are too distracted by their eventful, exploratory lives to take time for reflection and insight. Emotional maturity can occur earlier but such prodigies are usually young people who were removed from the hubbub by injury, illness or even prison.

People in their twenties have a tendency when they encounter an obstacle to slip back into the emotional state of childhood. They wear a multitude of personalities, unsure which one fits best. They bridle at criticism, demand love and loyalty while being imperfect at giving either and alternate between being disgusted at themselves and believing themselves to be quite wonderful.

This stage of emotional development shows most clearly how unevenly growth proceeds, overlapping and interacting with the stage behind and the level-to-be. "No phase is ever entirely given up," wrote Ruth L. Munroe in *Schools of Psychoanalytic Thought.* Sigmund Freud believed various systems of behavior exist simultaneously in every individual, who juggles them according to internal and external demands. The most prominent system becomes the personality and gains strength with use, while the weaker systems await their turn. He used the metaphor of an army which leaves garrisons behind as it advances, both to forward supplies to the front lines and to afford a refuge in case of retreat.

During their thirties, people begin a critical examination of their ruling system. They want it to be compatible with their heartbeat. Instinctively, they follow the Jungian maxim "Go with yourself, not against the grain."

They ask more questions of themselves: Why are you doing this? What was behind that nasty remark? They seek better answers. They are in another great emotional growth spurt: the first was when they were babies and toddlers; the next came just before puberty. Since then, everything has been confusion, broken by brief periods of consolidation.

There is a significant parallel: most of the greatest achievements of the human race were produced by people in their thirties. Harvey C. Lehman, who studied the lives of people of world prominence, found that people of genius made their major contributions between the ages of thirty and forty.

The thirties are the years when the creative fires burn at their brightest. People are ready to become their own projects. They are far enough from their childhoods to have finished the task of separation from parents that began when they were three. Their experiences have given them confidence in their survival skills. They know something of love; they are learning that unconditional love—love for its own sake, love that doesn't seek the attachments of dependence or domination—is not unsafe. They see the world as it really is, and not as it must be to preserve their sanity.

Many people skip the chore of self-assessment until later. The cultural anthropologist Ashley Montagu, in *Growing Young*, made an argument for old age, which he described as a time to get a second wind and enjoy a sense of youthfulness and beatific happiness. Since development is an unending state, humans at any age are unfinished. Only death marks the cessation of change. At any age, people are still working on growing themselves.

Emotional growth is a natural, inescapable force in much the same way as physical growth is. At a time when the organism is ready, it wants to improve. When babies wriggle out of their parents' arms, they are embarking boldly on a lifelong quest to be an independent being.

It is a human's early declaration of individuality, the first assertion that the person is unique and special and brave. That insistence on sovereignty not only propels the well-loved toddler toward self-reliance but also protects the less-loved toddler. Except for the most damaged and vulnerable few, most babies manage to keep a spark of faith in themselves and in a better fate. They wait, watchfully, for someone to come into their lives and confirm their own hunch that they are all right.

Some suspect that the quality of this spunkiness is acquired through the genes. Certainly some babies have it in abundance, apparently from birth, probably from conception, while others have little defense against the vagaries of their parenting. Along the family lineage there must have been warrior men and women who conquered their environments with the same steadfast belief in themselves.

Spinoza called this quality *cognatus,* which he defined as the tendency of people to persist, though the furies howl, in marching to their own drum. He believed that people are led in life "principally by the desire of honor." Whatever it is called, it is the sacred ingredient, the God-gift. It can't control destiny but it can determine whether the person will have a life worth living. It appears to be a compound of courage, resolution and attunement to self. Everyone has a measure of it; some people never tap their supply at all.

Paul Tillich termed the ability to see grandeur in all life a worship of "the God above God." The distinguished Roman Catholic intellectual M. C. D'Arcy wrote that "there is a last mysterious layer in the self that can never really be touched, an ultimate self." Abraham Maslow believed that at the core of everyone was "good behavior"—love, courage, creativeness, kindness, altruism—which is deeper and more natural than the "bad behavior" of hostility, fear and greed.

"Wonders are many," Socrates said, "and none is more wonderful than man."

Existence is the struggle between fear of going on and fear of going back, between the person's life-loving force and the death-pull of giving in to discouragements, rejections, fears, afflictions and frustrations. Many simply put in the years, like convicts doing time, and wait passively for parole. They want their unhappiness to disappear by magic. They dream of the dramatic moment when they will have an opportunity to shine, unaware that their war is one of small battles. Victories are achieved, almost casually, in acts of forgiveness, in small generosities, in invisible shifts of insight, in holding open a door for a stranger.

The scrappers buckle down and mature themselves. No one's method is much use to anyone else, though it is a common error to suppose that it is. Every human is unique and unrepeatable but there are some blazes on the trees to indicate the general direction.

One guide is to define the goal as a loving and useful self. Carl Jung described personality as a fluid state. It is not what a person is at the moment; that's transitory. Instead it is what the person is planning to become. Socrates said, "All he needs is the will to work out the truth and the courage to take the plunge. The important thing is to keep moving in the right."

A Canadian journalist, Eric Miller, over the space of a year or so seemed a man transformed. He had been, by his own report, opinionated, rude, impatient, quick-tempered and, on some occasions, obsequious—qualities he no longer possessed in marked degree. He explained, "Being nice is nicer than not being nice. It gets easier, I'm getting better at it. I tell myself every morning to watch myself. There's plenty of backsliding but I try again the next day. I just refuse to react the way I used to."

He considered: "It's pretty sickening, I suppose. But it works."

"By stating a belief, you can produce a belief," said Paul Mussen and Mark R. Rosenzweig, both of the University of California at Berkeley, in *Psychology: An Introduction.* Their unique research demonstrated that people respond better when the reward or threat is minor than when something significant is promised or threatened. A group of children warned not to touch a toy or the adults will remove all the toys will be inclined to touch the forbidden toy when the adults are out of sight. The same children asked not to touch a toy or the adults will be sorry will refrain from touching the toy.

Similar experiments produced the same results, suggesting that people address their behavior more sternly when mildly asked to be cooperative. The work of emotional development similarly begins, quite often, when people see a valued relationship in trouble. An easier disposition is constructed, slowly, slowly, to make life smoother.

Tenacity is essential. The early stages of self-maturing are as prone to a fall as the early stages of walking. No one notices the victories but the failures are in plain view. The process is an onion; it is Chinese boxes nesting in one another; it is Russian wooden dolls, each one containing a smaller and more vivid doll. The outer person conceals the secrets of someone else within. When this hidden person has been confronted and learned, there will be another oddity lurking underneath.

Eventually there is a sense of fragile unfolding. A belief in self emerges, trembling. What was once conceit is now pride; what was arrogance is self-confidence; what was possessive is loyalty; what was weakness is respect. The rest is consolidation.

The struggles of self-development are tedious and lonely, like getting-up exercises. People can't share invisible triumphs such as not arguing or giving up a grudge. One woman used to pretend when she was ironing that she was flattening her supervisor. When she stopped doing that, she felt pleased with herself—but who could she tell?

Emotional growth needs room. The person must have some privacy in order to reflect on behavior and wrestle with attitudes. Some friendships may be seen as destructive and should be dropped, while others are enriching and need devotion. A reordering of social engagements may be required. Small talk serves for communication in certain settings but on a regular basis it is a malnutrition diet.

Energy should go where it does the most good. If activities seem pointless and exhausting, they should be pruned. The heart of a life is a few essential relationships, recreation and good work; investment in those areas has a big payoff. Looking backward is bad for one's health if done to excess; the past is over. The brain would appreciate some delights: notice the fine clouds, hear music, see the tapestry, feel the waves, hug a baby.

Some behavior therapists believe that treating symptoms will make the disease subside: you are what you appear to be, or, rather, you will become what you appear to be, or, even, you won't really change but that won't matter if you change your behavior. Alcoholics Anonymous is an outstanding example of the latter. Its premise is not the cure of alcoholism; instead, the community uses mutual support in order to abstain from drinking.

A woman who suffered greatly from tension went to a doctor for tranquilizers. The doctor suggested that she try instead to pitch her voice lower. She sounded shrill, the doctor explained. The astonished woman took the advice. Her efforts to lower her pitch required concentration on breathing. Concentration on breathing led her to spend more time relaxed. Ability to relax allowed her to change her frantic schedule. Changing her frantic schedule resulted in a sense of spaciousness that she found even more relaxing. Relaxing . . . and so on.

An actor afflicted with ulcers embarked on a program of reading philosophy as a distraction. He became engrossed and could be found backstage with his head bent over Jung, Camus and Bergson. One day he realized he hadn't felt an ulcer pain for a long time. He went for an X ray and learned that his ulcer had disappeared.

The wife of an executive developed intense headaches at about the same time his job was changed, requiring him to travel a good deal.

Neurological tests could find no cause, so she sat down with herself and came to the conclusion that her headaches were her way of trying to keep her husband at home. She decided she should stop having headaches; anyway, the tactic wasn't working. Instead she went to work in a center for retarded children and never had a headache again.

A young man who hoped to be a concert pianist took a civil service job on a temporary basis in order to support his family. He turned out to be good at what he did and was steadily promoted. Each time he told himself he would stay only a year or so more, but the income was hard to resist. Eventually he was taken to the hospital vomiting blood. An ulcer had perforated his stomach. During his convalescence, he decided that the ulcer was the result of his thwarted longing to be a professional musician. Weighing the alternatives—a comfortable life against the risks of becoming a musician—he concluded ruefully that he wasn't a world-class pianist but he was a very good civil servant. He laid to rest the dream of a debut in Carnegie Hall and returned to work feeling cleansed.

Doctors have been known to instruct patients riddled by anxieties that they should stop worrying. They also tell people with a chronic cough to stop coughing, and people with leg injuries to stop limping. The principle is the same. Coughing irritates membranes and increases the need to cough; limping puts the spine out of balance; worrying is a worry in itself. People can make themselves walk normally, which hastens the return of normal gait. Similarly, a brain instructed to stop brooding and stewing over trifles has no choice but to make an effort to follow firmly meant instructions. Each person holds an on-off switch. It works imperfectly at first but eventually it may not even be needed.

It hurts to put weight on a sore knee and the effort to strangle a cough is a struggle. Not surprisingly, switching a mood of desolation or anger by determined effort is not a snap. Distraction provides only temporary relief from desolation, but temporary relief is not something to be dismissed. The long-term solution lies in hard self-analysis.

Something is wrong: too much stress (where? why?), too few people who care (so, how many are getting care?), too much mistrust (is it really justified?), too little meaning (get some meaning). "To love and be loved, to give and to receive, to work and to play and to rest —these are the bases of the emotional life," observed Leon J. Saul.

People in quest of maturity act on the evidence of their asssessment. They reorganize their attitudes and timetables. They switch emphasis. Because growth goes on so quietly its owner hasn't noticed, sometimes realization of progress comes in a flash of recognition: a click. Sometimes it takes ten years to forgive a father. Either way it is growth, and growth is a kind of divinity.

Erich Fromm called the North American obsession with popularity the "marketing orientation." It was confronted in the sixties by the flower-child movement which tackled human artifice. The new emphasis on honesty has resulted in a healthy skepticism of those who have nonstop smiles and never take offense. People are more willing to take the clock apart, examine all the queer wheels, give them a good bath and then, hopefully, put the machine together again to chime the hours.

This degree of candor takes courage and ought to be rewarded with quick results, like a crash diet, but it isn't. People are dismayed that after analyzing what causes them to be anxious or angry, they go on being anxious or angry anyway. They move forward, feeling good for weeks, and then plunge back into a depression.

One technique for feeling whole is to pretend to be intact. Anger gets submerged that way, but high blood pressure may result. Good works give the appearance of being a generous person, but the game falls apart if there is insufficient recognition. Emotions can be diverted and repressed but for lasting benefit they can only be counteracted by good feelings about oneself.

The objective is self-acceptance. People have to grow their own self-respect. Achievement, however extraordinary, can't do it alone. It is derived from the overall worthiness of the person's existence: the honesty, the integrity and love in relationships, the respect for life. The self can't be fooled with any other coin.

"It is always better to learn to bear with ourselves rather than to wage war against ourselves," said Carl Jung. "To forswear hypocrisy and to adopt an attitude of tolerance toward oneself can only have good results for the just estimation of one's neighbor, since men are all too prone to transfer to their fellow men the injustice and violence that they do their own natures.

"He who feels in a bad way with himself and wishes to improve

. . . must take counsel with himself. For unless a man changes inwardly as well, external changes in the situation are either unimportant or even harmful."

Abraham Maslow added, "Every person is, in part, his own project and makes himself."

North Americans have not shown a conspicuous talent for making themselves emotionally mature. In the 1980s, statistics indicate, one in every five adults has an emotional disorder severe enough to disturb normal living. The range of pain extends from violent behavior to attacks of panic in a crowd. Rates of emotional disability were found in a National Institute of Mental Health survey to be the same for women as for men, though it was believed for many years that women were more vulnerable to emotional breakdown than were men.

People who realize themselves, succeeding against the odds, piercing through their phoniness, excuses and illusions to the viable, creditable being inside, enjoy a sense of peace and unity. They are open to experience and finished with pointless hatred. They are, moreover, enthusiasts. "Above all, gentlemen," cried Talleyrand, "no *enthusiasm!*" Bernard Levin, the *Times* of London columnist, deplored the contained personality so much admired today and modern society's fear of feelings.

He wrote chidingly, "Societies like ours, undereducated and over-intellectualized, fear feeling as a Marxist fears freedom: because it undermines the structures we have devised and built to sustain the arbitrary and artificial nature of our world view."

People who haven't begun to grapple with their inner turmoil shrink from their feelings for less than global reasons. They are quite certain that if they opened themselves even a tiny crack, a fool might escape into view. By holding tight to what appears to be composure, their guilty secrets are safe. As they mature, however, they make the gratifying discovery that nothing inside is seriously amok after all.

They can be exuberant; they can be flexible, trusting that whatever follows will not be an irreconcilable disaster. Said Confucius in his old age, "I could follow what my heart desired, without transgressing what was right." They are social beings but pleased with solitude. Most important, they are assured of their sexual identity. They don't keep score. Copulation is egalitarian.

The feminist ideal of collaborative mating and democratic families fits mature women easily—it is upward mobility—but for men it is more difficult to give up habits of control. The principles of feminism offer androgynous development to both sexes. Mature women are not afraid of their anger or ambition and no longer feel compelled to be actresses; mature men can enjoy intimacy and don't deny their needs and capacities for tenderness and nurturing.

The new science of sociobiology, which examines how evolutionary pressures influence behavior, has been producing evidence that females have the same predisposition as males to assertiveness and competitiveness.

Carl Jung called the mastering trend of men *animus* and the nurturing, receptive trend of women *anima* and believed that both sexes were "in a way" bisexual. A male cannot successfully deny his *anima*, he wrote, or a woman her *animus*—"each must accept these attributes coherently for balance."

At the present stage of cultural male-female dichotomy, it is adolescent men and women who are most unlike one another. In old age, men and women become more alike.

"Emotional states," wrote Jerome Kagan in *The Nature of the Child*, "can be altered through information." One piece of information for both sexes to consider is that there are few real differences, beyond physiology, between men and women. The intuitive, sympathetic skills of women are acquired in a world where women still must negotiate and placate; the power and achievements of men are supported by cultural expectations.

One of the major research projects on sexual differences is the study of hundreds of children in Los Angeles being conducted by Carol Jacklin, director of the Program for the Study of Men and Women in Society at the University of Southern California, and Eleanor Maccoby. They report that the only difference which has withstood careful scrutiny is that girls are verbally brighter than boys and boys are more aggressive than girls. Even this may be culturally determined because other studies have shown that women talk more to their infant daughters than they do to their sons, and that sons are more encouraged to be active than are daughters.

(On the other hand, this is uncertain ground. Infant girls may vocalize more than little boys, which would provoke mothers to respond in kind; and infant boys don't seem to sleep as soundly and as long as infant girls, a possible indicator of a more restless nature.)

The first self-awareness of an adult is always unnerving. No one's insides are made of rose petals. In *World* magazine, Geoffrey Leytham wrote, "Few people are mentally sick and few people mentally well. The majority are just not hungry, their appetite for life has become dulled. It is as if the delights of childhood had been swamped by the cares of the adult. In the mature person, on the other hand, the wonderment and excitement of the child are combined with the experience and wisdom of an adult. The healthy person is a craftsman in the art of living."

Such craft in the art of living requires the elimination of excuses for bad conduct. People whose parents didn't love them certainly suffered a wrong, but to lament over it thirty years afterward is a death choice. A number of successful therapy programs now scrap the past and order patients to be accountable *this minute*. One such, widely imitated in adolescent treatment centers everywhere in North America, was a detention school in California where the psychiatrist was William Glasser. He declared, "The more delinquent children are convinced by traditional therapy that they are disturbed and have good reason to be so, the worse they will act in and out of custody."

He took no family history and was not interested in the stories of abuse which are the common currency of delinquents' lives. Instead he informed each new resident that he was not in custody because of emotional problems but only because he broke the law.

"We never excuse any action, past or present, directly or indirectly, by asking why or seeking the answer in the unconscious," explained Dr. Glasser. "No matter how severe the personality disorder, we maintain that removed from the atmosphere where excuses are accepted, the boy has adequate standards. We may admit he was mistreated, but we emphasize that he can't excuse his behavior because someone has rejected him."

An application of this is seen in the case of a woman whose behavior had deteriorated to a state of constant agitation, tears and temper tantrums. On her doctor's suggestion, she went for two weeks to a resort where no one knew her. During the vacation, she was a calm, social person who joined readily in beachside chats with other guests. As the period drew to a close, she realized that within the woman whose conduct was out of control was also a sane, well woman who could solve her problems in some other way than being sick.

Inside most people suffering from distorted emotions is a balanced personality which has been temporarily overwhelmed. Catherine Camp, senior social worker at the Toronto Psychiatric Hospital in the 1960s, told a conference in a report on reality therapy, "We take the approach that each person has the ability within himself or herself to handle things."

Erich Fromm addressed a packed meeting in a Toronto synagogue in 1963 at the height of his popularity as a humanist therapist. He was asked plaintively from the floor for a "practical solution" to the problems of living. He replied instantly, "Meditation for a half hour every day. Twice a day if possible." The audience groaned in disappointment. "I'm serious," Dr. Fromm insisted. "You have to stop in order to be able to change direction. Quietness, the experience of stillness, is an important requirement for mental health. Stop the rush and you will stop being a stranger to yourself."

No one admires solutions that take months, maybe years, to work, but most authorities agree that emotional development takes concentrated consideration. Harried, frazzled, tired people can scarcely hold their own emotionally; in a crisis, they are almost certain to regress into the coping systems that they used in childhood. The hard work of assessing a lifetime's debris of emotional memoirs, half-healed wounds and disfiguring scars needs some solitude and a rested, open mind. A matter as important as letting go of the need for parental approval can't be resolved by the drift of thought that streams beneath office work and waiting for a bus.

"The first distinguishing characteristic of thinking is facing the facts—inquiry, minute and extensive scrutinizing, observation," wrote John Dewey, nineteenth-century American philosopher-educator. Spinoza agreed. "The more an emotion becomes known to us, the more it is within our power and the less the mind is passive to it," he wrote.

Some emotions have to be challenged, pruned and diverted to where they will do no harm. Among these are anxiety, anger and fear. Others are so good for the person that they can be encouraged luxuriantly: affection and interest.

Intellect is of little help in emotional growth. "No emotion can be checked," warned Spinoza, "save by another emotion stronger than and contrary to the emotion to be checked." Intelligence can be a kind of straitjacket, in the same way that overdeveloped muscles can bind movement. The mind knows its own truth and welcomes its discovery. When people mature it is because they can. Unconsciously, they have been gathering the twigs and down for their own nests all their lives. A response someone made, an observed kindness, a bit of insight that came from nowhere, a casual shaft of comment, an experience or two of feeling good, all come together in an inexplicable way to create well-being. As Daniel Goleman explained in *Vital Lies, Simple Truths,* most emotional and mental activity goes on without people being aware of it. The material simply remains submerged until the person is able to make use of it.

The shading from dark to light is so gradual that most people aren't aware until long after they started feeling better about themselves that they no longer gnaw their fingernails. Sometimes a single event gives insight. For a man distracted by dislike of his job, it was the moment he looked up from reports he was angrily reading to see sympathy on the face of his four-year-old daughter.

The turning point can also be a decision taken: a letter or call to someone estranged, ending a relationship that has sapped confidence, moving on.

Mature people have given up the need to be perfect. They measure what they do against what they can do, rather than against a standard out of reach of any mortal person. They accept their mistakes, repairing everything that isn't irreparable. They don't believe any longer that there is nothing they can't fix.

"The greatest and most important problems of life are all fundamentally insoluble," wrote Carl Jung. "They can never be solved, but only outgrown."

Mature people are not spectacular to know. They follow all sensible rules, observe laws that do not conflict with honor, are untouched by fads and fevers, hold no radical beliefs. They are calm and affable, easy to like and trust; they appreciate. And occasionally they solve a problem by behaving like a full-fledged neurotic.

"Let not a man trust his victory over his nature too far," warned Francis Bacon, "for nature will lie buried a great time, and yet revive upon the occasion or temptation. Like as it was with Aesop's damsel, turned from a cat to a woman, who sat very demurely at the board's end, till a mouse ran before her."

Abraham Maslow created a fable in 1948 to illustrate the degrees of psychological health through which people pass to maturity. He imagined a dangerous jungle in which A manages to stay alive, but barely, by finding occasional food and water. B does not have such a difficult time, possessing a rifle and a cave with a closable entrance. C has all of these and two companions as well. D has the food, the gun, the safe cave, the allies and, in addition, the person D most loves. E, in the same jungle, has everything that D possesses but in addition is the well-respected leader of the group.

"For the sake of brevity," wrote Dr. Maslow, "we will call these men, respectively, the merely surviving, the safe, the belonging, the loved and the respected." Among the last are found the self-realized, the mature, the good.

SELECTED BIBLIOGRAPHY

Alexander, Franz and Francesca. *What Are You Afraid Of?* Chicago: Science and Research Associates, 1954.

Allport, Gordon W. *Becoming.* New Haven, Conn.: Yale University Press, 1955.

_____. *Pattern and Growth in Personality.* New York: Holt, Rinehart and Winston, 1961.

_____. *Personality and Social Encounter.* Boston: Beacon Press, 1960.

_____. *The Nature of Prejudice.* Reading, Mass.: Addison-Wesley, 1979.

Anderson, John E. Mooseheart Symposium on Feelings and Emotions, 1950.

Anthony, E. J. and Benedek, Therese, eds. *Depression and Human Existence.* Boston: Little, Brown, 1975.

Arcy, Martin C. d' *The Mind and Heart of Love, Lion and Unicorn: A Study in Eros and Agape.* New York: Meridian Books, 1956.

Ardrey, Robert. *The Territorial Imperative.* New York: Atheneum, 1966. With drawings by Berdine Ardrey.

Arendt, Hannah. *On Violence.* New York: Harcourt, Brace, Jovanovich, 1970.

Arnold, Magda Blondian. *Emotions and Personality.* New York: Columbia University Press, 1960.

Atkinson, John W. Nebraska Symposium on Motivation, 1954.

Balchin, Nigel. *Anatomy of Villainy.* London: Collins, 1950.

Beach, Frank A. Nebraska Symposium on Motivation, 1956.

Beauvoir, Simone de. *The Second Sex.* Translated and edited by H. M. Parshley. New York: Alfred A. Knopf, 1953.

Benedict, Ruth. *Patterns of Culture.* Boston: Houghton Mifflin, 1961. With preface by Margaret Mead.

Berrill, N. J. *Man's Emerging Mind.* New York: Dodd, Mead, 1955.

Blos, Peter. *The Adolescent Passage.* New York: International Universities Press, 1974.

Bolles, Robert C. Nebraska Symposium on Motivation, 1957.

Bowlby, John. *Child Care and the Growth of Love.* London: Penguin Books, 1965.

Bradburn, Norman M. *Structure of Psychological Well-Being.* NORC Monographs in Social Research Series, No. 15. NORC, 1969.

Brown, Judson S. Nebraska Symposium on Motivation, 1953.

Bruner, Jerome. *In Search of Mind.* New York: Harper and Row, 1983.

Candland, Douglas K. *Emotion: Bodily Change.* New York: Van Nostrand, 1962.

Cannon, Walter B. *The Wisdom of the Body.* New York: W. W. Norton, 1963.

Chesler, Phyllis. *Women and Madness.* Garden City, N.Y.: Doubleday, 1972.

Coleman, James C. *Contemporary Psychology and Effective Behavior.* Glenview, Ill.: Scott, Foresman, 1979.

Darwin, Charles. *The Expression of Emotions in Man and Animals.* Westport, Conn.: Greenwood Press, 1969, 1955.

Davitz, Joel R. et al. *The Communication of Emotional Meaning.* New York: Greenwood Press, 1976.

————. *The Language of Emotion.* New York, London: Academic Press, 1969.

Deutsch, J. A. *The Structural Basis of Behavior.* Chicago: University of Chicago Press, 1960.

Deutsch, Martin; Katz, Irwin; and Jensen, Arthur R. *Social, Class, Race and Psychological Development.* New York: Holt, Rinehart and Winston, 1968.

Dewey, John. *Human Nature and Conduct.* New York: Random House/Modern Library, 1930.

Dunbar, Helen Flanders. *Emotion and Bodily Changes.* New York: Columbia University Press, 1954.

Durant, William James. *The Story of Philosophy.* New York: Simon and Schuster, 1933.

Eccles, Sir John and Robinson, Daniel N. *The Wonder of Being Human.* New York: Free Press, 1984.

Ende, Robert N. et al. *Emotional Expression in Infancy.* Psychological Issues Monograph No. 37. New York: International Universities Press, 1976.

Farber, I. E. Nebraska Symposium on Motivation, 1954.

Farber, Leslie. *Lying, Despair, Jealousy, Envy, Sex, Suicide, Drugs and the Good Life.* New York: Basic Books, 1976.

Festinger, Leon. Nebraska Symposium on Motivation, 1954.

Fitch, Stanley K. *Insights into Human Behavior.* Boston: Holbrook Press, 1954.

Flugel, John Carl. *A Hundred Years of Psychology, 1833–1933.* With additional part *1933–1963* by Donald J. West. New York: Basic Books, 1964.

Freeman, Lucy. *The Cry for Love.* New York: Macmillan, 1969.

Freud, Sigmund. *Freud: On War, Sex and Neurosis.* Edited by Sander Katz. New York: Arts and Science Press, 1947.

Fromm, Erich. *The Art of Loving.* New York: Harper and Row, 1956.

————. *Escape from Freedom.* New York: Holt, Rinehart and Winston, 1941.

————. *Man for Himself.* New York: Holt, Rinehart and Winston, 1947.

————. *The Revolution of Hope Toward a Humanized Technology.* New York: Harper and Row, 1968.

Fulton, Robert, ed. *Death and Identity.* New York: John Wiley, 1965.

Garrett, Henry E. *Great Experiments in Psychology.* New York: Appleton-Century-Crofts, 1958.

Gilmore, John V. *The Productive Personality.* San Francisco: Albion, 1974.

Goertzel, Mildred G. and Victor. *Cradles of Eminence.* Boston: Little, Brown, 1962.

Goodenough, Florence L. *Anger in Young Children.* Westport, Conn.: Greenwood Press, 1975. University of Minnesota Institute of Child Welfare Monographs No. 9.

Greenacre, Phyllis. *Trauma, Growth and Personality.* New York: International Universities Press, 1969.

Harlow, Harry F. Nebraska Symposium on Motivation, 1953.

Heath, Douglas. *Maturity and Competence.* New York: Gardner Press, 1977. With foreword by M. Brewster Smith.

Highet, Gilbert. *Talents and Geniuses.* New York: Oxford University Press, 1957.

Hirsh, Selma G. *The Fears Men Live By.* New York: Harper and Row, 1955.

Horney, Karen. *The Neurotic Personality of Our Time.* New York: W. W. Norton, 1937.

———. *Our Inner Conflicts.* New York: W. W. Norton, 1945.

———. *Self-Analysis.* New York: W. W. Norton, 1942.

Hunt, Morton. *The Natural History of Love.* New York: Alfred A. Knopf, 1959. With dedication by Warren Chappell.

Huxley, Julian. *New Bottles for New Wine.* New York: Harper and Row, 1957.

Izard, Carroll E., with chapters coauthored by Edmund S. Bartlett and Alan G. Marshall. *Patterns of Emotions.* New York: Academic Press, 1972.

James, William. *Principles of Psychology.* New York: Dover, 1950. Reprint of 1890 edition.

Jenkins, R. L. Mooseheart Symposium on Feelings and Emotions, 1950.

Jersild, A. T. *Children's Fears.* New York: Columbia University Press, 1935. Monograph.

Jones, Howard Mumford. *The Pursuit of Happiness.* Ithaca, N.Y.: Cornell University Press, 1966.

Jung, Carl G. *The Development of Personality.* The Collected Works of C. G. Jung Vol. 17. Princeton, N.J.: Princeton University Press, 1981.

———. *Modern Man in Search of a Soul.* New York: Harcourt Brace World, 1933.

———. *The Undiscovered Self.* Boston: Little, Brown, 1958.

Kagan, Jerome. *Growth of the Child.* New York: W. W. Norton, 1979.

———. *Personality Development.* New York: Harcourt Brace Jovanovich, 1971.

Kenny, Anthony. *Action, Emotion and Will.* New York: Humanities Press, 1963.

Keyes, Ralph. *Chancing It: Why We Take Risks.* Boston: Little, Brown, 1984.

Kierkegaard, Sören. *The Concept of Dread.* Translated with introduction and notes by Walter Lowrie. Princeton, N.J.: Princeton University Press, 1957.

Klein, Melanie. *Love, Guilt and Reparation.* New York: Delacorte Press/Seymour Lawrence, 1975.

Klein, Melanie and Rivière, Joan. *Love, Hate and Reparation.* Two lectures by Melanie Klein and Joan Rivière. London: Hogarth Press and The Institute of Psycho-Analysis, 1937.

Krasner, Leonard and Ullman, Leonard P. *Behavior Influence and Personality.* New York: Holt, Rinehart and Winston, 1973.

Kurtz, Paul. *Exuberance: A Philosophy of Happiness.* Buffalo, N.Y.: Prometheus Books, 1977.

LaBarre, Weston. *The Human Animal.* Chicago: University of Chicago Press, 1954.

Larned, J. N. *A Study of Greatness in Men.* Freeport, N.Y.: Books for Libraries Press, 1972.

Laski, Marghanita. *Ecstasy.* Westport, Conn.: Greenwood Press, 1968.

Lehman, Harvey C. *Age and Achievement.* Princeton, N.J.: Princeton University Press, 1953.

Lewis, Helen B. *Freud and Modern Psychology.* New York: Plenum Press. Vol. 1, *The Emotional Basis of Mental Illness,* 1981. Vol. 2, *The Emotional Basis of Human Behavior,* 1983.

Lewis, Helen B. *Emotional Basis of Mental Illness.* New York: Plenum Press, 1981.

Liebman, Joshua L. *Peace of Mind.* New York: Simon and Schuster, 1946.

Lippmann, Walter. *A Preface to Morals.* New York: Macmillan, 1929.

Littman, Richard. Nebraska Symposium on Motivation, 1958.

Locke, John. *An Essay Concerning Human Understanding.* Edited with an introduction by John W. Yolton. New York: E. P. Dutton, 1964.

Lorenz, Konrad. *On Aggression.* Translated from the German by Marjorie K. Wilson. New York: Harcourt Brace Jovanovich, 1974.

Lund, Frederick H. *Emotions of Men.* New York: McGraw-Hill/Whittlesey House, 1930.

Maccoby, Eleanor and Jacklin, Carol. *The Psychology of Sex Differences.* Stanford, Calif.: Stanford University Press, 1974.

McClelland, David C. Nebraska Symposium on Motivation, 1955.

———. *Personality.* New York: Holt, Rinehart and Winston, 1951, 1967.

McDougall, William. *An Introduction to Social Psychology.* London: Methuen, 1908.

McGill, V. J. *The Idea of Happiness.* New York: Praeger, 1967.

Malmo, Robert B. Nebraska Symposium on Motivation, 1958.

Maslow, Abraham. *Motivation and Personality.* New York: Harper and Row, 1970.

———. Nebraska Symposium on Motivation, 1955.

———. *Toward a Psychology of Being.* Princeton, N.J.: Van Nostrand, 1968.

May, Robert. *Sex and Fantasy.* New York: W. W. Norton, 1980.

May, Rollo. *The Meaning of Anxiety.* New York: Ronald Press, 1950.

Mead, Margaret. Mooseheart Symposium on Feelings and Emotions, 1950.

Meerlo, Joost A. M. *Patterns of Panic.* Westport, Conn.: Greenwood Press, 1974.

Menninger, Karl with the collaboration of Jeanetta Lyle Menninger. *Love Against Hate.* New York: Harcourt Brace and World, 1942.

———. *Man Against Himself.* New York: Harcourt Brace World, 1938.

Menninger, William C. *Growing Up Emotionally.* Monograph. Topeka, Kans.: Menninger Institute.

———. *Self-Understanding.* Monograph. Topeka, Kans.: Menninger Institute.

Mill, John Stuart. *On Liberty.* Edited by Alburey Castell. New York: Appleton-Century-Crofts, 1947.

Montagu, Ashley. *The Concept of Race.* New York: Collier Books, 1969.

———. *Growing Young.* New York: McGraw-Hill, 1981.

———. *Human Heredity.* Cleveland: World Publishing Company, 1963.

———. *Touching.* New York: Columbia University Press, 1971.

Moran, Charles. *The Anatomy of Courage.* Boston: McMoran, Wilson, Baron, 1967.

Morris, Desmond. *The Human Zoo.* New York: McGraw-Hill, 1969.

———. *The Naked Ape.* New York: McGraw-Hill, 1967.

Mottram, V. H. *The Physical Basis of Personality.* New York and Harmondsworth, Middlesex, England: Penguin Books, 1944, 1952.

Mowrer, O. H. Nebraska Symposium on Motivation, 1953.

Munroe, Ruth. *Schools of Psychoanalytic Thought.* New York: Dryden Press, 1955.

Mussen, Paul and Rosenzweig, Mark R. *Psychology: An Introduction.* Lexington, Mass.: Heath, 1977.

Ortega y Gasset, José. *On Love: Aspects of a Single Theme.* New York: Meridian Books, 1957.

Peplau, Letitia Anne and Perlman, Daniel. *Loneliness.* New York: Wiley-Interscience, 1982.

Piers, Gerhart and Singer, M. B. *Shame and Guilt.* New York: Norton, 1971. With a foreword by Roy R. Grinken.

Pikunas, Justin. *Psychology of Human Development.* New York: McGraw-Hill, 1961.

Redl, Fritz and Wineman, David. *Children Who Hate.* New York: Free Press, 1951.

———. *Controls from Within.* Glencoe, Ill.: Free Press, 1952.

Reeves, John Wynn. *Body and Mind in Western Thought.* Harmondsworth, Middlesex: Penguin Books, 1958.

Reik, Theodor. *Of Love and Lust: On the Psychoanalysis of Romantic and Sexual Emotions.* New York: Farrar, Strauss and Giroux, 1984.

———. *Psychology of Sex Relations.* Westport, Conn.: Greenwood Press, 1973.

Richardson, Roy F. *The Psychology and Pedagogy of Anger.* Baltimore: Warwick and York, 1918.

Robbins, Caroline. *The Pursuit of Happiness.* Bicentennial Lecture Series. Washington, D.C.: American Enterprise Institute for Public Policy Research, 1974.

Ruckmick, Christian A. *Psychology of Feeling and Emotion.* New York and London, McGraw-Hill, 1936.

Russell, Bertrand. *The Conquest of Happiness.* New York: Liveright, 1958.

Ryle, Gilbert. *The Concept of Mind.* New York: Barnes and Noble, 1969.

Sailer, Randolph C. *Happiness Self-Estimates of Young Men.* Originally presented as the author's thesis, Columbia University, and published in New York by the university, 1931. Microform reprint, New York: AMS Film Service, 1972.

Saul, Leon J. *Emotional Maturity.* Philadelphia: Lippincott, 1971.

Scheidemann, Norma V. *Psychology of Exceptional Children.* Boston: Houghton Mifflin, 1931, 1937.

Schweder, Richard A. and LeVine, Robert A., eds. *Culture Theory: Essay on Mind, Self and Emotion.* Cambridge, Mass.: Cambridge University Press, 1984.

Seward, John P. Nebraska Symposium on Motivation, 1956.

Sherman, Mandel. *Basic Problems of Behavior.* New York, London: Longmans, Green, 1941.

Smith, Adam. *Powers of Mind.* New York: Random House, 1975.

Spielberger, Charles D., ed. *Anxiety: Current Trends,* 2 vols. New York: Academic Press, 1972.

Spinoza, Benedict de. *Ethics.* New York: Hafner Press/Macmillan, 1974.

Stern, Karl. *The Third Revolution.* New York: Harcourt Brace, 1954.

Suttie, Ian D. *The Origins of Love and Hate.* New York: Julian Press, 1952.

Szasz, Thomas S. *Pain and Pleasure: A Study of Bodily Feelings.* London, Tavistock, N.Y.: Basic Books, 1957.

Thoreau, Henry David. *Walden.* Garden City, N.Y.: Doubleday, 1970.

Tiger, Lionel and Fox, Robin. *The Imperial Animal.* New York: Holt, Rinehart and Winston, 1971.

Tillich, Paul. *The Courage to Be.* New Haven, Conn.: Yale University Press, 1952.

———. *Love, Power and Justice.* New York: Oxford University Press, 1954.

Tingbergen, Nikolaas. *Study of Instinct.* New York: Oxford University Press, 1969.

Tuan, Yi-Fu. *Landscapes of Fear.* New York: Pantheon Books, 1979.

Watson, John B. *Behaviorism.* New York: W. W. Norton, 1958.

White, Burton L. *The First Three Years of Life.* Englewood Cliffs, N.J.: Prentice-Hall, 1975.

Wittenborn, J. R. Nebraska Symposium on Motivation, 1957.

Woodworth, Robert S. *Psychology.* New York: Holt, Rinehart and Winston, 1962.

Wrench, David F. and Chris. *Psychology, a Social Approach.* New York: McGraw-Hill, 1973.

Zubek, John P. and Solberg, P. A. *Human Development.* New York: McGraw-Hill, 1954.